# COLLINS

# TIME FOR
# ENGLISH

## DAVID FOLL

## KENNETH CRIPWELL

## TERESA O'BRIEN

## BOOK 3

COLLINS
ELT

# ACKNOWLEDGEMENTS

The authors would like to thank the following for their assistance in the preparation of the book:
Aurèle J. Hedley (British Airways), Camilla Olsen, Howard Walwyn, Imanol Iriondo, John Morgan (Pilgrims Language Courses, Canterbury), Members of Pari Match, Milton Toubkin, Nancy Gross, Steve Castle, and especially Jan Keane for her help in writing materials.

The publishers would like to thank the following for permission to reproduce photographs or other visual material (page number in brackets):
Alan Patient (91), Alexander Turnball Library, Wellington (46), All-sport (82), Anthea Sieve King, Vision International (91), Architecture Design (84), The Australian Information Service, London (42, 43, 56, 60, 64), Australian News and Information Bureau (56), Axel Poignant Archive (46, 48), Barclay's Bank (82), Barnaby's (68, 82), BBC Enterprises Ltd (106, 110), BBC World Service (112), Bernice and Cliff Moon (55), BFI 20th Century Fox (34, 35), BFI United Artists (35), "Britain on View" (BTA/ETB) (83), British Council, Korea (111), The British Library (4), British Telecom (84), British Tourist Agency (83), Caroline Penn (108), Camera Press (52), Casio (86), Chris Ridgers (22, 86), Chris Webb (43), Christian Aid (108), Courtesy RCA, Pedosa (30), © DACS 1987, for *Wham* by Roy Lichtenstein (27), David Redfern (82, 83), Florida Division of Tourism (19), Frank Herrmann (108), Franklin Watts (56), GEC Electrical Projects Limited for photo of robot (86), Greg Evans (82), Greenhill (82, 95), S. E. Gunner and S. McCorky (50), Holt Studios Ltd (36–9, 48), Hutchison Library (111), Institute of Dermatology (36–9), Intermediate Technology (92), Jonathon Rutland (59, 61), Lufthansa German Airlines Photo-Archive Koeln (83), Madeleine Boyns (107), Marshall Cavendish Partworks (36–39, 90), Mary Evans (3, 4, 5, 46), M. C. Escher Heirs, c/o Cordon Art, Baarn, Holland (39), Metropolitan Museum of Art (27), Michael Busselle (66), Museum of Modern Art/Film Stills Archive (27), National Army Museum (4), National Film Archive (28), National Westminster Bank (86), New Zealand Publicity Photos and G. R. Roberts (43), Observer Colour Magazine (88), Oxfam (92), Oxford University Press, for permission to reproduce three illustrations from *Illustrated Human and Social Biology* by B. S. Beckett, illustrated by Brian and Constance Dear, published 1981 (96), Peter Charles Worth (108), Peter Newark's Western Americana (4, 5, 9, 10), Popular Food Service (3), Promotion Australia, London (60, 64), Ray Bird (31), Rediffusion (86), Rex Features (2, 3, 110, 111), Saatchi Collection, London (27), Save the Children (108), Science Photo Library (86), © 1986, Sea World of Florida, Inc. (20), Silver Burdett (9), Sophie Howard (36, 54), Spectrum Colour Library (50, 51, 84, 95), Tate Gallery (27), Teen Machine, 8490 Sunset Boulevard, LA, CA 90069 (36), Telecommunications Photo Library (82, 86), Thomas Nelson and Sons Ltd (18), Time-Life Films Inc. (34), Tourism Council (19), United World Colleges (98–9), © 1986, The Walt Disney Company (19), Warner Brothers, Inc. (70–72), Warner Brothers Music Limited for song "Blowing in the Wind", Wayland Publishers (50), Wellcome Institute Library, London (90), Whitney Museum of American Art (27), Zefa Picture Library (83).

The publishers would like to thank the following for their help in providing information or material used in this book (page numbers in brackets):
*Australia Now*, Australia, British Airways (23), David Werner: *Where there is No Doctor* (60), Dr June Goodfield (91), Flightrider Club, PO Box 150, High Wycombe, Bucks, England (22, 23), Food and Wine from France, 41 Piccadilly, London (55), Health Education Council (12, 94, 95), Leichner (72), Robert Creighton, United World Colleges (98–99), Samaritans (16), Usborne Book of Sewing and Knitting (52), *Woman's Day Magazine*, Australia (54, 58), Word in Action (Dorset) 1983 Ltd (102-104).

Collins ELT
8 Grafton Street
London
W1X 3LA

© David Foll, Kenneth Cripwell,
Teresa O'Brien,
Michael Beaumont 1987

First published 1987.

1 2 3 4 5 6 7 8 9 10

ISBN: 0 00 370402 5

Published by William Collins plc

Produced, designed and illustrated by SNAP Graphics, London.
Cover design by Richard Moon.
Printed in Spain by Mateu Cromo Artes Graficas, S.A.

# CONTENTS

# THE UNITED STATES OF AMERICA

### A WHAT'S IN A NAME?

The United States, the States, America, the USA, the US. The same country, but many names. Many images too. What do you think of when you hear or see these names?

Hamburgers   The Statue of Liberty
Mickey Mouse   The Stars and Stripes
Cowboys   Skyscrapers   Jeans

1 Identify the images round these pages.
2 Draw your own image of the USA and label it.

### B 🔲 FAMOUS PLACES

1 Match the names to the drawings on the map (a–e).

| WHAT? ■ |
| --- |
| The Golden Gate Bridge |
| The Kennedy Space Center*   The Statue of Liberty |
| The White House   Walt Disney World |

2 Match the cities (f–l) and states (m–p) to the places on the map.

| ● WHERE? ▲ | |
| --- | --- |
| CITIES: Boston  Dallas Los Angeles  Miami  San Francisco New York  Washington | STATES: California Florida  Kansas New York |

3 Check your ideas with your partner. Use questions like this:

What's this?
Do you know what this is?
What's the name of this city/state/thing?
This is Walt Disney World, isn't it?

Where is ................ ?

It's The White House.
Yes, it's ..................................... .
..................................... .
No, it isn't.
In the middle/south of the USA.

4 Listen to the cassette for the correct answers.

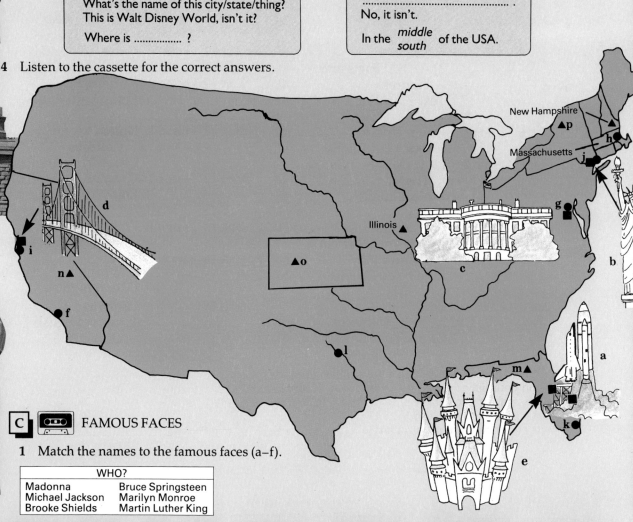

### C 🔲 FAMOUS FACES

1 Match the names to the famous faces (a–f).

| WHO? | |
| --- | --- |
| Madonna | Bruce Springsteen |
| Michael Jackson | Marilyn Monroe |
| Brooke Shields | Martin Luther King |

a   b   c   d   e   f

**2** Match the correct information to the Presidents (g–j).

| WHICH PRESIDENT? | |
|---|---|
| The 1st (1789-1797) | The 35th (1960-1963) |
| The 16th (1860-1865) | The 40th (1980-    ) |

**3** Check your ideas with your partner. Use questions like this:

g  h  i  j

Abraham Lincoln    Ronald Reagan    George Washington    John F. Kennedy

Who's this?
Which one of these is Martin Luther King?
This is Marilyn Monroe, isn't it?
Who was the thirty-fifth President?
Who was President from 1789 to 1797?

It's Madonna.
This one here.
Yes, it is.
.........................
.........................

**4** Listen to the cassette for the correct answers.

## D  GENERAL KNOWLEDGE QUIZ

**1** Write the answers in your notebooks.

a How many people live in the USA today?
  1 26 million    2 126 million    3 226 million

b Which US city is called The Big Apple?
  1 Los Angeles    2 New York    3 Washington

c When did Columbus land in America?
  1 1452    2 1492    3 1528

d When did the Pilgrim Fathers in the *Mayflower* land in America?
  1 1620    2 1683    3 1776

e How many stars are there in the US flag? Do you know why?

f Two of the 50 US states are separated from the other 48. Which two? Where are they?

**2** Check your answers with your partner. Then listen to the cassette for the correct answers.

## E ASSASSINATION!

The two assassins

John Wilkes Booth    Lee Harvey Oswald

There are several strange similarities between the lives and deaths of Presidents Lincoln and Kennedy. You can find out now. Here's how:

**1** *Preparation*
Student A look at page 9 for information on President Lincoln. Student B look at page 33 for information on President Kennedy. Do *not* show your list to your partner.

**2** *Communication Game*
Share your information like this:
Student A read your first sentence aloud to Student B. Student B find the similar sentence on your list and read it to Student A. Compare the information: how is it similar or different? Change over and continue.
Remember: you mustn't show each other your own lists.
(Note: all these facts are true!)

**3** *Writing*
Work together to write ten sentences about Presidents Lincoln and Kennedy. Join two pieces of similar information to make one sentence. Make sure that you use all these joining words:

  and
  and ..... also (use before the main verb)
  and ..... as well (use at the end of
  and ..... too      the sentence)
  both
  but
  who

*Example   Both* Presidents had wives *who* had dark hair, spoke French very well and were 24 when they got married.

## F GAME

How many new words can you make from these words?

THE UNITED STATES

**G** THE WAR OF INDEPENDENCE

1 How much do you know about American history? Do this quiz before you read the story.

1 In 1776 the Americans wanted to become independent from
the British / the Canadians / the French / the Indians.

2 The commander of the American army was called
Abraham Lincoln / Franklin Roosevelt / Harry Truman / George Washington.

3 The War of Independence took place in the
north east / north west / south east / south west of the North American continent.

2 Read the story of the War of Independence and check your ideas.

1 In 1764–5 the British Parliament introduced many new taxes. The Sugar Act* put a tax on sugar, the Stamp Act on legal documents and newspapers. These were very unpopular. In October 1765 a Colonial Congress met in New York to protest to King George III. So the next year Parliament repealed** the Stamp Act and changed the Sugar Act. But they introduced new taxes on paper, glass, paint and tea.

2 The American colonists especially hated the British soldiers ('redcoats'). One day (March 5th 1770) in Boston, people began to throw snowballs at some redcoats. They opened fire on the protesters and killed five people. This incident was called 'The Boston Massacre'.

3 Three years later the British introduced a Tea Act, which made British tea cheaper than American. Shopkeepers hated this and on December 16th colonists dressed in Indian clothes threw 342 chests of tea from a British ship into the sea. The British were very angry.

4 On September 5th 1774 the First Congressional Congress met in Philadelphia and decided to form groups of soldiers to fight the British. Seven months later, on April 19th, British and American soldiers met for the first time in Lexington, Massachusetts. This was the start of the War of Independence.

5 On July 4th 1776 in Philadelphia the thirteen colonies adopted the Declaration of Independence. This announced to the world the birth of a new, independent nation, the United States of America.

6 On October 19th 1781 Lord Cornwallis, the British Commander-in-Chief, surrendered to the American General George Washington. The war had lasted for six years. The British had lost, and the thirteen states were now free and independent.

* = Law
** = ended

A

D

F

B

IN CONGRESS, July 4. 1776.

The unanimous Declaration of the thirteen united States of America,

E

C

3 Match:
i) the titles (a–f) to the paragraphs (1–6).

a The end of the war   b The Boston Tea Party   c The Declaration of Independence   d The Sugar and Stamp Acts   e The start of the war   f The Boston Massacre

ii) pictures (A–F) to the paragraphs.

4 Choose the correct alternative.
these (para 1, line 4): the Sugar and Stamp Acts OR legal documents and newspapers?
they (para 1, line 8): a Colonial Congress OR Parliament?
They (para 2, line 4): the American colonists OR the redcoats?
This (para 4, line 6): The First Congressional Congress OR the meeting of British and American soldiers in Lexington?

5 Find the answers to these questions and write them in your notebooks.
1 Why did the British Parliament repeal the Stamp Act?
2 Why did the people in Boston throw snowballs at the redcoats?
3 What was the reason for the Boston Tea Party?
4 Why did the thirteen colonies adopt the Declaration of Independence?
5 Why are there thirteen stripes on the American flag?

# CHECK YOUR ENGLISH

## English for travelling: introducing yourself

**Jesse:** Hi, I'm Jesse.
**You:** Hi, my name's .....
**Jesse:** Excuse me?
**You:** ...............
**Jesse:** ............... How do you spell that?
**You:** ...............
**Jesse:** Well, pleased to meet you, .....
Where are you from?
**You:** ...............
**Jesse:** And are you over here on vacation?
**You:** Yes.
**Jesse:** How long are you here for?
**You:** Till ......      ..... more days.

1   *Listen, and mark the stressed syllables of the words in these phrases like this (')*

**Example:** from 'seventeen sixty 'four to 'five

1   the British Parliament
2   the Sugar Act
3   the Stamp Act
4   in October seventeen sixty-five
5   a Colonial Congress
6   New York
7   King George the third

2   *Listen and mark like this (/) the places where the reader pauses.*

*Example*   In 1764–5/the British Parliament/ introduced many new taxes./

The Sugar Act put a tax on sugar, the Stamp Act on legal documents and newspapers. These were very unpopular. In October 1765 a Colonial Congress met in New York to protest to King George III.

3   *There is one syllable in each phrase (between /   /) where the reader's voice changes. Listen and mark it like this ( ___ ).*

*Example*   In 1764–<u>5</u>/ the British <u>Parliament</u>/ introduced new <u>taxes</u>/.

4   *Listen and repeat phrase by phrase.*

---

KNOW YOUR GRAMMAR

---

**Review: the past tense; past time**

1   **Simple past**

**Form:**   *see Book 1, p.116, and Book 2, p.5 and p.29.*
**Use:**   *to fix an action/habit/state\* at a definite time in the past.*
*This time can be either a* **point of time** *(.) or a* **period of time** (|___|). *There is a gap between* now *and* then. *This means that the action/habit/state is finished.*

\* action (.)   Three years later the British introduced a Tea Act. (p.4)
habit (...)   From which two directions did the French come? (p.6)
state (|___|) The American colonists ... hated the British soldiers. (p.4)

**Exercise:**
1   *On p.4 find 12 expressions of definite time: 10* **points of time** *and 2* **periods of time**. *Make a list.*
*Example*   **On September 5th 1774** the First Congressional Congress met in .... (p.4)
2   *Other verbs on p.4 have no time words. Why not?*

2   **Past progressive**

**Form:**   *see Book 2, p.69.*
**Use:**   *for an action in the past which:*
1   *is happening at a definite time*
2   *is not finished* (|___.....|)
3   *is temporary* (|___|   )

*Example*   At 2 a.m. James Hopper was walking home. (p.8)
Oswald shot Kennedy when he was sitting in a car. (p.33)

```
    2 a.m.                      shot
      |                          |
|——....|                   |——....|
was walking                 was sitting
```

**Exercise:** *Use these words to make complete sentences about the San Francisco earthquake. (p.8)*
1   James Hopper/pass/hear
2   5.10 a.m./Bailey Millard/sit and paint
3   Jesse Cook/walk/see
4   John Barrett/work/hear
5   5.30 a.m./nearly 50 fires/burn
6   The wind/blow

# A NATION OF NATIONS

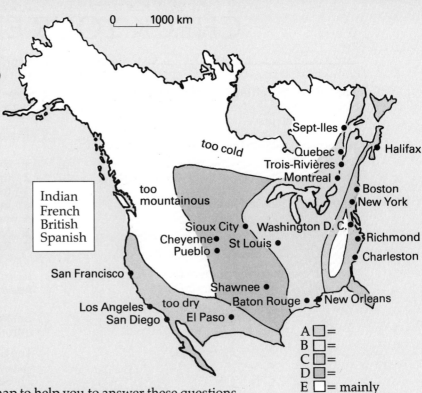

0    1000 km

Indian
French
British
Spanish

too cold
Sept-Iles
Quebec
Halifax
Trois-Rivières
Montréal
Boston
New York
too mountainous
Sioux City
Washington D. C.
Cheyenne
St Louis
Richmond
Pueblo
Charleston
San Francisco
Shawnee
Los Angeles
too dry
Baton Rouge
New Orleans
San Diego
El Paso

A ☐ =
B ☐ =
C ☐ =
D ☐ =
E ☐ = mainly uninhabited

## A WORKING WITH A MAP

1492 is an important date in European history. What happened then? People say 'the discovery of America' or when 'Columbus discovered the New World'. Europeans use words like 'discovery', 'discovered' and 'the New World'. But there had been people in America since 20,000–15,000 BC so there had been native Americans for thousands of years before Columbus' 'discovery'. These people didn't see things the same way as the Europeans.

1   Look at the place-names on the map. Use the words given in the box, and write which nationality settled where.

2   What do you think? Use the map to help you to answer these questions.
1   In which part of the continent did the British settle? Why?
2   From which two directions did the French come? Why?
3   Why did the Spanish settle mainly in the south west?
4   Where do the Indians live now? Why don't they live right across the continent?
5   Why did the Negroes come to the south east of America?

## B   THE LOSERS

Listen to this talk about the Indians and the White Man. There are seven different sections in this talk. The main ideas of each section are listed below (a–g). In what order does the speaker introduce these main ideas?

a   The Indians' idea of land.
b   The Indians in Hollywood films.
c   The name 'Indians'.
d   The Europeans and the Indians' land.
e   The fight between the Indians and the settlers.
f   The Indians and the early settlers.
g   Indian reservations.

## C IMMIGRATION

'The history of America *is* immigration.' From the first immigrants, the Indians, to the most recent, the Vietnamese, people from many different nations and races have made their home in America. Why did millions of Europeans emigrate from Europe to America in the nineteenth century? There were many reasons. We can divide the main reasons into two lists:

*PULL factors*
– The promise of employment for all
– The promise of better opportunities
– The hope of a better life

*PUSH factors*
– Overpopulation
– Unemployment
– Poverty
– Famine

Push or pull? Sort these factors into two lists:

– there were too many people and there was not enough land
– people wanted more land
– people were very poor
– there was no work
– people wanted better housing
– people wanted better-paid jobs

– people had no food
– people wanted a better future for their children
– people read travel books and newspaper articles about America
– people received letters from friends and relatives in the USA

## D THE AMERICAN LETTERS

The settlers in America wrote letters to their relatives and friends back in Europe; newspapers sometimes printed them for everybody to read. These letters were called the *American Letters*. Read these extracts from some American letters.

1 From a Norwegian in New York 1835:

*There is room for everybody here – work and good wages too. You can live well and have everything.*

2 From a Welshman in New York 1817:

*Dear wife, send the two eldest boys over to me here. I won't have to pay for their education until they are fourteen. The schools here are the best in the world, and the state pays for them.*

3 From a Swede in Illinois 1850:

*This is a free country. Everybody is equal: you don't have to take your hat off for anybody. The law is for both rich and poor.*

4 From a Dutchwoman in Massachusetts 1846:

*Nearly all people eat three meals a day. there are no poor here. Schools are free. there are no taxes. Everybody has good clothes. Nobody steals.*

5 From an Englishman in New Hampshire 1821:

*We have a comfortable house and acres of ground with potatoes, Indian corn etc. I have two pigs and two sheep. Cows in the spring were expensive, 33 dollars each, but I hope to buy one in the fall.*

What do you think life was like for each of these six people in his or her native country? Why do you think they left their homes for a new life in America? Use the ideas and language in **C** to help you explain.

## E ELLIS ISLAND

Every new arrival to the States passed through Ellis Island, New York. Here immigration officers questioned each new arrival closely.

Work in groups of three. Student A plays the part of a new arrival who wants to come in to the United States (look at p.25). Students B and C play the parts of immigration officers who interview Student A (look at p.73).

Where do you come from?

Where will you stay in the US?

How much money have you got with you?

Have you ever had any serious illness?

**IMMIGRATION FORM**

1 Name: ..................... .....................
   (forename)        (surname)
2 Nationality: .............................................
3 Native language: ........................................
4 Family in the USA?: yes ☐  no ☐
   (If yes, specify) .......................................
5 Reasons for leaving own country: ..................
6 Reasons for wanting to settle in the USA: .........
7 Address in the USA?: yes ☐  no ☐
   (If yes, specify) .......................................
8 Occupation in home country: .........................
9 Employment in the USA?: yes ☐  no ☐
   (If yes, specify) .......................................
10 Financial position: ....................................
11 Health:  poor ☐
         average ☐   (put H for heart trouble)
         good ☐
12 Knowledge of English:  poor ☐
                       basic ☐
                       average ☐
                       good ☐
                       native ☐

## F GO WEST, YOUNG MAN!

In 1910 approximately 30 per cent of the total population of San Francisco (417,000) was foreign-born. Two-thirds of these foreign-born people came from only six countries.
Use the pie-chart and the clues below to work out the names of the six countries (A-F).

**Clues:**
- The largest single group of immigrants was German.
- There was an equal number of Chinese and Swedish immigrants.
- There were five per cent fewer English than Italian immigrants.
- There were a thousand more German than Irish immigrants.

The foreign-born in San Francisco in 1910.

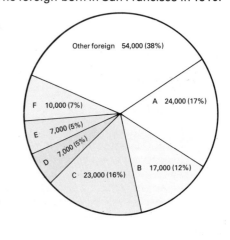

Other foreign 54,000 (38%)
A 24,000 (17%)
B 17,000 (12%)
C 23,000 (16%)
D 7,000 (5%)
E 7,000 (5%)
F 10,000 (7%)

# G COUNTDOWN TO DISASTER

**Wed April 18th 1906**
**2 am** James Hopper, journalist, walks home to bed. It is a quiet, peaceful night. In the harbour he sees the red and green lights and the dark shapes of the big ships. He passes a stable. As he passes, he hears a terrible sound: a horse is screaming. All the other horses start to kick their doors. Later he hears the dogs in the city dogs' home barking. He can't understand why.

**5 am** Bailey Millard, painter, starts work. He is sitting high on Russian Hill, painting the view over the city and bay. The sun is rising behind him and everything is golden.

**5.12** 90 miles north at Point Arena the first tremor comes out of the sea. It moves towards San Francisco at two miles per second. On its way it destroys villages, forests, hills, valleys and beaches.

**5.13–5.30** Nearly 50 fires start in the busy market area. There are only 38 fire-engines and most of the watermains don't work. The wind is blowing hard from the sea. The fire grows and the firemen can do nothing. For three days and nights the fire burns.

Market

Poin
Are

**5.20** The great Italian tenor, Enrico Caruso, opens his window in the Palace Hotel and begins to sing. People in the street stop to watch and listen. Another guest at the hotel says this is Caruso's bravest and best performance.

**5.12′.19″** Jesse Cook, police sergeant, actually sees the earthquake. He hears a deep sound and then sees it coming up Washington Street, moving smoothly like a wave.
John Barrett, journalist, hears the same sound. He runs to the window and sees the buildings dancing. Buildings begin to fall. Everywhere church bells are ringing. He thinks, 'This is the end of the world.'
There are three tremors, then silence – except for the hiss from broken gas pipes.

Washington St.

**Sat April 21st**
**7.15 am** The Great Fire of San Francisco stops. 450 people have died, 28,000 buildings have disappeared, an area six times greater than that of the Great Fire of London has burnt. It starts to rain.

1 Find the words for:
   – a building for keeping horses in
   – a shaking movement of the earth
   – a large underground pipe carrying water

2 Find in the text:
   – six words for movement
   – five words for occupations
   – five words for making a sound
   – five Christian names

3 Find the words in the text with the opposite meaning to:
   small   beautiful   low   high   worst
   quiet   softly

4 Use the ideas in the text to help you answer these questions. Why do you think . . .
   ...the horse screamed?
   ...the church bells rang everywhere?
   ...John Barrett thought, 'This is the end of the world'?
   ...Caruso sang from his hotel window?
   ...so many fires started?
   ...the fire lasted for three days?

## H IN THE PATH OF THE EARTHQUAKE

What happened to the Skinner farm when the tremor passed right under it? Copy the plan of the farm before the tremor. Then listen to Mrs Skinner's story. Show on your plan how everything moved. Then draw a new plan of the farm after the tremor.

### BEFORE THE TREMOR

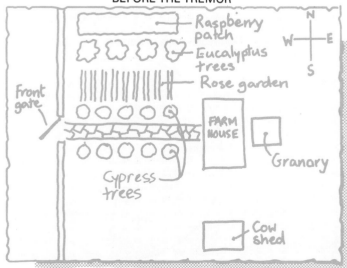

## I WRITE A NEWSPAPER REPORT

Copy and complete this newspaper report. Choose the correct words for the boxes and put the verbs in brackets in the correct tense (either Simple Past or Past Progressive).

| after the earthquake |
|---|
| then |
| at 5 this morning |

| and |
|---|
| and |
| because |
| but |
| when |

⬚ an earthquake [1](hit) the city of San Francisco. It [2](destroy) many buildings ⬚ [3](leave) many people without homes. John Barrett, a journalist, [4](say), 'I [5](work) in my office ⬚ I [6](hear) a terrible noise. I [7](run) to the window. All the buildings [8](dance) ⬚ ⬚ they [9](begin) to fall. Everywhere the church bells [10](ring). It [11](be) like the end of the world.'
   Nearly 50 fires [12](start) ⬚ ⬚ the firemen [13](can) do nothing ⬚ they [14](have) only 38 fire-engines and no water. The fire is now burning out of control.

# PROJECT ENGLISH

> **Did you know?**
> One of the 1.7 million Irish who emigrated to the States in the 1840s and 1850s was called Patrick Kennedy. He had lost his farm in Ireland and wanted to start a new life in Boston. His great-grandson John became the 35th President of the USA.

**1 Family research**

How much do you know about your grandparents? Find the answers to these questions about one grandparent:

Where and when was s/he born?
What nationality is s/he?
Where does s/he live now?
How long has s/he lived there?
Where did s/he live before?

**2 Your region**

Look at this advertisement from Rochdale, England. What is it advertising?
Prepare a similar advertisement for your own town/city/region. Think of all the positive things in your area:

1 Position: where is it? (by the sea/in the mountains/on a plain/by a lake/on a river).
2 Scenery: is it beautiful in any way?
3 Employment: is it good for business/farming/industry/tourism?
4 Services: has it got good shops/schools/hospitals/public transport?
5 Sport and leisure facilities: are there many sports centres/cinemas/swimming pools/libraries/museums?
6 Special features: is there anything special about your area? (think about things to see, places to visit, things to do).
7 Weather: which is the best season in your area?

Collect ideas with your neighbours and make an advertisement for the class noticeboard.

Why did s/he live there?
Where else has s/he lived (and worked)?

Make a list of the important dates and places in your grandparent's life. Ask your grandparent to lend you some photos, and perhaps some letters or other documents, and bring these and your list to school. Tell your class about your grandparent.

*"To the West, to the West, to the Land of the Free."*

## EMIGRATION
### TO
### IOWA and NEBRASKA, U.S.

The next Colony will leave Rochdale for Lincoln Nebraska, on Wednesday, June 28th, 1871.
The Burlington and Missouri River Railroad Company will provide the Colony with Through Tickets from Liverpool to Lincoln, at the following Rates:

| | | | | £ | s. | d. |
|---|---|---|---|---|---|---|
| Steerage on Steamer and 3rd class Railway | | | .... | 11 | 11 | 0 |
| Ditto | Ditto | 1st | Ditto | .... | | |
| Intermediate Ditto | | 1st | Ditto | .... | 15 | 2 5 |
| Cabin | Ditto | 1st | Ditto | .... | 18 | 5 5 |
| | Ditto | 1st | Ditto | .... | 24 | 11 5 |

A Guide will be furnished to accompany the Party from the Landing Port to their Destination, and every arrangement will be made for the care and comfort of the Colony, until they are finally settled in their New Home.

## HOMES FOR ALL!
More Farms than Farmers! More Landlords than Tenants!
### WORK FOR ALL WORKERS!
## 2,000,000 Acres of LAND for SALE
At from Four to Fifteen Dollars per Acre, on Ten Years' Credit, and only charged Six per Cent. Interest.

Those intending to join the Colony, should apply to the undersigned at once for full information and Copy of the Guide to Iowa and Nebraska.

### ASHWORTH & PARKER,
2, River-Street, Rochdale; and 4, Corporation-Street, Manchester,
Agents to the Burlington & Missouri River Railroad Company.
JOHN TURNER, PRINTER, DRAKE-STREET, ROCHDALE.

---

**STUDENT A**

1 Booth killed President Lincoln by shooting him in the head.
2 Booth shot Lincoln on a Friday.
3 Booth shot Lincoln in a theatre and then ran out into a shop.
4 Booth was born in 1839.
5 Lincoln's wife had dark hair, spoke French very well and was twenty-four when she married Lincoln.
6 Lincoln had a secretary called Kennedy.
7 Lincoln's son Robert was Ambassador to London.
8 After Lincoln's death Andrew Johnson, the Vice-President, became President.
9 Andrew Johnson was born in 1808.
10 Lincoln was sitting in a theatre when Booth shot him.

---

Full name: Helen Kathleen Cripwell
Born: 25th February 1968
Time in group: joined February 1985
Previous group(s): Children of the Dust, Cellar Ratz
Job(s): works in a bakery
Best friend: Annabel
Hero: James Dean
Heroine: Marilyn Monroe
Ideal holiday: to travel round Europe for a month
Ambition: to be a singer; to be a big name in the USA

# SCHOOL AND HEALTH

**A** EDUCATION IN THE USA

1 Look at these two pictures of American classrooms, one from the nineteenth century and one from the twentieth century. How many differences can you find?

2 Copy the diagram and notes about the American education system into your notebooks. Then read the text and complete the diagram. There is a mistake in the notes. Can you correct it?

There are three levels in the American education system: elementary, secondary and higher. Most American children go to public school where education is free.

The period of compulsory education – when by law children must go to school – is twelve years. These twelve years can divide in two ways: the older 8–4 plan, or the more common 6–3–3 plan (*see chart*). In the former, grades 1–8 are elementary school and grades 9–12 high school. In the latter, elementary school is in grades 1–6, junior high school in grades 7–9 and senior high school in grades 10–12.

In elementary school, children have one teacher for all subjects, but in high school there is a separate teacher for each one. Compulsory subjects in secondary education are: English, science, social studies, maths and physical education. Students can choose their other subjects ('elective') from areas such as foreign languages, the fine arts and vocational training.

The school year usually lasts for nine months, from early September to mid-June.

At the end of high school, students graduate with a high school diploma if they complete their studies satisfactorily. The grades go from A (=excellent) to F (=failing). In their last three years at school, students receive career advice and choose their subjects accordingly.

A child's introduction to the education system usually starts at the age of four or five. Kindergartens or nursery schools prepare the young child for life at elementary school.

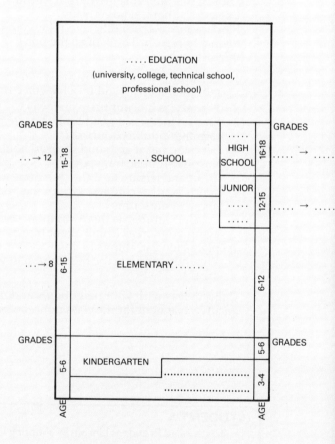

SUBJECTS:

| COMPULSORY | ELECTIVE |
|---|---|
| • English<br>• science<br>• social studies<br>• maths<br>• foreign languages | • fine arts<br>• physical education<br>• vocational training |

10

## B 🎞️ A TYPICAL SCHOOL DAY IN THE USA

Bonnie Reynolds is an American schoolgirl who is living and going to school in London at the moment. Here, reporter Deborah Tyler asks her about the American school day.

1 Read Bonnie's answers. What questions did Deborah ask Bonnie? Write them down in your notebooks.

2 Check your ideas with your partner. Then listen to the cassette for some possible answers.

3 Find in the text the American words for:

| GB | US |
|---|---|
| taking the register | |
| morning break | |
| biscuit | |
| term | |

### The Pledge of Allegiance

I pledge allegiance to the flag of the United States and to the Republic for which it stands, one nation under God, indivisible, with liberty and justice for all.

1 **What time does school normally start in the States?**
Between 8 and 8.30 in the morning.

2 .................. ?
Well, the normal ways – on foot, by car, by bus. If you live a long way from school – in the country for example – there are special yellow school buses which take you to school.

3 .................. ?
First, the teacher takes attendance – in England, that's called taking the register. Then, just before lessons start, the whole class stands together and says the Pledge of Allegiance to the American flag.

4 .................. ?
Yes – just like here – halfway through the morning. But we call it morning recess.

5 .................. ?
At about 11.30. Earlier than here. We get about 40 minutes.

6 .................. ?
No, it's not – you have to pay for it. Or you can take your own if you prefer. I take my own – I have sandwiches, fresh fruit, milk and a cookie – sorry, that's a biscuit.

7 .................. ?
Earlier than over here – at about 2.30.

8 .................. ?
No, we don't have to. Most children wear jeans and a T-shirt, something like that.

9 .................. ?
We have longer summer holidays in the States than you do here. But then our Thanksgiving, Christmas and Easter holidays are shorter than yours. Oh, and there's another word you should know – *semester* – that's *term* in England!

## C YOUR SCHOOL DAY

1 Is your school day the same as Bonnie's, or are there some differences? In groups of four make notes in two lists:

| Same | Different |
|---|---|
| .................. | .................. |
| .................. | .................. |
| .................. | .................. |

2 Write a new conversation between you and Deborah Tyler about your school day. Use questions 1–9.

Begin like this:

**Deborah:** What time does school normally start in your country?

**You:** ......................................................

## D AN AVERAGE FAMILY BUDGET IN THE USA

Note: a high percentage of a family's budget goes on medical care because there is no national health care programme (except for people over 65).

1 What do Americans spend most on?
2 Do Americans spend more on cars or on clothes and jewellery?
3 Homework: Make a similar pie-chart for your family budget. Ask your parents to help you.

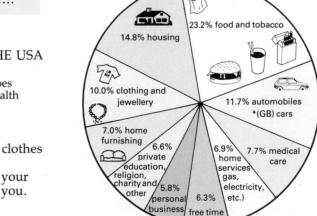

23.2% food and tobacco
14.8% housing
10.0% clothing and jewellery
11.7% automobiles *(GB) cars
7.0% home furnishing
6.6% private education, religion, charity and other
6.9% home services gas, electricity, etc.)
7.7% medical care
5.8% personal business
6.3% free time

**E** FLU

1 Look at the man in the picture. What's wrong with him?

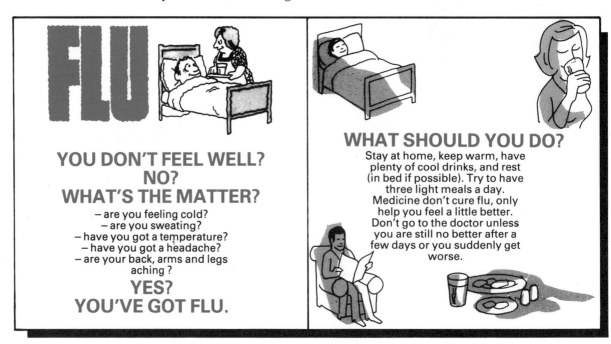

**FLU**

**YOU DON'T FEEL WELL?**
**NO?**
**WHAT'S THE MATTER?**

– are you feeling cold?
– are you sweating?
– have you got a temperature?
– have you got a headache?
– are your back, arms and legs
aching ?

**YES?**
**YOU'VE GOT FLU.**

**WHAT SHOULD YOU DO?**
Stay at home, keep warm, have
plenty of cool drinks, and rest
(in bed if possible). Try to have
three light meals a day.
Medicine don't cure flu, only
help you feel a little better.
Don't go to the doctor unless
you are still no better after a
few days or you suddenly get
worse.

2 Interview your partner and make notes. Ask and answer these questions.

Have you ever had flu?
↓
Yes, I have./No, I haven't.
↓
How did you feel?/How do you feel if you have flu?
↓
.......................................
↓
What did you do?/What should you do?
↓
.......................................
↓
How long did it take to get better?/How long does it take to get better?

3 Write a report about your partner and check it with him/her privately. (Or write about having flu.)

**F** GOING TO THE DOCTOR IN THE USA

1 Look at this chart about going to the doctor
in the USA.
Note: most people have health insurance in the
USA and see a private doctor.

2 Is going to the doctor the same in your country
or are there some differences? Make notes in
two lists:

**Same**      **Different**

3 Make a similar chart about going to the doctor
in your country.

**G** FROM THE NEWSPAPER

Read this newspaper article with the help of your
bilingual dictionary.

## Snakes alive – I'm cured!

PEKING: A young Chinese farmer has eaten more than 1800
live poisonous snakes to cure himself of convulsions. But now,
after two years, peasant Wang Biao from Jinlin province has
become addicted to the snakes and needs one before every
meal, reports the *Canton Daily*. He has started breeding them
to ensure he has enough to last him through the winter.

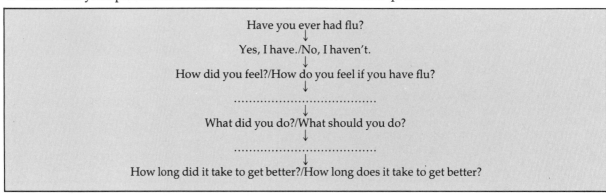

| Call the doctor's office* |
| :---: |
| ↓ |
| Make an appointment |
| ↓ |
| Go to your doctor's office and show your hospitalisation card to the nurse |
| ↓ |
| Wait in the waiting room |
| ↓ |
| Go into the doctor's examining room and tell him/her what is the matter |
| ↓ |
| S/he will examine you. Listen to his/her advice: s/he will give you a prescription if necessary |
| ↓ |
| Take this to the drugstore** and wait for your medicine (you have to pay unless your insurance covers this) |
| ↓ |
| Follow the instructions and take your medicine. |
| ↓ |
| For any emergency go to the emergency room of the nearest hospital – don't forget to take your hospitalisation card with you. |

*surgery (GB)
**chemist (GB)

# CHECK YOUR ENGLISH

## ENGLISH SPOKEN HERE 🎞

**English for travelling: at the doctor's**

Doctor: What's the matter?
You: I don't feel well.
Doctor: Can you describe how you feel?
You: ......................................................
Doctor: How long have you had this?
You: ......................................................
Doctor: Have you taken anything for it?
You: ......................................................
Doctor: Well, take these – one, four times a day – and come back if you don't get any better.
You: Thank you.
Doctor: I hope you get better soon.

1 *Listen and mark the syllable where the speaker's voice changes.*

*Example* What time does school normally <u>start</u> in the States?

a How does the day begin?
b Do you have a break?
c What time's lunch?
d Is it free?
e What time does school finish?
f Do you have to wear a uniform?
g And what about your holidays?

2 *Listen again and mark if the syllable goes up ( ↗ ) or down ( ↘ ).*

*Example* What time does school normally start in the States?

3 *With your partner, practise reading aloud the dialogue on p.11. Use questions a–g. Then change over and repeat.*

## KNOW YOUR GRAMMAR

REVIEW: **the present tense: present time**

**1 Simple present**
**Form:** *see Book 1, pages 14, 28 and 48*
**Use:** *for present*

  **1 states**
  *Example* There are three levels in the American education system. (p.10)

  *This includes facts in science*
  *Example* Medicines don't cure flu, they only help you feel a little better. (p.12)

  **2 habits**
  *Example* Most American children go to public school. (p.10)

  **3 instructions**
  *Example* Stay at home, keep warm, have plenty of cool drinks. (p.12)

**3 Action or state verb?**

1 *Find the 16 action verbs in the oval and match them to the action verbs in a–p.*
*Example* close–open

open see forget be make stand finish hear hate eat start know have got go snow prefer give push find read walk laugh listen return smell

2 *Put the other words in the correct lists. Note that the words in the lists are in alphabetical order.*

**2 Present progressive**

**Form:** *see Book 1, page 62*
**Use:** *for a present action which*    Now
    is happening now    |
    is temporary    ⊢———⊣
    is not finished    ⊢·····⊣

    *Example* Bonnie Phillips is living and going to school in London. (p.11)

**Exercise:**

Write some sentences about the three photographs on p.16.

*Example* Vivian is crying and her sister is asking her why.

| Action verbs | State verbs | | |
|---|---|---|---|
| | The Senses | Emotions and the Mind | Being or Having |
| a begin ..... | feel | believe | ..... |
| b close/open ..... | ..... | ..... | become |
| c come ..... | ..... | ..... | belong to |
| d cry ..... | seem | like | cost |
| e do ..... | ..... | love | ..... |
| f drink ..... | taste | ..... | |
| g leave ..... | | ..... | |
| h lose ..... | | remember | |
| i pull ..... | | understand | |
| j rain ..... | | want | |
| k run ..... | | | |
| l sit ..... | | | |
| m stop ..... | | | |
| n talk ..... | | | |
| o take ..... | | | |
| p write ..... | | | |

*Don't forget*

| State | Action |
|---|---|
| I have a bicycle. | I'm having lunch. |
| I think you're wrong. | I'm thinking about my holiday. |
| You look ill today. | What are you looking at? |
| *but*     I feel / I'm feeling | better today. / well today. |

# FRIENDS

**A** 🎞️ GANGS

**1** Look at the pictures of the boys and girls. How old do you think they are? Which one would you like to be friends with? When you read, find out this person's name. What else do you find out about him/her?

### Chapter One: An Introduction

My gang consists of three boys, two girls and a parrot. Our names are William, Jimmy, Jack, Kat the parrot, who is called Kiki and me, Bonnie. We are about thirteen, but William is the oldest. Some of us h nicknames: Kate's is Fatty, Jimmy's is Shorty and Ja is Ginger. We live in the same area in London but w don't go to the same school. The gang has existe for two years. The name of the gang is SECRET S and our password is XIS TERCES.

Kiki is a white parrot with a pink crest. She talk and is sometimes a bit rude. William is ta and well-built. He has short brown hair and w a blue jacket and a blue and white scarf and l everything about everything. He is fourteen year and talks like a professor and uses very long wo and reads a lot of books. Jimmy (or Shorty) is s but not fat at all. He has very fair hair, and quite short. He usually wears a camouflage ja and jeans. He also has a blue and white scarf He talks very fast and drops half the words His nose is usually red. He is thirteen years o

**2** Read about Bonnie's gang in England.

**3** Copy and complete this chart with information from Chapter One.

> Name of gang:
> Members of gang:
> boys ☐ girls ☐ other ☐ total ☐
> Age of members:
> Password:

**4** Identify the members of the gang from the pictures (1–6). Don't forget their nickname if they have one.

1 ..... ('Fatty')  2 ..... ('.....')  3 ..... ('.....')
4 .....  5 William  6 .....

**5** a Can you explain the nicknames?
b Who do you think the leader of the gang is? Why?
c Can you explain the password?

**6** The Hideout
The gang has its hideout in a small park called Victory Park. Look at the map and listen to Bonnie's directions. Which of the four places marked on the map (a–d) is the Secret Six hideout?

## B ALL ABOUT YOU

How well do you know your partner? Ask these questions to find out all about him/her. Make notes of the important information and then write a description in four parts. Check it with your partner privately.

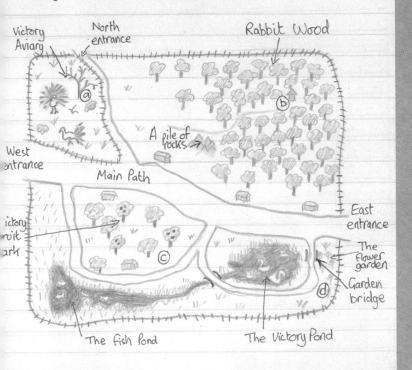

Jack is of average height and wears normal clothes, but he has bright red hair. That's why he's called Ginger. I'm thirteen years old and I have blonde hair. I'm quite good at school. I like adventures and animals. And Kate is just fat. The gang always has a lot of adventures.

**A**

HOME
1 What's your position in the family?
2 How many people live in your home?
3 What jobs do you do in the home?
4 Do you have your own bedroom?

**B**

SCHOOL
1 What subject are you best at?
2 What subject are you not very good at?
3 Are you better at games than academic subjects?
4 Do you prefer arts subjects to science subjects?

**C**

SELF
1 What clothes do you like wearing?
2 What colours do you like wearing?
3 What do you want to be when you grow up?
4 What are you most afraid of?

**D**

FRIENDS
1 What things do you like doing with your friends?
2 What's your best friend's Christian name?
3 When's his/her birthday?
4 What colour are his/her eyes?

## C WHO INFLUENCES YOU?

These people could influence you:

| Entertainers | Parents | Teachers |
| --- | --- | --- |
| | ↘ ↓ ↙ | |
| Religious figures → | You ← | Friends |
| | ↗ ↑ ↖ | |
| Strangers | Neighbours | Relatives |

1 Copy the diagram into your notebook and put a photo of yourself in the middle.
2 Who influences *your* opinions? Put the names of the people who influence you in the correct place on your diagram.
3 Which three people do you listen to most? Why are they so important? How do they influence your opinions?

**D** OPINIONS AND FEELINGS

1 Read about these opinions and feelings.

1 All war is wrong
2 All boys think about is girls, football and showing off
3 All girls think about is clothes, love stories and looking pretty
4 I can smoke if I want – it's my own decision
5 My parents treat me like a baby
6 Women can't have babies *and* a job – they must choose one or the other
7 Fathers should help to look after children as much as mothers do
8 We shouldn't kill animals for food

3 What do your partners think?
Work in groups of four. Find out and record the opinions and feelings of your group.

2 What do you think?
Copy this chart into your notebooks and put a mark in the correct column for your own opinions and feelings about the statements on the left.

|   | Agree strongly | Agree | Not sure | Disagree | Disagree strongly |
|---|---|---|---|---|---|
| 1 |  |  |  |  |  |
| 2 |  |  |  |  |  |
| 3 |  |  |  |  |  |
| 4 |  |  |  |  |  |
| 5 |  |  |  |  |  |
| 6 |  |  |  |  |  |
| 7 |  |  |  |  |  |
| 8 |  |  |  |  |  |

A 'All war is wrong'. What do you think, **B**?
B I agree. What do you think, **C**?
C I'm not sure. What about you, **D**?
D I disagree. And you, **A**, what do you think?
A I agree strongly.
B So that's I *agree strongly*, I *agree*, I *not sure* and I *disagree*. Now, Number 2. 'All boys think . . .'

**E** PERSONAL PROBLEMS

1 Match the speeches (a–c) to the pictures (1–3).

a I only asked her to the cinema – she didn't need to laugh at me.
b Oh shut up – I don't know what's the matter with me.
c You're my best friend, you know how much I love him. How could you go out with him?

2 Read about the organisation called The Samaritans. Is there a similar organisation in your own country?

# the samaritans

If things get too much for you, and you feel worried and lonely, then maybe we can help.
The Samaritans are there when things are too much. We'll listen to you and try to help with your problems.
We won't tell you what to do. We won't tell anyone about you. You don't even have to tell us your name.
You can phone or write or call in at the nearest Samaritan centre (you'll find the address and number in the local telephone book).
Samaritan volunteers can be any age from 17 to 70. They're all good listeners who care about people – so if you want to talk, call us. We're open 24 hours a day, 7 days a week, and it'll cost you nothing.

Scott had never had a girlfriend . . .

It was the worst night of Sally's life . . .

John loves me now. It's not my fault, is it?

Vivian's sister was unhappy again . . .

What are you crying about now?

1

2

3

**Red River Valley**

From this val - ley they say you are go - ing, we will

miss your bright eyes and sweet smile, For they say you are ta - king the

sun - shine that bright - ens our path - way a while.

## Joke spot

1 **Boy:** Can I hold your hand?
  **Girl:** It's not *so* heavy. I can hold it myself.

2 **Brother:** If you have ten Easter eggs and I ask you for five, how many do you have left?
  **Sister:** Ten.

3 John had a present for all his girl-friends. He put them on the table and saw one present between two presents, one present behind two presents, and one present in front of two presents. How many girl-friends did he have?

4 What's always coming but never arrives?
  ˙ʍoɹɹoɯoꓕ

5 Two men robbed a bank. They decided to bury the money they stole. If it takes two men five days to dig a hole, how many days will it take them to dig half a hole?

**Nobody knows the trouble I see**

No - bo - dy knows the trou - ble I see, No - bo - dy knows but

Je - sus, No - bo - dy knows the trou - ble I see,

Glo - ry hal - le - lu - jah. Some - times I'm up some-times I'm down,

Oh yes Lord, some - times I'm al - most to the ground, Oh yes Lord.

# HOLIDAYS

## A  YOUR NEXT HOLIDAY

1  Work in groups of four. Find out about your partners' plans for their next holiday. Then write a short report. Use the models on the right.

> Where are you going to spend your next holiday?

> I don't know.
> .....

2  Group leaders report to the teacher. Use the frames to help you give your information.

| is | going to spend | his | next holiday in . . . |
|---|---|---|---|
| are | | her | |
| | | their | |

| One member | of our group |
|---|---|
| Two members | |

| doesn't | know where | he | is | going to spend | his | next holiday. |
|---|---|---|---|---|---|---|
| | | she | | | her | |
| don't | | they are | | | their | |

## B  FLORIDA – THE SUNSHINE STATE

1  Look at the picture. Would you like to go on holiday there? Why do you think Florida is a good place for holidays?

2  Use the words in the box to fill in the gaps in this extract from a geography book. Use each word once only.

> autumn  blue  good  high  international
> long  private  sandy  warm  wide

RECREATION AND TOURISM

### Florida – the Sunshine State

▽ **Figure 3**  Tourist attractions in Florida

*Miami (see fig. 1) is a major resort for the following reasons:*

**Natural advantages**

- □ [1]..... summer temperatures and [2]..... hours of sunshine :fig. 2) but not too humid because of sea-breezes
- □ [3]..... winters (January 16°C) because of sub-tropical location
- □ Warm, clear, [4]..... seas
- □ Natural sandbars which give 24 km of ..... beaches
- □ A lagoon which gives shelter for yachts against [6]..... hurricanes

**Man-made attractions**

- □ Luxury hotels and [7]..... luxury flats on sandbar (see fig. 1)
- □ Large marinas in lagoon
- □ [8]..... roads
- □ An [9]..... airport (one of the busiest in the world) which makes journeys from North America and Europe easy
- □ A [10]..... range of entertainments e.g. nightclubs, aquariums, zoos, marinas and golf courses
- □ Near to other attractions e.g. Walt Disney World, the Kennedy Space Centre, the Everglades and the coral islands of Key West (see fig. 3)

△ **Figure 1**  Miami Beach
▽ **Figure 2**  'Sunny Florida'

| | April | May | June | July | Aug | Sept | Oct |
|---|---|---|---|---|---|---|---|
| Average monthly temperature (°C) | 25 | 28 | 30 | 31 | 31 | 30 | 28 |
| Average hours of sunshine | 9 | 9 | 8 | 8 | 8 | 7 | 7 |

3  Find the words in the text for these six definitions:

1..... / briːz / n  a light gentle wind
2..... / ləguːn / n  a lake of sea water, partly or completely separated from the sea
3..... / sændbɑː / n  a bank of sand at the mouth of a harbour or river
4..... / hʌrɪkeɪn / n  a storm with a strong fast wind, especially in the West Indies
5..... / ʃɛltə / n  protection
6..... / jɒt / n  a light sailing boat

4  What do you think?
1  In which season is it perhaps better not to go to Miami?
2  What are the three best reasons for going on holiday to Miami? Use the ideas in 2 to help you. Explain your choices.

*Examples*
I think the international airport is very important because then you can travel to Miami very easily.

I don't think the good roads are very important when you are only there on holiday.

## C CHOOSING A PACKAGE HOLIDAY

1 Here is an example of a British holiday company's package holiday to Florida.

Find the words which mean: **a** free **b** meets you and takes you somewhere

2 Work it out
1 How many full days do the holiday-makers have in Miami?
And in Orlando?
2 How many nights do the holiday-makers spend in Miami?
And in Orlando?
3 How many days do the holiday-makers spend travelling?

### Miami + Orlando,
#### 2-Centre Holiday

A relaxing week at the beach in the Florida sunshine, then a week of fun and variety at Orlando. That's a favourite combination and it makes a great holiday.

| | |
|---|---|
| Day 1 | Fly from London to Miami. Hotel representative meets you at the airport and takes you to your hotel. |
| Days 2–7 | At leisure in Miami. |
| Day 8 | Hotel representative takes you to airport. From here you fly to Orlando. Hotel representative collects you. |
| Days 9–14 | At leisure in the Orlando area. |
| Day 15 | Morning transfer to Tampa airport for your homeward flight. |
| Day 16 | Arrive at London airport in the morning. |

## D 🎞 WHAT TO DO ON HOLIDAY

1 These are some of the places you can visit in Florida. Match the pictures to the texts and sort them into two lists – Miami and Orlando. Use the map on p.18 to help you.

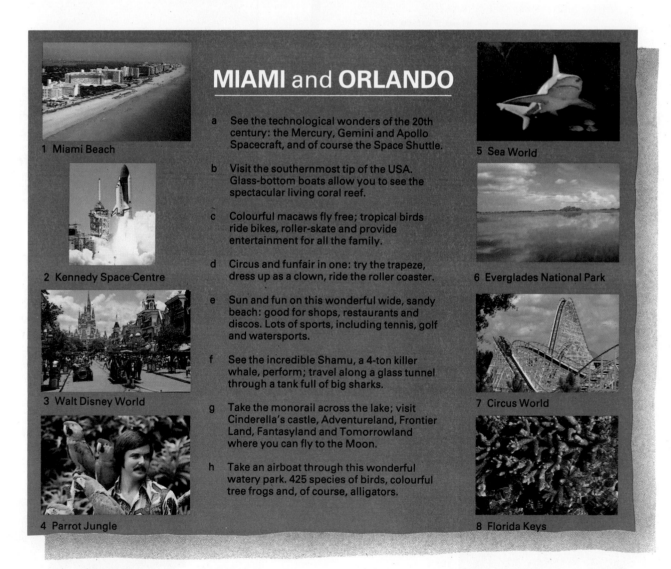

# MIAMI and ORLANDO

1 Miami Beach

2 Kennedy Space Centre

3 Walt Disney World

4 Parrot Jungle

a See the technological wonders of the 20th century: the Mercury, Gemini and Apollo Spacecraft, and of course the Space Shuttle.

b Visit the southernmost tip of the USA. Glass-bottom boats allow you to see the spectacular living coral reef.

c Colourful macaws fly free; tropical birds ride bikes, roller-skate and provide entertainment for all the family.

d Circus and funfair in one: try the trapeze, dress up as a clown, ride the roller coaster.

e Sun and fun on this wonderful wide, sandy beach: good for shops, restaurants and discos. Lots of sports, including tennis, golf and watersports.

f See the incredible Shamu, a 4-ton killer whale, perform; travel along a glass tunnel through a tank full of big sharks.

g Take the monorail across the lake; visit Cinderella's castle, Adventureland, Frontier Land, Fantasyland and Tomorrowland where you can fly to the Moon.

h Take an airboat through this wonderful watery park. 425 species of birds, colourful tree frogs and, of course, alligators.

5 Sea World

6 Everglades National Park

7 Circus World

8 Florida Keys

2 Listen to these young people talking about their interests. Choose the best place for them to visit (from a–h).

1 Rosalind    3 Robert
2 David       4 Deborah

3 Choose three places which you would like to visit. Put them in order of preference. Find out about your partner's choices and explain your own.

**E** MAKING ARRANGEMENTS

1 Read this postcard from a penfriend in Fort Lauderdale, Florida.

> Hi!
> I'm so happy you're coming to Miami for your vacation. Fort Lauderdale, where I live, is near Miami, so at last we can meet!
> What shall we do together? Do you want to go anywhere special. There are lots of interesting things to do here. Shall I meet you at the airport? Send me the details of your vacation — when you're coming where you're staying, etc.
> See you soon, I can't wait!
> Maria

2 Reply to Maria's postcard. Use the information in the letter from the travel agent's.

## TRAVEL AGENTS

This is to confirm your flight to Miami Florida on April 11th. You leave London Gatwick at 09.30 and arrive in Miami at 12.30 local time. Flight number BA 123. You are booked into the Miramar Hotel for 7 nights and fly back April 17th. Flight number BA 124 departs 16.30 arrives in London 05.30 April 18th.

Thank Maria for her postcard
Give her the details of your vacation
Refuse (nicely) her offer to meet you at the airport
Suggest how you will meet
Finish

> ..............................................
> I'm arriving on ......... at ..........
> My flight number ...................
> I'm staying for...... nights at ......
> I'm going back ...................
> Don't worry about the airport — there is a special bus to the hotel.
> ..............................................
> ..............................................

**F** SEA WORLD, ORLANDO

Read this extract from a report Maria made at school after an excursion to Sea World.

## A VISIT TO SEA WORLD

At Sea World, Orlando, there is a special exhibit called Shark Encounter where you can come face to face with a large shark. You can see sharks swim past you, next to you, even over you, and all from a distance of only a few metres. It's completely safe too!

This is a picture of Shark Encounter from above. You can see a huge tank filled with sharks. The tank is the size of four tennis courts and it cost $6 million to build. It contains 3 million litres of sea water.

At the bottom of the tank there is a special walkway. This walkway moves through a glass tunnel across the bottom. It is 42 metres long and gives you a fantastic view of sharks swimming all round you. The glass is ten centimetres thick, this is five times thicker than necessary. 3 million people pass along the walkway each year. Twice a week divers move the sharks to one side with nets and then they vacuum and polish the glass to keep it clean for the visitors.

DID YOU KNOW — some of the scenes from Jaws 3 were made there?

# CHECK YOUR ENGLISH
ENGLISH SPOKEN HERE 🔲

**English for travelling:   cashing travellers cheques**

**You:** I'd like to cash some travellers cheques please.
**Teller:** OK. You need two pieces of identification.
**You:** I've got my passport.
**Teller:** And something else with your photo on.
**You:** I've got an identity card. Is that OK?
**Teller:** Can I see it?
**You:** Yes, here you are.
**Teller:** OK. And can I see your travellers cheques? Are they in dollars?
**You:** Yes.
**Teller:** Fine. So, how much do you want?
**You:** $50 please.
**Teller:** OK. Sign the cheques please.
**You:** Here you are.
**Teller:** And here's your money. Have a nice day.
**You:** Thank you.
**Teller:** You're welcome.

## Statement or question?

*Listen to these sentences. Write down if they are spoken as a statement (s), or as a question (q).*

a   BC 4202
b   13.30
c   New York
d   P-H-I-double L-I-P-S
e   going out on December 15th
f   coming back BC 4203

## Polite or impolite?

*Listen. Mark if the speaker's voice goes up (↗) or down (↘). The first two are done for you.*

a   Hallo   ↗
b   Sit down   ↘
c   No
d   Goodbye
e   Give me your passport
f   Where's your boarding-pass?
g   Go to gate thirty-two
h   Yes

*Which sounds more polite? Rise or fall?*

---

KNOW YOUR GRAMMAR

---

REVIEW: **future time**

### 1   'Going to'

**Form:** *see Book 2, p.21*
**Use:** *for plans or ambitions for the future Example Where are you going to spend your next holiday? (p.18).*
**Exercise:** *Look at your group sentences about the members of the group.*

### 2   Present progressive

**Form:** *see Book 1, p.62*
**Use:** *for fixed plans, which are going to happen soon. We usually include a time word or phrase. Example I'm arriving on April 11th at 12.30 (p.20).*
**Exercise:** *Look at the ticket on p.22. Make sentences about this traveller.*

### 3   Will/shall

**Form:** *see Book 2, p.21*
**Use:** *1   for a 'neutral' future (which the speaker cannot control) Example What will the weather in Orlando be like on Sunday? (p.24) 2   for suggestions and offers Example What shall we do together? (p.20) Shall I meet you at the airport? (p.20)*
**Exercise:** *1   Look at the map on p.24 and make sentences about the weather in other 2   US cities on Sunday. How many examples of Use 2 above can you find on p.24?*

### 4   Simple present

**Form:** *see Book 1, p.48*
**Use:** *For a fixed timetable in the future (for example a travel agent's or a school's) Example Hotel representative meets you at the airport . . . (p.19).*
**Exercise:** *Find four more examples of this way of expressing the future on p.19.*

# GOING ABROAD

## A PACKING

What should you put in your suitcase for a holiday in Miami? Look at the objects in the picture and make a list. Can you think of any other things to take?

*Example*   toothbrush, wallet

## B MONEY

### Currency
The basic unit of currency is the dollar bill* ($1 equals 100 cents). Paper bills also come in $2, $5, $10, $20, $50, $100, $500 and in $1,000 denominations. Although all denominations are of the same color,** the amounts are clearly printed on the bills. Coins are minted in 1¢, 5¢, 10¢, 25¢, and 50¢ denominations.

Penny (1 cent)
100 Pennies = $1.00

Nickel (5 cents)
20 Nickels = $1.00

Dime (10 cents)
10 Dimes = $1.00

Quarter (25 cents)
4 Quarters = $1.00

*note (GB)
**colour (GB)

**currency** / kʌrənsɪ / n    the particular type of money in use in a country: the German currency is among the strongest in the world

**denomination** / dɪnɒmɪneɪʃən / n    a standard of quantity, size, measurement, or especially of value: coins of many denominations

**mint** / mɪnt / v    to make (a coin)

## C  COLLECTING YOUR TICKET

Look at the information on this passenger ticket and baggage check.

Listen to the conversation between a passenger and the travel agent and make notes about the ticket. What is wrong with the ticket?

## D TAKING A PLANE

1   What happens when you take a plane? Complete the flow-chart by adding the missing arrows.

| Go to terminal 90 minutes before departure |

| Check in | ← | Find correct airline desk |

| Say goodbye to your family/friends | Go through passport control and security check |

| Wait in departure lounge for flight call | Go to correct boarding gate |

| Board aircraft and take your seat | Take off (on time, if there has been no delay) |

2   Have you ever travelled by plane? Tell your partner what happened. If you haven't been in a plane, tell your partner what you remember from the flow-chart.

 **E** UP, UP AND AWAY

**1** Look at the picture. Where is the girl? Why is she there? Read below to find out.

Have you ever wanted to go through that special door at the front of the plane? Have you ever wanted to sit next to the captain and watch him fly the plane?

This girl is one of the lucky ones who have been up on the flight deck. That's because she's a member of a special club for young fliers – the British Airways Flightrider Club. And after her visit the captain signed a special certificate for her, and she filled in the details of the flight in her own log book.

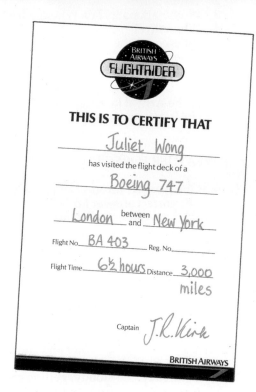

**THIS IS TO CERTIFY THAT**

_Juliet Wong_

has visited the flight deck of a

_Boeing 747_

_London_ between _New York_
and

Flight No. _BA 403_  Reg. No. ___

Flight Time _6½ hours_ Distance _3,000 miles_

Captain _J.R.Kirk_

**BRITISH AIRWAYS**

| Your British Airways Hours and Mileage | | | | | | | |
|---|---|---|---|---|---|---|---|
| Date of Flight | Aircraft & Registration | From | To | Hrs. Mins. | Statute Miles | Seat No. | Crew Signature |
| 11 Feb | Boeing 747 VB-EEK | London | New York | 6.30 | 3,000 | 26A | J.R.Kirk |

**2** Find the answers to these questions in the certificate and log book.

1 Where was Juliet flying to?
2 How far is it from London?
3 How long does it take to get there?
4 What type of plane was she flying?
5 Where did she sit?
6 What was the captain's surname?

**3** Would you like to join the Flightrider Club? Write to this address: Flightrider Club, PO Box 150, High Wycombe, Bucks, England.

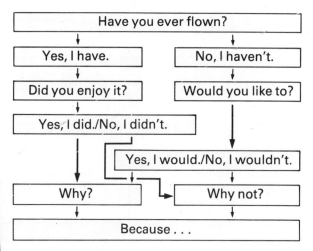

**BRITISH AIRWAYS FLIGHTRIDER**
**APPLICATION FORM**

Please enrol me as a member of the British Airways Flightrider Club. I enclose the 'one-off' subscription fee of £5. This covers my membership of the club from the day of joining until my sixteenth birthday.

NAME
HOME ADDRESS

AGE | DATE OF BIRTH
| DAY MONTH YEAR

POST CODE    COUNTRY    I AM A (Boy/Girl aged 16 or under)

**F** FLYING

**1** Interview your partner and then write a short report. Use the frame below.

```
         Have you ever flown?
          ↓              ↓
   Yes, I have.      No, I haven't.
          ↓              ↓
  Did you enjoy it?  Would you like to?
          ↓              ↓
Yes, I did./No, I didn't.
                  ↓
          Yes, I would./No, I wouldn't.
          ↓              ↓
        Why?          Why not?
          ↓              ↓
            Because . . .
```

**2** Check your report with your partner.

23

## G AT THE AIRPORT

This is a copy of part of the Arrival Record for the United States. You fill it in when you land and you show it to the Customs Official at Immigration. When you leave the country you give it back.

**1** With your partner, write seven questions for the Customs Official for sections 1–7 of the record.
Use the words below to make your questions.
1 What/family name?
What/first name?
2 When/born?
3 What/nationality? OR Where/born?
4 Where/live?
5 Where/stay/the US?
6 Where/get/visa?
7 What/flight number?

**2** Copy the Arrival Record into your notebooks and fill it in for yourself.

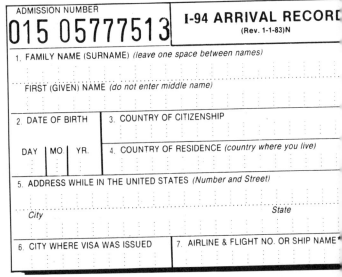

ADMISSION NUMBER
015 05777513    **I-94 ARRIVAL RECORD**
(Rev. 1-1-83)N

1. FAMILY NAME (SURNAME) *(leave one space between names)*

FIRST (GIVEN) NAME *(do not enter middle name)*

2. DATE OF BIRTH    |    3. COUNTRY OF CITIZENSHIP

DAY | MO | YR.    |    4. COUNTRY OF RESIDENCE *(country where you live)*

5. ADDRESS WHILE IN THE UNITED STATES *(Number and Street)*

City    State

6. CITY WHERE VISA WAS ISSUED    |    7. AIRLINE & FLIGHT NO. OR SHIP NAME*

## H WEATHER FORECAST

Look at the weather forecast for January 12th and choose the correct answer for 1–5.
What will the weather in Orlando be like . . .

1 ... on Sunday?     cloudy/fine/hot/wet
2 ... on Monday?     fine but cold/sunny and fine/
                     warm and dry/wet and
                     windy
3 ... on Tuesday?    cloudy and cold/
                     cloudy and warm/
                     fine and warm/fine but cold
4 ... on Wednesday?  cloudy and cold/fine but
                     cold/hot and sunny/warm
                     and wet
5 ... on Thursday?   cloudy, getting colder/
                     fine, getting colder/
                     fine, getting warmer/
                     wet, getting warmer

**3** Role play. Student A look at p.25, Student B look at p.73. When you have finished, change over.

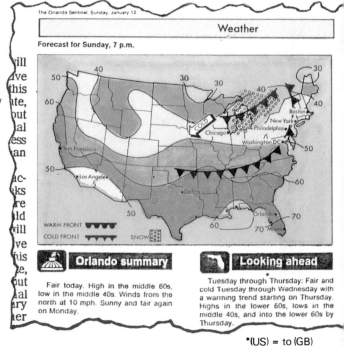

The Orlando Sentinel, Sunday, January 12

Weather

Forecast for Sunday, 7 p.m.

WARM FRONT
COLD FRONT    SNOW

**Orlando summary**
Fair today. High in the middle 60s, low in the middle 40s. Winds from the north at 10 mph. Sunny and fair again on Monday.

**Looking ahead**
Tuesday through Thursday: Fair and cold Tuesday through Wednesday with a warming trend starting on Thursday. Highs in the lower 60s, lows in the middle 40s, and into the lower 60s by Thursday.

*(US) = to (GB)

## I WHAT TO DO?

You have two free days to spend with your penfriend. Make plans for those two days. Look at p.19 for ideas of what to do. Use the frame below to help you.

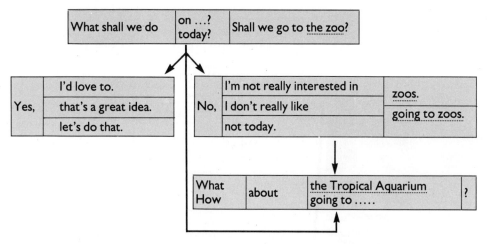

| What shall we do | on ...? today? | Shall we go to the zoo? |

| Yes, | I'd love to. |
| | that's a great idea. |
| | let's do that. |

| No, | I'm not really interested in | zoos. |
| | I don't really like | going to zoos. |
| | not today. | |

| What How | about | the Tropical Aquarium going to ..... | ? |

## J BRITISH? AMERICAN?

Match the British English words to the American English words.

| American English | British English |
|---|---|
| apartment | underground |
| automobile | chemist |
| bathroom | holiday |
| drugstore | motorway |
| elevator | petrol |
| freeway | toilet |
| gas | car |
| subway | flat |
| truck | lift |
| vacation | lorry |

# PROJECT ENGLISH

## TOURISM – A GOOD OR BAD THING?

1   Look at what happens when a country develops its tourist industry (Points 1–10). Do you think these things are good or bad? Give each statement a score.

| Very good | Good | Neither good nor bad | Bad | Very bad |
|-----------|------|----------------------|-----|----------|
| +2 | +1 | 0 | −1 | −2 |

1   Tourists spend money: this brings in foreign money. The country can use this to buy foreign goods.
2   Local craftsmen make things for tourists to buy.
3   Political problems in a country can stop tourists coming.
4   Tourism means airports, roads and hotels.
5   Foreigners own many of the hotels and much of the profit goes abroad.
6   Tourists see little of the real life of the ordinary people.
7   The tourist industry employs many people.
8   Tourism brings social problems with it (e.g. crime, drugs).
9   Hotels buy a lot of local farm produce.
10  Many jobs in the industry are seasonal (e.g. only in the summer).

Now add up your score. Do you think that tourism is a good thing?

2   What else happens to the country? Collect some more ideas – from your partner, your friends, your parents. Add them to points 1 to 10.
    Find out what an adult thinks about tourism. Compare the adult's opinions with your own – are they the same or different?

3   With your teacher's help take a class vote on the question, 'Is tourism a good thing or a bad thing?'

4   Visit your local tourist office. Collect the figures for the foreign visitors to your region or your country in the last year. Make a pie-chart of nationalities for the noticeboard with the title

    FOREIGN VISITORS TO . . . . . IN 19 . .

## Student A role-cards for immigration role-play

♀ 1
Your name is Alicia Gonzalez. You come from Oviedo, Spain. You want to join the family of your grandchild in Florida. All your children are in the United States now.
    Your husband has just died and you can't live by yourself any more.
    Your husband was a baker and you helped him, but you are too old to work any more.
    You have a little Spanish money with you and some pieces of gold jewellery.
    Your health is not bad for your age but you have had two bad falls – on one occasion you broke a leg. You were very sea-sick on the journey but you're feeling better now.
    You know very little English.

♂ 2
Your name is Abraham Mankes. You come from Amsterdam, Holland. You have a sister in Massachusetts (the writer of letter 4 on p. 7). She has written to you telling you to come and join her.
    Business is not very good and people say that the United States is a land of opportunity. You'd like to open another tobacco shop there and you know that Virginian tobacco is very good.
    You have sold your shop and brought all your money with you.
    Your health is all right, but you have had a lot of problems with your teeth.
    You speak a little English. When you were young you were a sailor and so you learned several languages.

### Student A – Passenger

Give your Arrival Report to the Customs Officer. Answer his/her questions politely. It is very important to give him/her the correct information. Remember – s/he can refuse to let you enter the country.

## Word puzzle

Fill in this word puzzle with the British/English form of the words in the clues.

*Example:* truck (US)   lorry (GB)

1   Gas
2   Bill (as in 'five dollar bill')
3   Subway
4   Cookie
5   Apartment
6   Semester
7   Drugstore
8   Elevator
9   Automobile
10  Bathroom
11  Vacations

# POETRY AND ART

 **A** COLOUR

**1 Preparation**

1 Look through Units 1–3 of this book. How many examples of these colours can you find in five minutes?

pink red blue white yellow violet orange

Make lists for each colour.

2 What colours do you associate with the four seasons? Choose two colours for each season.

3 Look at the illustrations round the poem below. Do you know the names for these things in English? (If not, you will find them in the poem.)

**2 Reading a poem**

1 Listen to the poem and follow in your books.

2 Find the names of the things in the illustrations and add them to your colour lists.

**3 Dictionary work**

Find the words in the poem for these five definitions:

**Example:**

**mellow** / mɛləʊ / adj   sweet and ready to eat

1 ..... / brɪŋk / n   the edge
2 ..... / fləʊt / v   to move on water or in the air without falling
3 ..... / raɪp / adj   (of fruit and vegetables) ready to pick and eat
4 ..... / twaɪlaɪt / n   the time when day becomes night

**4 Rhyme and stress**

1 In the poem find the pairs of rhymes for these vowel sounds:

/e/  /ɪ/  /iː/  /uː/  /aɪ/

How many different spellings can you find for the same sound?

2 Look at the rhythm pattern for the first two lines.
What is <u>pink</u>? A <u>rose</u> is <u>pink</u> __ v __ v __ v __
<u>By</u> the <u>fountain's</u> <u>brink</u>   __ v __ v __

Underline the stressed syllables in the rest of the poem. Then listen again and check your ideas.

3 With your partner, practise reading the poem aloud.

**5** What did you think of the poem?
Work in groups of four. Group leaders collect the votes for your group.

very good   good   all right   not very good   terrible

---

**WHAT IS PINK?**

*What is pink? A rose is pink*
*By the fountain's brink.*

*What is red? A poppy's red*
*In its barley bed.*

*What is blue? The sky is blue*
*Where the clouds float through.*

*What is white? A swan is white*
*Sailing in the light.*

*What is yellow? Pears are yellow*
*Rich and ripe and mellow.*

*What is green? The grass is green*
*With small flowers between.*

*What is violet? Clouds are violet*
*In the summer twilight.*

*What is orange? Why, an orange,*
*Just an orange.*

*Christina Rossetti*

---

**Did you know?**
About 8 per cent of men and 0.4 per cent of women are slightly colour-blind. (This usually means it is difficult to see the difference between red, green and brown).
Our eyes are able to see nearly 8,000,000 shades of colour.

1 Look at these examples of American Art. Can you find something
  a amusing  b frightening  c colourful  d stupid?

1

2

3

4

5

6

2 Sort the words in the two boxes into positive (+) and negative (−).

| Impressions | Feelings |
|---|---|
| amusing  boring  colourful  crazy  exciting  frightening  interesting  nice  stupid  violent | afraid  angry  bored  cheerful  happy  peaceful  sad  worried |

3 What are your impressions and feelings about this kind of painting and sculpture? Tell your partner. Use the words in the boxes and this frame to help you.

| I (really) | hate<br>don't like<br>like<br>love | it.<br>this one. | I think it's ......<br>It makes me feel ...... |
|---|---|---|---|

4 Class vote
  1 Choose your three favourite works of art. Give three marks to your first choice, two for your second and one for your third.
  2 Work in groups of four. Organise your group's three favourites (in order of preference).
  3 Group leaders work with your teacher to decide the class vote.
  4 Record the class vote. Do you agree with this? Tell your partner what you feel.

**C**  ENTERTAINMENT

**1** Ask yourself these questions.
Answer **Yes** or **No**.

Have you ever been to ...

a an art gallery?
b the ballet?
c a classical concert?
d an exhibition?
e a folk concert?
f the opera?
g a pop concert?
h the theatre?

**2** Our reporter, Deborah Tyler, is at the Brooklyn
Academy of Dramatic Arts. She is interviewing
two students there, Benny and Kimberley,
about their favourite forms of entertainment.

  1 Listen to the two interviews and make notes
    about the two students' likes and dislikes.
  2 Put the list of forms of entertainment in
    order of importance for each student.

**3** Interview your partner using the questions
in **1** above.

**4** Write a report about your partner and then
check it with him/her. Use these examples to
help you.

*Benny has never been to a pop concert.*
*Kimberley has been to classical concerts.*
*Benny likes going to photographic exhibitions.*
*Kimberley doesn't like folk music.*

**D** GOING OUT

There are two dialogues here. In one, a person is asking about tickets
for a pop concert, in the other about a special exhibition. Choose one
dialogue and copy it into your notebooks.

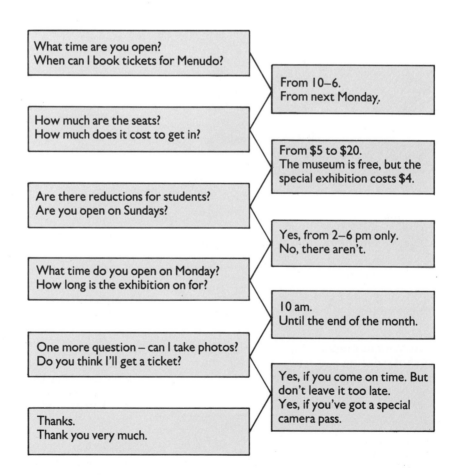

| | |
|---|---|
| What time are you open?<br>When can I book tickets for Menudo? | From 10–6.<br>From next Monday. |
| How much are the seats?<br>How much does it cost to get in? | From $5 to $20.<br>The museum is free, but the special exhibition costs $4. |
| Are there reductions for students?<br>Are you open on Sundays? | Yes, from 2–6 pm only.<br>No, there aren't. |
| What time do you open on Monday?<br>How long is the exhibition on for? | 10 am.<br>Until the end of the month. |
| One more question – can I take photos?<br>Do you think I'll get a ticket? | Yes, if you come on time. But don't leave it too late.<br>Yes, if you've got a special camera pass. |
| Thanks.<br>Thank you very much. | |

Read your dialogue through with your partner. Then try to memorise it.

# CHECK YOUR ENGLISH

 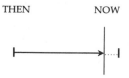

**English for travelling: talking about English**

| | |
|---|---|
| **Jesse:** | You speak English very well. |
| **You:** | Really? |
| **Jesse:** | Yes, I mean it. |
| **You:** | Thank you. |
| **Jesse:** | Where did you learn it? |
| **You:** | ................................................ |
| **Jesse:** | How long have you been learning it for? |
| **You:** | ................................................ |
| **Jesse:** | And do you like learning English? |
| **You:** | ................................................ |
| **Jesse:** | Can you understand us Americans? |
| **You:** | ................................................ |

**A  Finished or unfinished?**
*In the following sentences does the speaker's voice go down ( ↘ ) or down and up ( ↘↗ )? The first two are done for you.*

a  It's grèat  →
b  This one's nice ↘↗
c  I like it
d  I like it
e  It's all right
f  I think folk music is awful
g  I don't really like opera
h  This one's OK

**B**  *Are these sentences finished? If not, finish them in your own way.*

*Example*   Menudo's nice.
   Menudo's nice (but I prefer Pari Match).

1  The poem's all right
2  This picture makes me feel happy
3  I've never been to the ballet before
4  The museum is free

————————— KNOW YOUR GRAMMAR —————————

REVIEW: **the present tense: past time**

**1  Present perfect**

**Form:**  *see Book 2, p.61*
**Use:**  *for actions, habits and states*
   1  *which begin in the past (THEN) and continue up to the present (NOW)*
   2  *which happen some time before NOW but we don't know when*

| THEN | NOW |
|---|---|
| 1 | ————————→ |
| 2 | ?←———————— |

*Examples*
The members of the group have always been the same age. (p.30)
I've started wearing make-up.
I've loved music all my life.
They have made songs against drugs.(p.30)

   3  *with expressions of indefinite time:*
   *e.g.* ever, never, yet, already, just *(or* recently), for, since, before

*Examples*
Have you ever been to an art gallery? (p.28)

I've never been to the opera before. (p.28)

He's already recorded a Spanish language version of *She Works Hard for the Money.* (p.30)

*Differences between the present perfect and the simple past:*
1  *there is no gap between* THEN *and* NOW. *If there is a gap you must use Simple Past.*
2  *you can't use expressions of* **definite** *time* (**point of time** *or* **period of time** *expressions*) *with the present perfect. If you want to use these expressions, then you must use the simple past.*

**Exercise:**
*Find examples of the present perfect in Unit 4, Lesson 2.*

**2  Present perfect progressive**
**Form:**  *have/has (not) + been + the 'ing' form*
*Example* We've been rehearsing hard.

**Use:** *for an action verb (see p. 30) which*
   1  *started in the past and is continuing now*
   2  *is temporary*
   3  *is not finished*

| THEN | NOW |
|---|---|
| ⊢————————→ ⊣ |

*Example* They have been making records and bringing pleasure to millions of fans since then.

# MUSIC

## A FACTS, FIGURES AND MENUDO

Read about Menudo, then copy and complete these facts about the group.

Do you know this group? If you have heard their music or bought their records, you will know that they are very special. And not just because of their music.

Menudo started in 1977 in Puerto Rico. The five guys in the group have always sung the same sort of music. They have also always been the same age. 'How?', you ask. Because the boys who sing and play in the group don't stay there for long. They change all the time – when one reaches his sixteenth birthday, or when his voice breaks, he has to leave and another boy takes his place. That way everything stays the same – except for the boys themselves! There have been more than fifteen boys in the group and the numbers are rising all the time.

There is even a fan-club for the ex-members of the group.

Menudo signed their first recording contract in November 1983. Since then they have been making records, appearing on television, touring and bringing pleasure to millions of fans. They have fans in the States, in Central America, in South America and in Japan.

These are some of the highspots of Menudo's career:

– they have recorded over 65 songs and made seven albums

– they have had a Saturday morning TV series in the States

– they have made songs against drugs

– they were the first International Youth Ambassadors for UNICEF

– they took part in the Tokyo Music Festival, a yearly competition for artists from all over the world

1 There are . . . . . guys in the group.
2 Menudo started . . . . . years ago.
3 No boy in the group can be older than . . . . . .
4 There have been more than . . . . . boys in the group.
5 They have recorded . . . . . songs.
6 They have made . . . . . albums.

## B MEET A MENUDO MAN

Now meet Ray Acevedo, the newest addition to the group. His dream has just come true and now he's a Menudo Man! In case you don't know it already, Ray is five feet five inches* tall, and weighs 82 pounds**, with brown hair and eyes. His favorite*** sports are basketball, baseball and volleyball and he just *loves* comic books. He has been in showbusiness for a while now. He's already recorded a Spanish language version of the Donna Summer hit 'She Works Hard For The Money' and that was a hit on radio stations all over Puerto Rico. But that success was nothing like this. 'I feel on top of the world,' he says. 'Watch out – the Fiery Five are on their way!'

Find the words for:
a   for some time
b   fantastic

* one inch = 2.5cm
** one pound = 0.45kg
*** favourite (GB)

## C GAME: WHO IS IT?

Look at the description of Ray Acevedo. Write a similar description of your favourite pop star. Include: physical description, nationality, and the name of one hit but *not* the name of your star. Work in groups of four. Read each others' descriptions: can you guess who the other pop stars are?

Helen sings in a band called Pari Match.
Listen to her story about how the group started
and put these eight pictures in the correct order.
Look through the pictures before you listen.

A

B
Have you heard anything yet?

Nothing.

C
We've been rehearsing hard and we want to make a demo-tape.

D
Here are your copies.

Thanks.

E
SIX WEEKS LATER
Did you have a good holiday?

Yes, great thanks.

F
I know these two boys – they're looking for a singer.

G
I've written some songs – shall we try them?

H
Hi, I'm Helen, Ruth's sister.

I'm James.

I'm Al.

**E** MAKING A RECORD

1   Do you know how a record is made? Look at the picture sequence to find out.

1    2    3    4    5    6

2   Match the sentences (a–f) to the pictures.

a   . . . . . you put down the vocals.
b   . . . . . you explain your ideas to the producer.
c   . . . . . the sound engineer sets his instruments and checks the sound levels.
d   . . . . . you book a recording studio.
e   . . . . . you put down the instrumentals.
f   . . . . . the producer mixes the sound.

3   Write about making a record. Follow the order of the pictures. Use sentences a–f and put the correct time word or phrase from the box below in the gaps. Begin with d. Don't forget to give a title to your description.

at that time / first / and lastly / then / after that / on the day of the recording

31

**F** POP STAR INTERVIEW

Student A – interviewer – copy out this form.
Student B choose one member of Pari Match (for
Helen, look at p.9; for James p.33; for Al p.57).

> How long have you been in Pari Match?

> Have you been in any other groups before?

> Have you ever had another job?

> Have you visited the USA yet?

**PROFILE (for Pari Match)**
Full name:
Born:
Time in group:
Previous group(s):
Job(s):
Ambition:
Ideal holiday:
Best friend:
Hero:
Heroine:

**G** MENUDO OR PARI MATCH?

**1** Sort these adjectives into the columns below.

| wonderful | horrible | nothing special | fantastic | good |
|---|---|---|---|---|
| lovely | OK | bad | ugly | awful |
| not very good | great | no good | terrible | all right |

| − − − | − − | − | + | + + | + + + |
|---|---|---|---|---|---|
| . . . . . | . . . . . | . . . . . | . . . . . | . . . . . | . . . . . |
| . . . . . | . . . . . | . . . . . | . . . . . | . . . . . | . . . . . |
| . . . . . | . . . . . | . . . . . | . . . . . | . . . . . | . . . . . |

**2** Listen to these American boys and girls talking about Menudo or Pari Match. Which does each prefer?

a Jack
c Bobby
b Valerie
d Eileen

**3** Which do you prefer? Why? Work in groups of four: use the language on page 27 and the words in **1** to help you.

**H** COULD YOU BE A POP STAR?

What does it take to be a pop star? Look at the following list. Give each statement a score.

| very important | 2 |
|---|---|
| quite important | 1 |
| not important | 0 |

If you think something is not important, give an example of a pop star who *can't* sing, who *hasn't* got a beautiful voice, etc.

**To be a pop star you must**
1 be able to sing
2 have a beautiful voice
3 be good-looking
4 be tall
5 be able to play an instrument
6 be able to read music
7 be able to dance well
8 have a lot of money
9 be unmarried
10 be able to write songs
11 want to be a star
12 know the right people

**I** HOW I'VE CHANGED

**1** Find two photos of yourself: one when you were 10 or 11, and a recent one. Stick them on a piece of card.

**2** How have you changed? Make notes under the headings.

|  | THEN 19__ | NOW 19__ |
|---|---|---|
| 1 *Size* (Height) | .................... | .................... |
| (Weight) | .................... | .................... |
| 2 *Looks* (Clothes) | .................... | .................... |
| (Style) | .................... | .................... |
| 3 *Friends* (Boys) | .................... | .................... |
| (Girls) | .................... | .................... |
| 4 *School record* | .................... | .................... |
| 5 *Favourite things* | .................... | .................... |
| 6 *Interests* | .................... | .................... |

**3** Tell your partner about the changes in your life.

> 1 I've grown ... cm.
> 2 I've stopped wearing .....
> 3 I've made a new friend, .....
> 4 I've started learning .....
> 5 I've become interested in .....
> 6 I've read .....

# ENJOY YOUR ENGLISH

**Blowing in the wind**

How many roads must a man walk down before you can call him a man? Yes 'n' how many seas must a white dove sail before she sleeps in the sand? Yes 'n' how many times must the cannon-balls fly before they're forever banned? The answer my friend is blowin' in the wind, the answer is blowin' in the wind.

Full name: James Alexander Seldman (or Jay Alex in conversation)
Born: 6th February 1968
Time in group: joined April 1985
Previous group(s): Cats Under Pressure
Job(s): none
Best friend: myself
Hero: Boy George
Heroine: Boy George
Ideal holiday: six months on a Greenpeace ship
Ambition: to meet Kate Bush; to have a Number 1 in the States

## STUDENT B

1 Kennedy's wife had dark hair, spoke French very well and was twenty-four when she married Kennedy.
2 Kennedy had a secretary called Lincoln.
3 After Kennedy's death Lyndon Johnson, the Vice-President, became President.
4 Oswald killed Kennedy on a Friday.
5 Oswald killed Kennedy by shooting him in the head.
6 Oswald shot Kennedy from a shop and then ran into a theatre.
7 Oswald was born in 1939.
8 Lyndon Johnson was born in 1908.
9 Kennedy's father Joseph was Ambassador to London.
10 Kennedy was sitting in a car when Oswald shot him.

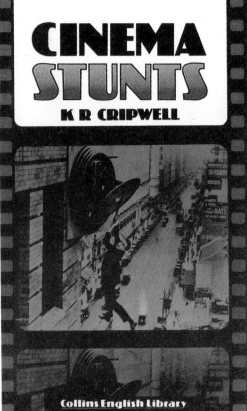

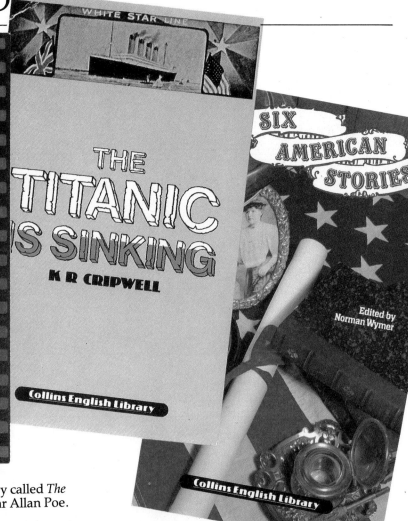

**1** This is an extract from a short story called *The Murders in the Rue Morgue* by Edgar Allan Poe.

'STRANGE MURDERS: During the night people living in the Rue Morgue were woken from sleep by fearful cries. They came from a large house where two women lived – Madame L'Espanaye and her daughter, Camille.

'Neighbours broke into the house. At once the cries stopped. Instead, two angry voices from a floor above were heard. These sounds then suddenly stopped. The men ran up the stairs and looked in all the rooms on three floors. All were empty.

'Then they came to a large room at the back of the house. The door was fastened *inside*. They broke open the door – and a fearful sight met their eyes.

'The room was a wreck. Furniture was destroyed. A knife, covered with blood, lay on a chair. A woman's long grey hair, pulled out by the roots, hung over a bed. On the floor, there were jewels, silver spoons, and three bags of gold coins.

'The body of the daughter, Camille, was found in the chimney. It was pushed hard up that small hole through the roof, and the head was hanging downwards. It took six strong men to pull the body out of the chimney. Round the woman's neck there were deep finger marks of a very large hand.'

There are many unanswered questions in this extract. Which questions are important? Make a list. Then turn the book upside-down and look at the list at the bottom of the page.

Are there any other questions you would like to ask?

So, what do you think has happened and why? If you want to know the answers, you'll have to look in *Six American Stories*.

– Where was Madame L'Espanaye?
– How was this possible?
– Who pushed Camille's body up the chimney?
– Why were there jewels, silver spoons and three bags of gold coins on the floor?
– Who pulled the woman's hair out?
– Whose knife was covered with blood?
– Why was the furniture destroyed?
– Who fastened the door from the inside?
– Why did these sounds suddenly stop?
– Who did the two angry voices belong to?
– Why did the cries stop when the neighbours broke into the house?
– Why did these two women live together?

**2**  This is an extract from a book called *Cinema Stunts* by K. R. Cripwell.

1

Canutt fixed a ring under the underlined saddle of a horse. Then he took a rope and fastened it to a post in the ground. He took the other end and passed it through the ring on the saddle. Then he tied the rope in turn to each leg. The rope looked like a W under the horse. This is why the stunt is called the Running W.

2

What do the underlined words mean? Use the pictures to help you explain.

Can you see the **W** under the horse? In which picture can you see it? What do you think happened after Picture 2?

Here are some more famous cinema stunts.

If you are interested in knowing how these stunts were filmed, read the book!

**3**  This is an extract from a book called *The Titanic is Sinking* by K. R. Cripwell.

One after another the lifeboats dropped into the sea.

One old woman cried out, 'Don't put me in the boat. I don't want to go in the boat. I've never been in an open boat before.'

'You must go,' said an officer.

Most people went quietly. Some of the passengers could not speak English. They could not understand the officers and the officers could not understand them. Many of the third-class passengers became afraid. Some got into boats but many did not. They ran from one place to another. They asked questions and did not wait for answers.

Most of the boats were now gone. One by one they left the side of the *Titanic*. From the boats all eyes were on the ship. They could see the people. They could see the lights. And they could hear the music of the ship's band. It was happy dance music.

1  What's happening?
Is the ship leaving harbour?
        going down?
        coming into harbour?

2  Do you know this story? If so . . .
   a  which country is the ship going to – England? Russia? Spain? the USA?
   b  Who are the third-class passengers? Why can't some of them speak English? Where have they come from and where are they going?
   c  Why is the ship's band still playing?

# TEEN Machine

## MENUDO

MENUDO AND GIRLS – WHAT DO THEY LIKE BEST?

Roy Rosello

**Ricky Martin** – I love girls who smile all the time. Laughing and having a good time is very important to me and I like to share that with a girl. Which girl? Well, I love Brooke Shields movies . . .

Ricky Martin

**Roy Rosello** – I like friendly girls. I don't like proud girls at all. I haven't dated a fan yet, but maybe . . . The best thing for a girl who wants to meet me is just to be friendly.

Charlie Rivera

**Charlie Rivera** – Right now I'm not thinking about marriage. But in the future I'll look for a girl who is sincere, intelligent and knows how to cook! Cooking is very important in my house, because I love to eat.

Ray Reyes Leon

**Ray Reyes Leon** – I like a girl who is sincere, friendly and happy. When I say happy I mean a girl who likes laughing and who makes me laugh. I also like girls who are feminine in the way they dress and look.

**Robby Rosa** – If I date a girl she has to like me for myself and not because I'm famous and in Menudo. I respect sincerity and I like girls who respect it too. Of course it's nice if she's intelligent, kind and makes me laugh too!

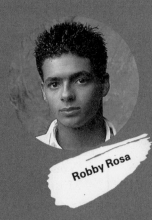
Robby Rosa

Dear *Teen Machine*,
Hi! I am 16 years old and in the 10th grade. I love your magazine a lot. Keep it up! I love Menudo very much! I am a real big fan of Roy Rosello! Can you give me some information about him? I would really love it!
Monika Lamontagne
Sanford, Maine

Dear Monika,
Here's the lowdown on our boy Roy. His mom's name is Miriam Diaz, and his pop answers to Juan Rosello. Roy has two brothers and one sister. He's really into soccer. As a matter of fact, he was in Puerto Rico's Children's National Soccer Team! Feed him corned beef, and he'll be a very happy guy. As for music, Pink Floyd's his fave group. Roy plans to go on singing no matter where life takes him.

Girls – which Menudo guy is the one for you?    Boys – which Menudo guy do you agree with most?

36

## ● THE COLOUR TEST

*You need:* seven coins this size

*What to do:* Look at the eight colours in the paintbox. Which do you like best? Write the name of the colour next to (a) in the chart below. Cover the colour in the paintbox with one of your coins. Which colour do you like best now? Write the name next to (b) and cover the colour with a coin. Continue until you have filled in the chart.

Now turn the book upside-down to find out about your personality.

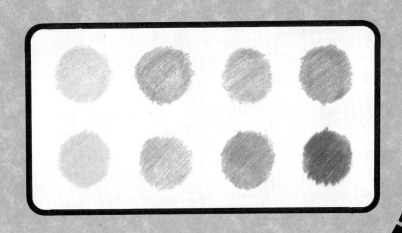

| 1 | 2 | 3 | 4 |
|---|---|---|---|
| a ......... | c ......... | e ......... | g ......... |
| b ......... | d ......... | f ......... | h ......... |

# FIND OUT ABOUT YOUR PERSONALITY

## ● FIND THE STARS

Find the American and British singers and groups in this puzzle. There is a prize-winning name – the one diagonal name. The rest are either vertical or horizontal. There are at least 15 including the prize-winning name.

```
D T S P A U L Y O U N G G
A U P P A R I M A T C H H
V S R F B R A E P T Y N
I I I A H A D Z R I W O
D V N D N O E K I N G T
S L G M A D O N N A L N
Y E S E J U U F C T E O
L B T S A N W R E U A S
V R E M G E H A A R H K
I U E I G M A L R N C C
A C N C E T M G O E I A
N E X K R W E S T R M J
```

## HOW TO INTERPRET THE COLOUR TEST

Note: the meaning of each colour depends on its position in the four pairs 1–4. Find out about your personality now!

Note: there are over 40,000 different ways of putting these colours in order of importance. Each way shows a different personality. It takes a whole book to interpret individual choices properly. The meanings here are approximate. Don't take them too seriously!

**GREY**
1st pair: you don't like being active
2nd pair: it's difficult for you to get what you want
3rd pair: you like being active, but you won't fight with anyone
4th pair: you are impatient

**BROWN**
1st pair: you don't like any difficulties in your life
2nd pair: you feel uncomfortable and helpless
3rd pair: you like food and drink and the good things in life
4th pair: you want other people to like you

**BLACK**
1st pair: you find life difficult
2nd pair: you are not happy with things
3rd pair: you don't get everything you want
4th pair: you want to be independent

**VIOLET**
1st pair: you are romantic
2nd pair: you need to express yourself carefully
3rd pair: you get angry easily
4th pair: you like people who tell the truth

**YELLOW**
1st pair: you want a change in your life
2nd pair: you like anything new
3rd pair: you need to have your friends with you
4th pair: you can't get what you want

**RED**
1st pair: you like to be active and to enjoy yourself
2nd pair: you want to be more successful than you are
3rd pair: you need peace and quiet
4th pair: you feel helpless

**GREEN**
1st pair: you want to be independent
2nd pair: you must get what you want
3rd pair: you are optimistic
4th pair: you can be negative and passive

**BLUE**
1st pair: you are looking for peace and quiet
2nd pair: you are quiet and responsible
3rd pair: you like to be independent
4th pair: you are never still

37

## *Fashion Tips*
### Accessories

**How to make them work for you**

**If you're short,** wear a lot at head or neck level: this brings people's eyes up and makes you look taller. Try hats, big earrings, lots of necklaces, men's ties, lots of brooches, a lace scarf in your hair or at your neck.

**If you're tall,** bring people's eyes down by wearing accessories below the waist. Wear low belts and exciting socks, shoes and boots.

**If you're heavy,** don't wear belts and keep your accessories small and elegant. Don't wear accessories near the heaviest part of your body.

**If you're thin,** wear as many accessories as possible. Belts, scarves, jewellery, everything.

# Acne

ACNE — 'spots*' — is very common in adolescence: four out of five teenagers suffer from it in some way. But for most teenagers it is not serious and sooner or later it gets better. If you have acne, you can do several things to help the problem.

## WHAT TO DO ABOUT SPOTS

**DO**
- regularly wash problem areas with hot water: rub your skin vigorously and dry yourself with a rough, dry towel
- wash your hair often, and keep it off your face
- keep brushes, combs, towels etc, as clean as possible
- stop wearing make-up if possible
- get as much sunshine as you can

**DON'T**
- use too much soap when you wash — your skin will produce too much oil
- use oily shampoos and cosmetics
- put creams on dirty skin
- leave make-up on overnight
- eat foods which seem to give you spots

### DANGERS
1   If you pick and squeeze spots, you can cause secondary infection: this may leave severe scars on the skin.
2   Acne can also cause psychological problems: it can make a normal, happy teenager worried and depressed.

### REMEMBER
Acne doesn't last for ever. Usually there is one bad year and then things get better.

## *Dear Doctor*

Q   I have very bad acne. Should I go to the doctor?

A   Yes. Your doctor can give you antibiotics to control the secondary infection. S/he can also give you advice about what to do.

Q   Does chocolate cause spots?

A   It can do. Some foods can cause spots and you should stop eating them if possible. But other things, apart from diet, cause acne.

Q   Do boys get worse spots than girls?

A   Generally yes, because male hormones can help to cause acne. Female hormones can help to stop it.

*pimples (US)

## *Ways of seeing*

When you go to the optician, s/he tests just your sight.

If you can read all the lines on the card from a distance of two metres, your eyesight is very good.

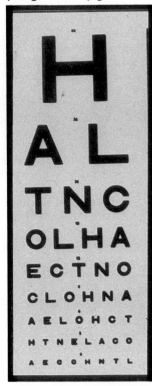

But s/he doesn't test how your brain interprets what it sees. What is this for example?

It can be difficult to recognise familiar objects from an unfamiliar angle.

---

People who are colour-blind can't see the numerals on this card.

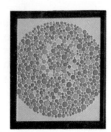

What do you see here – two faces or a vase?

Sometimes the brain makes mistakes because of its habit of seeing things together.

Can you see an animal here?

## *Tricks which the eye can play*

◄ What is wrong with this picture?

▼ And a trick for your eye.

Look at this strange-coloured US flag for 30 seconds without blinking. Then look at a piece of white paper. You should see the flag in its true colours. (This is called an 'after-image'.)

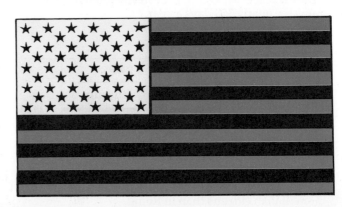

# THE USA: FACTS AND FIGURES

## A FACTS IN BRIEF

**Capital:**
Washington, D.C.

**Area:**
9,371,839 square kilometres. The USA is the fourth largest country in the world (after The Soviet Union, Canada and China).

**Population:**
226,545,805

**National Holidays:**

| | |
|---|---|
| Jan 1st | New Year's Day |
| Jan 20th | Martin Luther King's Birthday |
| Feb 17th | Washington's Birthday |
| May 26th | Memorial Day |
| July 4th | Independence Day |
| Sept (1st Monday) | Labour Day |
| Nov 11th | Veterans Day |
| Nov (4th Thursday) | Thanksgiving Day |
| Dec 25th | Christmas Day |

## B PEOPLE

**Populations of major cities:**

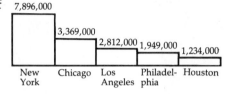

**Religions:**
Of the most common religions in the USA there are:

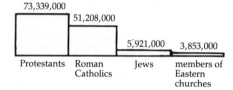

**Languages:**
The principal foreign languages spoken in the USA are:

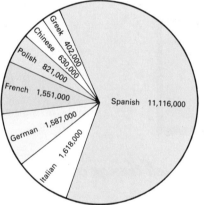

**Entertainment:**
*TV* – 99 per cent of American homes have a TV. There are about 150 million TV sets in the USA. In some places you can choose from more than 12 channels. Some of these are on the air 24 hours a day.
*Cinema* – the *drive-in cinema* is something very American. You watch the film from your car: you drive in to the cinema car park and park near a post with a speaker. You pull the speaker into your car to hear the sound. The largest drive-in in the world is in New Haven, Connecticut with room for 4,000 cars.
There are also drive-in restaurants (with waiters and waitresses on roller skates), banks and even churches.

**Travel:**
*Automobiles* – in 1984 there were 124,821,000 automobiles in the USA for 147,075,000 drivers. There are over six million kilometres of road; many of the highways have between four and 12 lanes.
*Air* – the world's busiest airport, O'Hare in Chicago, handles more than one take-off or landing every minute, 24 hours a day.

> **Did you know?**
> There are no thirteenth floors in American buildings. The Americans are very superstitious and so the lift* goes from the 12th to the 14th floor.

*(US) elevator

## C CLIMATE

Hottest temperature ever recorded: 56.7°C Death Valley, California, July 10th 1913.

Coldest temperature ever recorded: −60°C Tanana, Alaska.

Wettest place: Mt Wai-'ale'ale in Hawaii where it rains for nearly 360 days a year.

Did you know?

| The world's | largest | garage | is in | Chicago (O'Hare airport). |
|---|---|---|---|---|
| | | museum | | New York (the Museum of National History). |
| | highest | shop | | New York (Macy's). |
| | | building | | Chicago (the Sears Roebuck Tower – 443 metres high, 115 storeys). |

In New York City there are more Irish citizens than in Dublin, more Jewish citizens than in Tel Aviv and more Italian citizens than in Rome.

# TEST YOUR ENGLISH

## A 📼 WHAT DO YOU SAY?

Listen to the question on the cassette and choose the correct answer a, b or c.

1. a No, it's in Florida.
   b Yes, it is.
   c Miami's in Florida.

2. a I had breakfast.
   b I've had breakfast.
   c I was having breakfast.

3. a Yes, I did.
   b Yes, I have.
   c Yes, I was.

4. a For three days.
   b Three days ago.
   c I was ill last night.

## B 📼 CORRECT THE MISTAKES

Listen to this news report about the Mexican earthquake of September 20th 1985. Then correct the mistakes in Sentences 1–5 and write out the correct sentences in full.

*Example* The earthquake in Mexico was smaller [bigger] than the San Francisco earthquake of 1906.

1. First reports say that thousands of people have died.
2. Mexico City, with a population of 15 million, is the world's largest city.
3. The only news coming out of Mexico at the moment is by telephone.
4. The earthquake hit Mexico at 7.19 this evening just as people were getting ready to leave work.
5. It lasted for 15 seconds.

## C COPY AND COMPLETE

Choose the correct words for the boxes and put the verbs in brackets in the correct tense.

### The start of the American Revolution

[____] British soldiers in Boston [1](want) to go to Concord to take away the colonists' guns. [____] [2](want) to arrest two colonial leaders, Samuel Adams and John Hancock.
[____] the colonists [3](find out) about the British plans. [____] [4](have) just one problem: they [5](not know) which way the British would come – by land or by sea?
[____] [6](agree) on a signal: one light in a Boston church tower if the British were coming by land, two if they [7](come) by sea.
[____] a colonist [8](watch) the church tower. His horse [9](be) ready. [____] he [10](see) two lights in the church tower. [____] [11](get) on his horse and [12](ride) through the night. He [13](tell) the colonists that the redcoats [14](come) by sea.
[____] the American soldiers [15](be) ready to meet the British at a small village called Lexington. Someone [16](fire) a shot and the American War of Independence [17](begin). The American soldiers [18](not fight) for long [____] when the British [19](arrive) in Concord they [20](can not) find any guns, nor the two men.

| but | so they |
|-----|---------|
| but | suddenly |
| he | that night |
| in 1775 | they |
| so | they also |

## D TRUE OR FALSE?

Read the information extracts about the two big London airports and then do Questions 1–8

### Heathrow
Heathrow is the world's busiest international airport with 29 million passengers a year – 24 million international and 5 million domestic. It has four terminals: Terminal 1 – British Airways, UK carriers, and domestic shuttles. Terminal 2 – European airlines. Terminal 3 – Intercontinental services. Terminal 4 – Concorde.

The site lies 15 miles to the west of London, just off the M4, linked to the London Underground network by the Piccadilly line. It occupies 2,958 acres, employs 45,000 people, and enables 74 airlines to operate over 260,000 air movements a year.

*Trains and Underground*
Heathrow is linked to central London by the Piccadilly Line. Underground trains run every four minutes. The first train leaves London at 05.46 (Sunday 07.36) and the last at 00.11 (Sunday 23.37). The fare is £1.50 single from central London. British Rail also operate a coach service connecting Heathrow with Reading and Woking stations and stopping at all terminals.

*Taxis*
The average fare from Heathrow to central London is £12 to £15, but if you wish to travel to a district outside the Metropolitan police district, you must agree the fare with the driver *before the journey starts*.

### Gatwick
Gatwick is the world's fourth busiest international airport with 14 million passengers a year – 12.9 million of these are international and 1.1 million domestic.
It is about 28 miles south of London, and is easily accessible from the M23 and A23. The Gatwick Express train operates non-stop between Gatwick and Victoria, London, every 15 minutes during the day and hourly at night. Journey time: 30 minutes. Express coaches operate between Gatwick and many parts of Britain.

The airport site covers 1,876 acres and employs 15,050 people. It is used by 60 airlines, for a total of 152,842 flights per year.

*Trains*
The Gatwick Express is a regular service which runs between Victoria, London and the airport. Departs every 15 minutes between 05.30 and 22.00 hours, with an hourly service through the night. Fares: £4.20 single, £8.40 return.

*Buses*
The Green Line Flightline 777 express coach service between Victoria, London, and Gatwick takes 70 minutes and costs £2.75 single, £3.50 day return and £4.50 period return.

True or false?

1. Heathrow has 29 million more passengers a year than Gatwick.
2. More airlines use Heathrow than Gatwick.
3. Gatwick employs more people than Heathrow.
4. Heathrow is nearer central London than Gatwick.
5. If you take a taxi from Heathrow to central London, it will not cost you more than £12.
6. It is quicker to take the express coach from Gatwick to Victoria than the train.
7. You cannot reach Heathrow direct by a British Rail train service.
8. You cannot reach Gatwick by underground

41

# DOWN UNDER

## A  QUIZ

What makes Australia and New Zealand different from Europe? Think of three things that are different or unusual for each of these three categories:

1 weather and climate
2 physical geography
3 animal life

## B  CLIMATE

1 What's 'upside down' about Australia and New Zealand?

1 Look at the towns on the Weather Table and find them on the map.
2 Write a list of the towns. Are they in the north or south of the country? Write *N* or *S* next to each one.
3 Mark with a star (*) the town that has the highest number of hours of sunshine.
4 Mark with a cross (×) the town that has the lowest number of hours of sunshine.
5 Mark with two stars the town that has the lowest average temperature for the hottest month.
6 Mark with two crosses the town that has the lowest average temperature for the coldest month.

2 Use the information in the table and on the map to help you write about the Australian climate:

In Europe the hottest places are in the south but in Australia and New Zealand, the south is_____than the north. So, for example, Melbourne, in the_____, has_____hours of sunshine each day while Darwin, in the_____, has_____hours of sunshine. Similarly, Hobart, in the_____, has the lowest average _____for the hottest month while Darwin has the_____. Darwin also has the_____average temperature for the coldest month while Canberra, in the_____, has the_____.

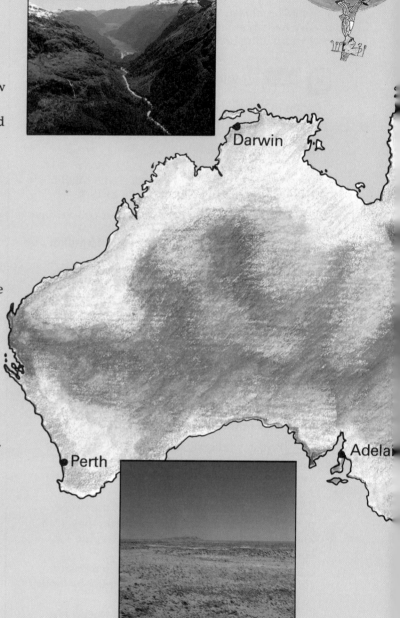

## C  SEASONS

Many Europeans think that the seasons are upside down in Australia and New Zealand!
Match the months and seasons 'down under'.
Which months are missing? Compare your answers with your partner's.

spring

autumn

winter

summer

December to February

? to ?

? to ?

June to August

### Weather in Australia's capitals

| | Average daily hours of sunshine | Average temperature for hottest month (°C) | Average temperature for coldest month (°C) |
|---|---|---|---|
| Adelaide | 6.9 | 23.0 | 11.1 |
| Brisbane | 7.5 | 25.0 | 14.9 |
| Canberra | 7.2 | 20.3 | 5.4 |
| Darwin | 8.5 | 29.6 | 25.1 |
| Hobart | 5.9 | 16.7 | 7.9 |
| Melbourne | 5.7 | 19.9 | 9.5 |
| Perth | 7.9 | 23.7 | 13.2 |
| Sydney | 6.7 | 22.0 | 11.8 |

* A rain day is a day on which rainfall is 0.2 mm or more

3

4

5

Great Barrier Reef

N
W←→E
S

Brisbane

berra  Sydney
bourne

Hobart

Auckland

Wellington

Christchurch

Pacific ocean

Dunedin

## D COMMUNICATION GAME

1 Match the words to the definitions.

island / aɪlənd /
mountain / maʊntɪn /
volcano / vɒlkeɪnəʊ /
– a piece of very high land made of rock
– a mountain (with a large hole at the top) which
  sometimes pours out hot, melted rock
– a piece of land with water all around it

2 Match the names to the pictures. (1–5)
a volcano       the Great Barrier Reef
hot springs     the desert     a fjord

3 Pair work
Student A  look at the information about Australia on
page 57.
Student B  look at the information about New Zealand
on page 105.
Read your list. Do *not* show your list to your partner.
Student A, read one sentence aloud. Student B, find a
similar sentence on your list. Compare the information.
Are the two countries similar or different? Take it in
turns to read your sentences.

4 With your partner, write each pair of sentences as one
sentence about Australia and New Zealand. Write ten
sentences. Begin each one with information about
Australia. Use *but*, *both* or *and*.

*Example*  Australia is about 25 times larger than Great
Britain but New Zealand is about the same size as Great
Britain.

5 Use the new sentences to write a passage called
*Australia and New Zealand – a Comparison*. Organise it
like this:
Paragraph 1: size, islands, distance from the sea
Paragraph 2: height of land
Paragraph 3: interesting geographical features

## E ANIMALS

Danny's uncle has just come back from Australia and New
Zealand. He is showing Danny his photos of Australian
and New Zealand animals.

Listen to their conversation. Copy the table and write the
number of the correct picture next to the name of the
animal. Then listen again and mark with a tick (✓) the way
or ways in which these animals are different or strange.

1     2     3

4     5     6

| | Picture number | Baby grows outside the mother | Eats at night | Can't fly | Colour |
|---|---|---|---|---|---|
| kangaroo | | | | | |
| koala | | | | | |
| wombat | | | | | |
| kiwi | | | | | |
| emu | | | | | |
| swan | | | | | |

1 Try to match the names of these explorers to their nationalities and the parts of the world that they explored. Compare your answers with your partner.

| Marco Polo | Spanish | China and the Far East |
| Dirk Hartog | English | Western Australia |
| Captain Cook | Italian | New Guinea and Manila |
| Luis de Torres | Dutch | Australia and New Zealand |

2 What do you know?
Answer as many of the questions as you can.
1 Who lived in Australia before the explorers arrived?   a the Maoris   b the Aborigines   c the Polynesians

2 When did English-speaking people start living in Australia?
a in the 19th century   b in the 15th century
c in the 18th century   d in the 13th century

3 Was gold ever found in Australia?

3 Now read the text and find the answers you didn't know.

## WHO DISCOVERED AUSTRALIA?

40,000 years ago the only people who lived in Australia were the Aborigines. They had probably come there across the sea from Asia. When the British arrived in Australia, the Aborigines had already lived there for thousands of years. It was their country.

Before the British discovered the east of Australia, explorers from several different countries had tried to find the 'unknown Southland', as they called it. In the second half of the sixteenth century several Spanish explorers set out from Peru to try to find it because they thought that there was probably gold there. However, they found nothing and sailed away again.

Then, in 1606, a Spanish sailor who was called Torres sailed from Peru to the New Hebrides. After that he went on to Manila via the Moluccas. He had passed through the narrow piece of sea between New Guinea and northern Australia

which is now called the Strait of Torres. In his letters, however, he did not say anything about a piece of land to the south.

The Dutch also looked for the unknown southland. In 1623 some Dutch seamen sailed from Jakarta into the Gulf of Carpentaria. They found no gold so they sailed away again. (In fact, many years later, people did find gold in Australia.) Seven years earlier Dirk Hartog had landed on an island in Shark Bay on the west coast. This is now called Hartog Island. In 1642 Abel Tasman, the greatest of the Dutch explorers, discovered Tasmania, a large island just south of mainland Australia. On a later journey in 1644 he made maps of the northern coast of Australia. The Dutch decided not to continue their explorations, however, because the land seemed too poor. For a long time, though, the western part of Australia was called New Holland.

Much later, in the second half of the eighteenth century, Captain Cook, an Englishman, discovered the east coast of Australia, almost by accident. He claimed it for his king, and soon after that the British began to live there.

(You can find out more about Cook's explorations in Unit 8).

4 Read the text again.
1 Match these names to the coloured routes on the map. Write a name and a colour.

Cook   Tasman
16th-century Spanish explorers
Torres   Hartog
17th-century Dutch seamen

2 Match these places to the numbers on the map. Write a name and a number.

The Strait of Torres   Tasmania
Hartog Island   Gulf of Carpentaria

5 Tell the story.
1 With your partner, put the sentences in order to tell the story of the exploration of Australia. Write the letters of the sentences in the correct order.

Note: if we talk about something out of chronological order in the past we use had + verb.

a The Spanish had tried earlier but they were unsuccessful.
b In the seventeenth century the Dutch discovered parts of the northern and western coasts.
c The Aborigines, the first inhabitants of Australia, probably came across the sea from Asia forty thousand years ago.
d Finally, Captain Cook found the east coast of Australia and claimed it for King George III of England.
e Many centuries later, Europeans tried to find a large rich land in the south.

2 Check your answers with your teacher.

3 Write the sentences in the correct order in one paragraph.

# CHECK YOUR ENGLISH

ENGLISH SPOKEN HERE 〔▭▭〕

### Read it aloud

Away out in the Mungalongaloo Mountains in the middle of Australia there is a wonderful waterhole called Willawallawalla.

Willawallawalla is the only waterhole for hundreds and hundreds of miles. It is in the dead centre of the Deadibone Desert.

For hundreds and thousands and millions of years nobody knew that the Mungalongaloo Mountains were in the dead centre of the Deadibone Desert. No-one had discovered them.

### English for journeys

**Friend:** Hi! How was the journey?
**You:** Not bad. A bit tiring.
**Friend:** How long did it take?
**You:** About <u>six</u> hours.
**Friend:** Which way did you come?
**You:** We took the <u>Barcelona road</u> and came through Tarragona and Valencia.
**Friend:** Did you stop anywhere?
**You:** Yes, we stopped at <u>Castellón</u> for a coffee.
**Friend:** Come in and have something to eat.
**You:** Thank you.

### How to talk about the points of the compass

Spain is to the southwest of France.
Greece is to the east of Italy.
Paris is in the northeast of France.
Ireland is to the west of Britain.

### Sounds and spelling

/e/

dead    weather    measure

*How many more words can you find with the letters* ea *and the sound* /e/*? Make three lists.*

WE STOPPED AT CASTELLON FOR A COFFEE.

---

WORD WORK

---

**1** *Copy and complete this verb table.*

| Present | Past | Past Participle |
|---|---|---|
| arrive |  | arrived |
| come |  | come |
| cross | crossed |  |
| discover |  |  |
| explore |  | explored |
| find |  | found |
| forget |  | forgotten |
| go |  | gone |
| leave | left |  |
| lose | lost |  |
| pass | passed |  |
| put |  |  |
| reach |  | reached |
| sail |  | sailed |
| set out | set out |  |
| stop |  |  |
| try | tried |  |

**2** *Match the prepositions with the diagrams*
across   in   round/around
through   up   down

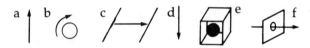

**3** *Use your dictionary to find the difference between these 'journey' words.*
journey   trip   voyage   flight   cruise

*Complete the sentences with the correct word.*
1 The_____from England to Australia took a long time in the eighteenth century.
2 Today, the_____from Australia to England takes less than a day.
3 Of course, if you want to see half the world on the way to Australia, you can take a_____.

---

KNOW YOUR GRAMMAR

---

### The past perfect

| Affirmative ⊕ | | Negative ⊖ | | Interrogative ⑦ | | | Short answers |
|---|---|---|---|---|---|---|---|
| I<br>You<br>He<br>She<br>It<br>We<br>You<br>They | had closed. | I<br>You<br>He<br>She<br>It<br>We<br>You<br>They | had not closed. | Had | I<br>you<br>he<br>she<br>it<br>we<br>you<br>they | closed? | Yes, he had.<br>No, she hadn't. |

Note: *had* can be written *'d*.

If we are already talking about the past, we use the past perfect to go back to an *earlier* past time to talk about things that happened before the time we are talking about.

```
├─────────────┬─────────────┤
past           past          NOW
perfect        simple
```

*Find these key sentences.*

When the British started to live in Australia, the Aborigines *had* already *lived* there for thousands of years.
Seven years earlier, Dirk Hartog *had landed* on an island in Shark Bay.

# HOW DID THEY GET THERE?

**A** THE FIRST PEOPLE

**1** Read and find out.

   1 Which people have lived in New Zealand for the longest time?

   2 From which direction did the Aborigines come?

**2** Match the texts to the pictures.

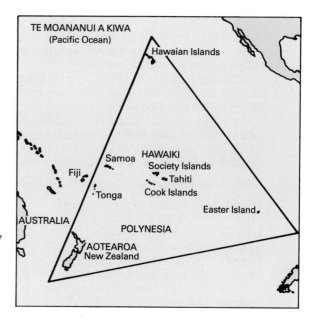

1 When white people first went to Australia they called all the people who were already there 'aboriginal'. This means people who have lived in a place from the earliest known time. No-one is quite sure when the Aborigines first arrived. Many people believe that they walked to Australia from New Guinea about 40,000 years ago. (At that time there was no sea between New Guinea and Australia.) They had probably come across the sea from the north in canoes to escape during the Ice Age.

2 No humans lived in New Zealand until about 1,000 years ago. Then the first canoes arrived, with the first people, the Maoris. They had tied two canoes together for extra strength and had put a small cabin between the two, to keep food dry.

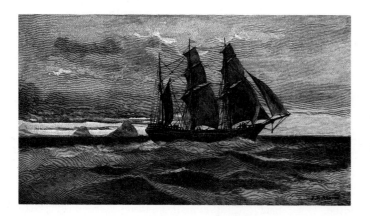

3 Why did these first Maoris go to New Zealand? The work of archaeologists and other scientists, and the old stories of the Maoris themselves solve some of this puzzle. The Maoris are Polynesians, part of the great family of peoples who live in the Pacific Ocean. So they are related to the islanders of Tahiti and Hawaii and Easter Island. We know this because their languages are similar and the people look alike. The islanders had probably decided to go in search of a new land and a better life.

**3** 1 Read Paragraph 1 again and find a noun for a type of *boat*.

   2 Read Paragraph 3 and find:
     – an adjective that means *almost the same*
     – a noun for *someone who studies things from the past*
     – a noun for *a problem*.

**4** Put these sentences in the order in which they happened.

*Paragraph 1*
a The Aborigines walked to Australia.
b The Aborigines sailed from the north to New Guinea.

*Paragraph 2*
a They put a small cabin between the two canoes.
b The Maoris arrived in canoes.
c The Maoris tied two canoes together.

**5** Write three questions about each paragraph and ask your partner to answer them. Begin your questions:
1 What did . . . ?
2 When did . . . ?
3 How did . . . ?
4 Why did . . . ?

## B CONVICTS

**1** Read about this link between the history of the United States of America and the history of Australia.

Before you read, look at page 4 and find the date on which the British surrendered to the Americans.

> Before America became independent, Britain used to send its criminals (or convicts) there to work. In the eighteenth century, laws were very severe and people went to prison for very small crimes. As a result of this, the prisons in Britain were full of people. One way of dealing with this problem was to send prisoners out of the country to America. This was called transportation. The newly independent USA, however, decided that it did not want to receive British convicts any more.
>
> The British government therefore decided in 1786 that it would start a new colony in southeast Australia, or New South Wales as they called it. So, on May 13th 1787, a fleet of 11 ships left Britain to make a journey half way round the world. The ships arrived at Botany Bay on January 20th 1788. The journey had been very difficult. The fleet of ships sailed under the command of Captain Arthur Phillip. On board there were 1,030 people and 736 of these were convicts. Their job was to make a colony from nothing.

**2** Read the first paragraph and decide what these words refer to:

| line 2 | *its* | Britain's or America's? |
|---|---|---|
| line 3 | *there* | Britain or America? |
| line 6 | *this* | a) very severe laws |
| | | b) people went to prison for small crimes |
| | | c) laws were very severe in the eighteenth and nineteenth centuries and people went to prison for small crimes |
| line 8 | *this* | a) severe laws |
| | | b) too many people in the prisons |
| line 10 | *This* | a) this problem |
| | | b) sending people out of the country |

**3** True, false or don't know?

1 People began to live in Australia because the USA did not want British criminals in their country.
2 It took the ships less than six months to travel from Britain to Australia.
3 More than half the people on the first ships were convicts.
4 A group of ships that sail together is called a fleet.

## C STARTING A COLONY

**1** Make a list of six things you would need to start a colony. Put the most important things first and decide on the percentage of money you would spend on each thing, e.g. spades for digging – 10 per cent.

**2** Do not look at your partner's list.
Ask questions to find out what she or he has written. Note the answers. Use questions like these:

What did you put first?
How much of the money would you spend on that?

**3** When you have both asked questions and taken notes, discuss and agree on one final list. Write a paragraph with the title *Things we would take to start a colony*. Give your reasons. Start like this:

> We would take ..... because ...... We would spend ..... per cent of the money on it/them. We would also take ......

**4** Work it out.
On the right is a list of the things Captain Phillip and his men took to Australia.

| | |
|---|---|
| Clothing and bedding | £ 4,939 |
| Food for convicts and sailors for two years | £ 16,205 |
| Wine | £ 381 |
| Handcuffs and irons for convicts | £ 42 |
| Writing paper, envelopes, etc | £ 63 |
| Tools and farming equipment | £ 3,056 |
| Large tents for officers | £ 389 |
| Portable house for the Governor | £ 130 |
| Medicines, doctor's instruments, etc | £ 1,429 |
| Seed grain | £ 286 |
| Old canvas for tents for the convicts until huts can be put up | £ 69 |
| Saucepans and cooking equipment | £ 118 |

Student A
1 Work out the total amount of money that they spent on the first six items on the list.
2 Work out the percentage of the total that they spent on each of the first six items on the list.

Student B
1 Work out the total amount of money that they spent on the last six items on the list.
2 Work out the percentage of the total that they spent on each of the last six items on the list.

Students A and B: Make a table and fill in your total and your percentages. Ask your partner for his or her total and for the other percentages.

**D** 🔲 NEW AUSTRALIANS

1 Copy these notes. Listen to the interviews and complete the notes.
Use the words in the box.

| Nationalities: | Italians | Greeks | Chinese |
|---|---|---|---|

| Reasons: | a to work on sugar cane fields |
|---|---|
| | b to find work |
| | c to escape political imprisonment |
| | d to work in vineyards |
| | e to find gold |
| | f to open cafes |
| | g to fish |
| | h to work in coalmines |

2 Use your notes to write two paragraphs for the school noticeboard about *why people went to live in Australia.*
Write one about the Italians and one about the Greeks. Begin them like this:

> Between 1852 and 1870 many Italians went to live in Australia to ...... They were not the first, however. In 1851 some Italians had ...... Then, in 1891, .....
>
> After 1945 many Greeks went to live in Australia to ...... They were not the first, however. In 1830 some Greeks had ...... Then, later, .....

| Dates | Nationalities | Reasons |
|---|---|---|
| 1830–90 | | |
| 1851 | Chinese | |
| 1852–70 | | to escape political imprisonment |
| 1891 | | |
| 1899 | | |
| 1945 – | | |

**E** MAORIS AND ABORIGINES

1 Pair work. Your partner will interview you about your research for a school project.

Student A: read the encyclopaedia entry about Maoris on page 49. Make notes to answer these questions about Maoris.

| QUESTIONS | ANSWERS | |
|---|---|---|
| | MAORIS | ABORIGINES |
| Do they have their own language? | | |
| Do they have their own religion? | | |
| Do they have their own arts? | | |
| What is their political position? | | |

Student B: read the encyclopaedia entry about Aborigines on page 49. Make notes to answer these questions about Aborigines.

Student A ask Student B about Aborigines and write the answers beside your own answers about Maoris.

Student B ask Student A about Maoris and write the answers beside your own answers about Aborigines.
First make sure you can say the words Maori and Aborigine.

*Maori* is pronounced / ˈmaʊrɪ /
It rhymes with "flowery".
*Aborigine* is pronounced / ˈæbəˈrɪdʒɪnɪ /
It has five syllables.

2 Can you guess these place names?

Which names are Maori?
Wellington    Rotorua    Tokoroa
Auckland    Wairakei    Hamilton    Te Kuiti

Which names are Aboriginal?
Wollongong    Brisbane    Woomera
Victoria    Wagga Wagga

**F** MINI-DISASTERS

1 Read the first story. Complete the second and third stories. Write a fourth story yourself.

a

b

c

Peter wanted an evening paper.
He rushed to the shop.
It had just closed.

Jane was tired. She had had a bad day.
She arrived home and opened her bag.
She had _ _ _ _ _ her key.

Ricky was late.
He rushed into the classroom and sat down.
He had _ _ _ _ _

2 Write a three-line story about a mini-disaster that happened to you.

# PROJECT ENGLISH

## USING AN ENCYCLOPAEDIA TO FIND FACTS

Can you find the answers to these questions by passing your eyes very quickly over the texts? You do not have to read every word. See how quickly you can answer them. Time yourself.

Remember the texts (they are called 'entries' in an encyclopaedia or dictionary) are in alphabetical order.

QUESTIONS

1　How many toes does a koala have?
2　Is coral a plant or an animal?
3　New Zealanders are sometimes called by the name of their national symbol. What is that?
4　Which animal uses its big tail to help it move very fast?
5　Where did the Aborigines come from?
6　List three important things about the capital city of New South Wales.
7　Where did Captain Cook die?
8　In which year was gold first found in Australia?
9　In which century did the Maoris arrive in New Zealand?
10　Which animal is now protected because there are very few of them left?

**ABORIGINES** These are the people who have lived in Australia for thousands of years. They probably originated in south east Asia and migrated across land which is now under water. They lived by hunting. When the Europeans arrived, they killed many of the Aborigines and many more died because they caught European illnesses. The population decreased but it is now increasing. The Aborigines are not happy about their political position. They want their own services and schools. The situation is slowly getting better. There are many different Aboriginal languages and many place-names in Australia are Aboriginal. They also have their own religion. They believe that life started in the Dreamtime and they have many stories about this time. Some of the most interesting things to see in Australia are the very old Aboriginal rock paintings and beautiful pictures about their religion.

**COOK, CAPTAIN (1728–79)** The son of a Yorkshire farmer, he began work at the age of 18. He worked on coal ships before joining the navy in 1775. He became famous for his chart (or map) making, especially of New Zealand and Australia. He was the first person to sail around the world from west to east. He was killed in Hawaii when he was trying to settle a dispute.

**CORAL** Tiny animals that live in the sea. They gradually build a hard substance that may take many different shapes. (See illustration.) The substance, often red or pink, is valued for its beauty and is often used in making jewellery, e.g. rings, ear rings, necklaces, etc. The Great Barrier Reef in Australia is made up of coral islands.

**GOLD RUSH** In the mid-nineteenth century there was a series of discoveries of gold and people 'rushed' or hurried from all over the world to find their share. In 1849 there was a rush to California in the United States. Then in 1851 there was the rush to Victoria in Australia. Finally, gold was discovered in New Zealand in the 1860s.

**KANGAROO** The kangaroo is a marsupial and a native of Australia. It has long back legs and a very strong, muscular tail that is used for support when the animal is sitting and for balance when it is jumping along at high speed. The female kangaroo has a pocket (or pouch) at the front of its body. The baby kangaroo (or joey) puts its head into the pouch to drink its mother's milk. It can also sleep in the pouch.

**KIWI** A bird that is native to New Zealand. It has an extremely long, narrow beak. It feeds at night and cannot fly. It is the national symbol of New Zealand and can be seen at Rainbow Springs on the North Island.

**KOALA** The koala is a marsupial and is native to Australia. Its fur is grey. It has 20 toes and very sharp claws which it uses for climbing eucalyptus trees. It feeds at night. The female koala often carries her baby on her back. The number of koalas has decreased so it is now a protected animal.

**MAORIS** These are the people who arrived in New Zealand about 1,200 years ago, travelling by canoe across the Pacific. The arrival of the Europeans in the eighteenth century led to wars over land in the 1860s and 1870s. Since then, there has been a slow but steady integration of white New Zealanders and Maoris and today they live in relative harmony. They have their own language and many place names in New Zealand are Maori. The early Maoris had their own religion. It had many different gods and spirits. Today many of them are Christians, but they have many traditions which go back to the old religion. Maoris like to decorate everything in a very detailed way. They carve wood and weave material. Maoris are not completely happy about their political position in New Zealand. There are some important Maoris in politics but they would like to have more.

**SYDNEY** The capital of the State of New South Wales. It is on the southeast coast of Australia. Sydney is Australia's largest city and the main port. It has a beautiful harbour with a famous bridge. Looking over the harbour is the Opera House, an extremely interesting example of modern architecture.

Now make some questions to ask your friends.

# THE OUTDOOR LIFE

## A LIFE ON A SHEEP FARM

1 Answer these questions then read the text and check your answers.
  a Is that a girl or a boy on the motorbike?
  b How old is he or she?
  c What is the name for a baby sheep?
  d What is the name of the material that we get from sheep?

The King family live on a sheep farm in the state of Victoria. Colin and his wife, Ellen, have two daughters – Sarah, who is twelve, and Jo, who is ten – and a baby son called Alex.

The Kings have 1,000 hectares of farmland, which is not very big by Australian standards. They have 200 beef cattle and 5,000 merino sheep. Merino sheep are bred specially for their wool, which is of very good quality. About 1,500 lambs are born on the farm every year. Unfortunately, not all of them live. Some are killed by the winter frost.

The two girls often help their father on the farm. Both of them ride motorbikes and they use them to round up the sheep (with the help of sheepdogs, of course). Sarah also drives the tractor and the pick-up. She is only allowed to drive on the farm. You have to be 18 to drive on the roads in Australia. While Sarah is taking hay to the cattle, Jo is feeding the five farm dogs. They are kept outside in special pens. If you treated them like pets, they would be no good for working with the sheep, so they have to be kept outside.

2 True or false?

  a The Kings' farm is big for Australia.
  b The Kings keep more sheep than cattle.
  c The cold weather kills some of the lambs every year.

  d The farm dogs are kept inside the house.
  e You can have a driving licence for the roads at the age of 15 in Australia.

## B  SHEEP SHEARING

1 Listen to Mr King talking about sheep shearing. Look at the pictures. Put them in the right order. Then find the right caption for each picture.

  a Then the sheared sheep is freed.

  b The fleeces are put into large bales. These are then pressed down and stitched up ready for sale.

  c A sheep is taken by its front legs and is held firmly.

A

B

C

## C FROM SHEEP TO SHOP

**1** Match one verb group to each stage of the process shown in the drawings.
*Example* Number 1: is washed

| | | |
|---|---|---|
| are spun | is sent | is rinsed |
| is divided | is dried | are wound | is dyed |

How does dirty wool from sheep become a lovely woollen jumper? Natural wool carries oil as well as dirt and dust, grass seeds and bits of plants. The wool must first be cleaned so it is put into a series of washbowls and is washed in soapy water. It is then rinsed in plain water and dried in a drying machine.

Next the wool is put into a carding machine, the largest machine used in the wool industry. This machine has a series of large cylinders and rollers with thousands of fine wire teeth, rather like a comb. With the help of these teeth, the wool is divided into thick strands and these are wound on to spools ready for the spinning process.

The thick strands are then spun into fine wool – the kind that you buy in a wool shop. The wool is still a rather dirty white so it must be dyed before it is sent to the knitting factory. This is done in another big bowl. The wool has now been processed and dyed and it is ready to be made into hundreds of different jumpers, which will be sold in many different places.

1

2

3
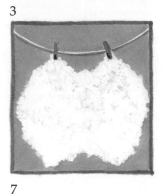

4

5
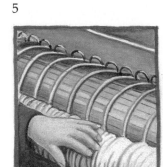

6

7

8

---

d  The fleece is sheared off in one piece.

e  The fleece is then spread on a table and is graded.

f  The sheep are rounded up.

**2** Mr King, the farmer, used two verbs together when he was talking about the shearing process.

*Example*  The sheared sheep *is freed*.

Listen again and write down the other verb groups like *is freed* in your notebooks. You should find 11 more, but be careful – sometimes two verbs are joined, e.g. caption b.

D

E

F
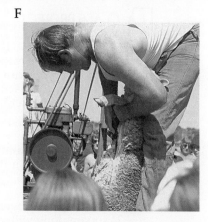

**CASTING ON**
(Making the first row of stitches)

Wind the wool around your finger and pull a loop through it. Slip it on to a knitting needle and pull it to make a stitch.

Hold this needle in your left hand. Put your right needle into the stitch and wind the wool under and around it.

Then pull the loop of wool through with the point of the right needle to make a stitch. Slip it on to the left needle.

To make the next stitch, put the right needle between the two stitches, wind the wool around it and continue as before.

Make 18 more stitches in the same way. Start each one by putting the needle between the two last stitches.

**MAKING THE KNIT STITCH**

With the wool at the back, slip the right needle into the first stitch on the left needle. Put the right needle under the left one. Wind the wool around the right needle.

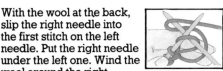

Pull the loop of wool towards you through the stitch on the left needle.

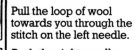

Push the right needle forwards and slide the old stitch off the left needle, keeping the new stitch on the right needle.

Continue to the end of the row. To start a new row, turn the knitting round and hold the full needle in your left hand.

 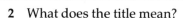

**CASTING OFF**
(When you have finished your knitting)

Knit the first two stitches in the row. With the wool at the back of the work, put the left needle into the first stitch.

Lift the first stitch over the second one and drop it off the needle so that only the second stitch is left.

Knit another stitch, then lift the first stitch over the second one as before. Continue like this along the row.

When you reach the last stitch, break off the wool, slip it through the stitch and pull it, to tighten the loop.

---

**E**  A POEM

1 Dogs are very important in the running of sheep farms. They help to collect or round up the sheep. This is known as 'heading' or 'mustering'. Read this poem from New Zealand.

*LAST RUN*

*He'd fallen over a cliff*
*And he'd broken a leg,*
*Just a mustering dog.*
*And he looked at me, there on the hill,*
*Showing no hurt, as if he'd taken no ill,*
*And his ears, and his tail,*
*And his dark eyes too,*
*Said plainly,*
*'Well, Boss, what do we do?*
*Any more sheep to head?*
*Give me a run.'*
*But he'd never head sheep any more.*
*His day was done.*
*He thought it was fun*
*When I lifted the gun.*

2 What does the title mean?

3 How did you feel when you read the poem? (Look at p.27 for some suitable adjectives).

4 Discuss these questions with your partner in English.
   a Did the dog feel any pain?
   b Can you think of another way to say, 'His day was done' in English?
   c Why do you think the farmer did what he did?

5 Often English poems have words that rhyme at the end of lines. How many rhyming words can you find? Write the phonetic symbols /ɪ/, /uː/ and /ʌ/ in your notebook. Under each symbol write a list of the words with that sound in them. Remember, they may not be spelt the same way. Write three lists.

6 *He'd fallen; he'd broken; he'd taken.*
   What does *'d* mean in these verb groups?

**F** CLASS PROJECT

FAMINE IN ETHIOPIA

Frequently there are disasters in different parts of the world. Everyone can help in some way. Blankets are always useful. Follow the instructions and knit a class blanket.

1 With size 3mm needles cast on 25 stitches.
2 Knit one row.
3 Turn the knitting and knit another row.
4 Continue like this until your knitting measures 8 cm.
5 Cast off.
6 Sew the squares together – 24 squares wide by 24 squares long will make a good blanket.

# CHECK YOUR ENGLISH

**How to talk about schoolwork**

a Have you finished?
b I can't do number 3.
c What did you put for number 1?
d I put Australia.
e I got that one wrong.
f What should we put here?
g Should we use the passive?
h Yes, I think so.

**Sounds and Spelling**

*Silent letters* b *and* k.
*Match the words to the definitions on tape.*

a comb    d knee    g knock
b lamb    e knife    h knot
c limb    f knit    i know

## WORD WORK

**1** *Match the abbreviations to their meanings.*

|        | Latin |              | English             |
|--------|-------|--------------|---------------------|
| e.g.   | a     | nota bene    | take special note of |
| n.b.   | b     | ante meridiem | before noon        |
| i.e.   | c     | exempli gratia | for example       |
| a.m.   | d     | post meridiem | after noon         |
| p.m.   | e     | id est       | in other words, that is |

**2** *Copy and complete this verb table.*

| Present | Past | Past Participle |
|---------|------|-----------------|
| allow | allowed | |
| be | | |
| bring | brought | |
| dry | | |
| keep | kept | |
| sell | | |
| send | | |
| spread | spread | |
| take | | |
| wind | wound | |

## KNOW YOUR GRAMMAR

**The present passive**

| Affirmative ⊕ | | |
|---|---|---|
| I | am | called. |
| He/She/It | is | called. |
| You We They | are | called. |

| Negative ⊖ | | |
|---|---|---|
| I | | am not called. |
| He/She/It | | is not called. |
| You We They | are not | called. |

| Interrogative ? | | |
|---|---|---|
| Am | I | called? |
| Is | he/she/it | called? |
| Are | you we they | called? |

| Short Answers |
|---|
| Yes, I am. No, I am not. |
| Yes, he/she/it is. |
| No, | you we they | are not. |

**1** *The present passive is often used when we do not know who is doing an action, for example, in a factory.*

**2** *It is also used when we are more interested in the action than in who is doing it. Compare these sentences:*
Someone frees the sheared sheep.
The sheared sheep is freed.

**3** *If we want to use the passive and say* who *is doing an action, we use* by.

*Example* The grapes are picked by people from the village.

### *Don't forget*

The present passive usually has two verbs,
*be + past participle*, but when there are two actions together the verb *be* is not always repeated.

**With modal verbs**

| I He She It You We They | can may will must | be called. |
|---|---|---|

**The infinitive**

| to be called |
|---|

*Find these key sentences:*

The bush is the Australian word for land that
*is* not *cultivated*.
Then the sheared sheep *is freed*.
It *is* then *rinsed* in plain water and *dried* in a drying machine.

> **Did you know?**
> The *bush* is the Australian word for land that is not cultivated.
> The *outback* is the Australian word for the parts of Australia far away from the sea, where very few people live.

# WORK AND PLAY

## A   A HAT FOR THE BUSH

Hats with corks, like these, are often worn by Australians in the bush.

1   What do you think the corks are for?
**a** decoration   **b** fun   **c** keeping the flies away   **d** holding the hat on

## B   A YOUNG WINEMAKER

1   Read very quickly through the magazine article about Rosalind and write down all the words that are connected with wine, e.g *vintage*.

# Vintage gold for Rosalind

Rosalind Ritchie, chief winemaker at her parents' winery, Delatite Wines, near Mansfield in Victoria's north-eastern highlands, is one of the youngest and most successful women working in the industry.

The quietly spoken 26-year-old gained a degree in oenology at Roseworthy College in South Australia before returning home to make the 1982 vintage which won a number of gold and silver medals.

'Getting awards for our first vintage helped put us on the map,' said Rosalind. 'Winning a gold medal doesn't always mean the wine is exceptional but getting three gold medals from three different judges in three different places, well . . . it's pretty good.'

Both a Rhine Riesling and a Cabernet Sauvignon collected three gold meals, a Gewurztraminer won two gold medals and two silver, a Shiraz won a silver and a late-picked Rhine Riesling won two silver medals.

Rosalind was not wholly comfortable talking about herself and her acheivements, and it was obvious she would have preferred to be in the vineyard, pruning vines and instructing her father, Robert, brother David and a German winemaker, Heidi Schon, who was staying with the Ritchies for work experience.

There is plenty of work to be done when you are a winemaker and Rosalind said she enjoyed it. 'It's not a difficult job but the hours are long . . . you work seven days a week.

'I love vintage time – getting the grapes in and processing them, making sure everything is just right going into the tank. I don't really like processing, refining and filtration, but it has to be done. I can do the job well but it's not a joy for me. When the wine is in the bottles, then I feel a sense of achievement,' she said.

While making her first vintage, Rosalind called on a South Australian-based wine consultancy, Oenotec. 'It's a firm that helps set up small wineries and runs them through procedures for the first couple of years. I couldn't have done without their advice. I was on the phone to them every day and had consultants visit when I had a problem,' she said.

Rosalind was ten years old when the first grapes were planted and she and her older brother, Stuart, now a computer systems analyst, enjoyed helping. Her younger brother David, 22, has recently left university to work in the business while the youngest, 15-year-old Charlie, is at Geelong Grammar School.

'I had always wanted to be a winemaker until I was in my last year of school at Geelong Grammar, when I had a change of heart and wanted to be a vet,' Rosalind explained. 'Then I thought that I wouldn't do well enough in my exams, and I was right, so I applied to Roseworthy College, to study the science of wine,' she said.

In 1983, the small vineyard was awarded three gold and two silver medals for its Rhine Riesling and one gold and three silver medals for its gewurztraminer.

For such a young winemaker to produce award-winning wines is quite an achievement. Rosalind is optimistic there'll be plenty of excellent vintage years ahead.

2   Match these words in the text with one of the meanings a–f: oenology   a medal   vintage time   a sense of achievement   consultants   optimistic
   a   a piece of metal which is used as a prize or reward for being the best at something
   b   the science of winemaking
   c   a feeling of happiness because something has been well done
   d   people who know a lot about something and who can give advice
   e   hopeful that something good will happen
   f   the time when the grapes are picked from the vines

3   Read the text again and answer these questions.
   1   How many medals has Rosalind Ritchie won since 1982?
   2   How many brothers has Rosalind got?
   3   How many days a week does Rosalind work?
   4   Put these sentences in the correct time order.
      a   Rosalind wanted to be a vet (an animal doctor).
      b   Rosalind wanted to be a winemaker.
      c   Rosalind became a winemaker after all.
      d   Rosalind applied to Roseworthy College to study winemaking.
      e   Rosalind did not think that she would pass the exams to go to Veterinary College.

4   Use the five sentences in **3**.4 about Rosalind to write a short passage with only two sentences. Do not use Rosalind's name more than once.

When she was quite young, ........
.................................... but ..........
.................... Then, at about the
age of 17, ................................ so
.................... and ............................

## C THE WINEMAKING PROCESS

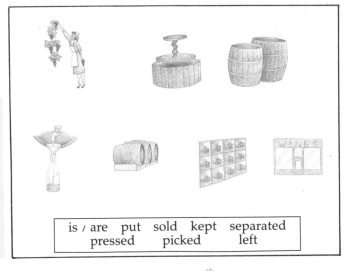

1 Complete the captions for this wall poster. Use the words in the box. You will usually need two verbs for each blank.

    a  The grapes _____ in late summer.
    b  Then, they _____ so that the juice runs out.
    c  Next, the juice _____ from the skins and pips.
    d  It _____ into large containers and _____ to ferment.
    e  Later, it _____ into smaller containers.
    f  After about a year, it _____ into bottles.
    g  If it is a good wine, the bottles _____ for several years.
    h  The cheaper wines _____ immediately.

| is / are | put | sold | kept | separated |
|---|---|---|---|---|
| pressed | | picked | | left |

## D WOMEN'S WORK?

1 Match the words to the pictures.

2 Divide the types of work into three lists. Put **M** for men's work, **W** for women's work and **MW** for work you think can be done by both.

3 Pair work
Compare your lists with your partner's. Take notes about your partner's lists.

4 In groups of three: tell Student **C** what you think and what your partner thinks.

5 In groups of six: Write a report of your opinions for the noticeboard. Use sentences like these:

> We all agree that *x* is women's work.

> Three of us think that *x* is men's work.

> I don't think that *x* is women's work because …

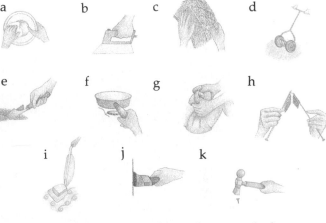

knitting   painting a room   hoovering   gardening

changing a nappy   mowing the lawn   washing up

hammering a nail   changing a tyre   cooking   ironing

## E LIVING IN AUSTRALIA – THE GOOD THINGS

Marco    John    Nicky    Alan

1 Copy the table.

| Name | Place of birth | Family's country of origin | Happy? | Reasons |
|---|---|---|---|---|
| Marco | | | | |
| John | | | | |
| Nicky | | | | |
| Alan | | | | |

2 Look at reasons a–h.

    a  he likes living near the sea
    b  he likes Melbourne
    c  he likes boats and water skiing
    d  he likes Australian Rules Football
    e  he likes good weather
    f  he likes living on a cattle station
    g  he likes surfing every day
    h  he likes riding horses

3 Listen to these young Australians.
Student A: fill in the chart for Marco and Nicky.
Student B: fill in the chart for John and Alan.

4 A: ask B about John and Alan and fill in your chart.
B: ask A about Marco and Nicky and fill in your chart.

Use these questions:

> Where was ————— born?
> Where does he live now?
> Where does his family come from?
> Is he happy in Australia?
> Why?

5 Write a caption for each of the photographs. The first one has been done for you.

Marco was born in Australia and lives in Melbourne but his family comes from Greece. He is very happy in Australia because he likes Melbourne and he likes Australian Rules Football.

**F** SPORTING AUSTRALIA

1 Read and find out if these sentences are true or false.
   a Surfing originated in Australia.
   b Over half the population of Australia play sports.
   c Surf lifesavers pay to belong to a surf club.
   d A swimmer in danger wears a harness.

# SPORT FOR ALL

*Jane Ross reports on the outdoor life enjoyed by Australians thanks to their weather.*

Australia is a great place to live. One reason is that the weather is so good. Australia has a lot of sun, so people enjoy spending time outside. Sport is very popular, especially water sports because most Australians live near the sea. About six million Australians play sports, including tennis, cricket, various types of football, bushwalking, fishing, sailing, swimming and surfing.

Say 'Australia' and 'sport' and most people think of surfing. I went along to a beach near Perth to find out about it. I always thought that surfing was invented in Australia, but I was wrong! It wasn't. It began in Hawaii, I'm told. Captain James Cook sailed to Hawaii from England in the 1770s. He watched the islanders surfing and admired their skill. Captain Cook was the first Englishman to land in Australia. But we don't think he began surfing in Australia! Surfing became a popular sport in Australia only in the twentieth century.

I knew that surfing was a dangerous sport but I didn't know about the special surf lifesaving service that you find on every surfing beach in every area where surfing is popular. Gerry Miller is a surf lifesaver. He told me that lifesavers often risk their own lives to save people in danger. I asked him if he was paid for lifesaving. 'No, just the opposite. We pay to be members of the surf club,' he said. He told me that there are 14,000 lifesavers throughout Australia. 'They make Australia's beaches among the safest in the world.'

I was lucky enough to be in Perth for the annual surf carnival. There were competitions in lifesaving, swimming and surfing. The photo shows the lifesavers on parade. They are carrying the equipment that they use in rescue attempts. It's quite a complicated procedure: the lifesaver wears a harness, a kind of belt with straps round the neck. The harness is attached to the line. Then the line is wound around the reel. When the lifesaver reaches the swimmer in danger the line is pulled in by the other lifesavers on the beach. Thanks to these strong men, a risky sport is made a little safer.

NEXT WEEK: Gerry Miller with advice on surfing safety.

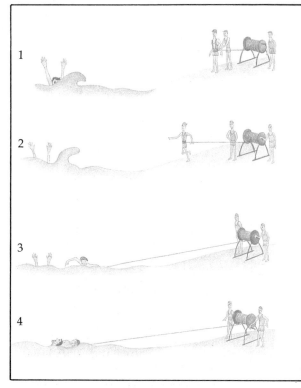

2 Use the sentences a–h to complete a Wallchart for Lifesavers. The sentences are in the wrong order.

   a The line must be unwound smoothly from the reel.
   b The drowning person must be taken firmly under the chin.
   c The chosen lifesaver must run to the sea as quickly as possible.
   d The rest of the lifesavers must make sure that the safety line is firmly attached to the harness.
   e The lifesaver must swim strongly but safely to the person who is drowning.
   f The line must be wound in as rapidly as possible.
   g The lifesaver must put on the safety harness.
   h The lifesaver must be watched carefully in case help is needed.

**Waltzing Matilda**

Once a jol - ly swag - man camped be - side a bil - la - bong,— un - der the shade of a cool - i - bah tree, And he sang as he sat and wait - ed till his bil - ly boiled,— Who'll come a - Walt - zing Ma - til - da with me?

CHORUS

Walt - zing Ma - til - da, Walt - zing Ma - til - da, Who'll come a - Walt - zing Ma - til - da with me? And he sang as he watched and wait - ed till his bil - ly boiled,— You'll come a - Walt - zing Ma - til - da with me.

# J●ke sp●t

1 Patsy's birthday is in winter. But she was born in summer.
How?

2 Dora hit a tennis ball as hard as she could. It came back to her just as fast. But the ball didn't touch anything on its journey.
What happened?

3 The flight time between London and Paris is one hour. Every minute, a plane leaves London for Paris. And every minute, a plane leaves Paris for London.
One fine morning, a pilot left London for Paris. How many planes from Paris did he meet?

4 How many words in the dictionary? A dictionary is full of words. Even the *word* DICTIONARY is full of them. Tina was looking at the name on the front of her dictionary one day, and she asked herself, "How many words can I find, even *before* I open the dictionary?"
So she made a list of all the words she could make from the letters of DICTIONARY. Her list had more than 40 words. How many can you find?

Full name: Alasdair Scott-Goddard or Al in conversation
Born: 22nd December 1967
Time in group: joined December 1984
Previous group(s): Cats Under Pressure, Vogue
Job(s): computer programmer, electrician in recording studio
Best friend: my dog, Muttley
Hero: David Bowie
Heroine: Joan of Arc
Ideal holiday: six months in New York or Hong Kong
Ambition: to make Pari Match a worldwide name.
To work in film, TV and music production

Student A
1 Australia is about 25 times larger than great Britain.
2 In Australia only 5 per cent of the land is very high.
3 Australia is made of one enormous island and one small one.
4 Australia is a very flat country.
5 The mountains in Australia are near the east coast.
6 Australia has a small island to the south.
7 People who live in the centre of Australia are 3,000 kilometres from the sea.
8 The highest mountain in Austalia is 2,228 metres high.
9 Australia has some interesting geographical features.
10 Australia has an enormous desert and the Great Barrier Reef.

# THE ROYAL FLYING DOCTOR SERVICE

**A** MELISSA – A TRUE STORY

**1**  1  How old is the girl in the picture on the left?
    2  Does she look  happy?  ill?  lonely?

3  Read the magazine article and check your answers.

## THE FLYING DOCTOR SERVICE TO THE RESCUE

### The story of a very courageous girl

*Melissa Davies with her sister and mother*

A remarkably courageous girl, Melissa Davies has succeeded in doing what doctors considered quite impossible. She has gone back to Alcoota Cattle Station, north of Alice Springs, to work again as a private tutor.

Last June, an unconscious Melissa was flown from Alice Springs to Royal Adelaide Hospital, near death, or, to quote the surgeon, Dr North, 'fighting impossible odds'.

The story began when Melissa was riding on the distant cattle station north of Alice Springs. She fell off her horse and was kicked in the head. *Fortunately*, the station owner's wife, Wendy Webb, found Melissa very soon after the accident. She contacted the Flying Doctor by radio. An hour later he had flown Melissa to Alice Springs hospital. There she had an operation. The next day she was flown to Adelaide Hospital. She was *unconscious* for nearly a month and had to have an operation to help her breathe.

Quite simply, this Sleeping Beauty, as Melissa was called in the hospital, was lucky to be alive. 'The death rate for people with Melissa's injuries is about 50 per cent,' said Dr North. 'Melissa's one of the lucky ones. And I've no doubt that her courage, determination, and will of steel pulled her through.'

Everyone who knows Melissa knows about the 'will of steel', especially her mother. It was 22-year-old Melissa's independence that took her to Alcoota in the first place. She had just graduated in science and biochemistry from Adelaide University and was impatient as she could not find a job immediately. Then one day she saw an advertisement asking for someone to teach two *teenage* children on a *distant* cattle station. She had always liked climbing and walking in the bush so she applied.

Melissa's recovery was greatly helped by the constant care and attention of her mother, her younger sister, Priscilla, and her university friends but above all it was due to her own courage and *determination. Gradually* she got stronger.

Melissa's *employers* at Alcoota Cattle Station were *delighted* when they heard that she was getting better. They said that they didn't want anyone else to work with their children and that they would wait for her.

Now she is happily back at work at Alcoota.

**2**  True or false?
  a  Melissa did not complete her university studies.
  b  Melissa had a riding accident.
  c  Mrs. Webb is Melissa's employer.
  d  Melissa had an operation at Alice Springs hospital.
  e  The Flying Doctor Service helped to save Melissa's life.
  f  Another tutor did Melissa's job while she was in hospital.

**3**  Match the words in *italics* in the magazine article with the meanings a-h.
  a  happily or luckily
  b  a long way off *or* far away
  c  aged thirteen to nineteen
  d  not knowing what is happening around you
  e  a strong will to do what you want to do
  f  very pleased
  g  people who pay you to work for them
  h  little by little

**4**  1  Compare this text written in reported speech with paragraph 4 of the article which includes direct speech. Look carefully at the punctuation and the verbs. Make a list of the differences.

> Doctor North said that the death rate for people with Melissa's injuries was about 50 per cent. He added that Melissa was one of the lucky ones and said that he had no doubt that her courage, determination, and will of steel had pulled her through.

  2  Compare your list with your partner's.

  3  Paragraph 7 of the article about Melissa is written in reported speech. Read it again and then rewrite it using direct speech.

**HOW THE FLYING DOCTOR SERVICE WORKS**

Many people in Australia live far away from towns in the outback. If they become ill they have to send a radio message to the Flying Doctor Service. They are then given advice or, if they are very ill, a doctor flies out in a light aircraft to see them.

Flying doctors lead very dangerous lives. They can suddenly find themselves caught in the middle of a large dust cloud or a thunderstorm, or blown about by gale force winds. Sometimes a pilot has to tie down his plane to stop it being blown away. The rainy season is a very difficult time for pilots. They have to keep their eyes on the ground and be very careful where they land. Otherwise the plane could be grounded for months. It is a very difficult life indeed.

| Flying Doctor Service Report Sheet | |
| --- | --- |
| 1. Time of call | |
| 2. Name of caller | |
| 3. Address | |
| 4. Symptoms of patient | |
|    Temperature | |
|    Place of pain | |
|    Able to eat? | |
|    Able to walk? | |
|    Length of illness | |
|    Any other symptoms | |
| 5. Details of runway | |
|    Position | |
|    Direction | |
|    Lights? | |
|    Vehicles for light? | |
|    Any obstacles? | |
| 6. Action to be taken | |
|    Give instructions | |
|     about medicine | |
|     about first aid | |
|    Keep in radio contact | |
|    Fly immediately | |

1 Copy the report sheet. Listen to the radio call to the Flying Doctor. Fill in the details.

2 Complete the doctor's report for the Flying Doctor Base using a word from the box to fill each space. You can use a word more than once.

| had | wouldn't | won't | has |
| --- | --- | --- | --- |

Mrs Johnson at Horseshoe Creek reported that her little boy ..... a temperature of 39°, that he ..... eat and that he ..... bad stomach pains. She added that he..... been like that for twenty-four hours.

Who's ill? Over.
How old is he? Over.
What's wrong? Over.
How long has he had it? Over.
Has he got a sore throat? Over.
A high temperature? Over.
Is there blood in his spit? Over.
Does he smoke? Over.
I need to examine him.
I'll fly out this afternoon. Over.

My father, Mr James Arthur. Over.
He's nearly 72. Over.
He has a very bad cough. Over.
He's had it for the past month. Over.
Yes, he has a very sore throat. Over.
Yes. It's been over 38° since yesterday. Over.
Yes, there's a lot of blood in his spit. Over.
He was a heavy smoker, but not now. Over.
Thank you, Doctor. I'd be very grateful.
Over and out.

3 Look at the conversation between the Flying Doctor and Mrs Andrews. In pairs take turns reading it aloud.

4 Write the Flying Doctor's report on the radio conversation. Use the frame below.

Flying Doctor Case History —Mr James Arthur
Mrs Andrews reported that her father,
Mr James Arthur, aged ....., had a very bad
cough. She said that ..... He also......
She said that ..... She reported that.....
but ......

## C DIAGNOSIS

Read the descriptions of pneumonia, flu, strep throat and bronchitis. Follow the diagnosis chart and match an illness to paths A, B, C, and D.

Pneumonia is an infection of the lungs. The signs of this illness are: a bad cough often with lots of mucus, a high temperature, chest pain and sores around the mouth. Treatment with antibiotics can make the difference between life and death. A lot of water should be drunk.

Influenza or 'flu' is a virus which attacks the lungs. The signs of the illness are: a cough with lots of mucus, a high temperature, a sore throat, aches all over the body, a runny nose. The illness spreads easily from person to person. The treatment is fairly simple. Patients should rest, drink a lot and take aspirin.

Strep throat is a very bad throat infection. The signs of the illness are: some coughing, a high temperature, and a sore throat. The back of the mouth will be very red and there may be some swelling under the jaw. Antibiotics should be given.

Bronchitis is an infection of the tubes that carry air to the lungs. It causes a noisy cough, often with mucus. The patient will wheeze and will feel a tightness in the chest. The illness is often the result of heavy smoking. It can be treated with antibiotics. Smokers should stop smoking.

## D ROLEPLAY

Take turns to be the Flying Doctor and a radio caller. The Flying Doctor should use the diagnostic chart. The radio callers should use the role cards on page 65.

## E HOW TO USE A THERMOMETER

Every family should have a thermometer. You should take the temperature of a sick person four times a day.

1 Match the instructions to the pictures.
 a Put the thermometer either under the patient's tongue, (the mouth should then be kept shut)
 b Clean the thermometer well with soap and water.
 c or under the armpit if you think the patient will bite the thermometer.
 d Shake it hard until it shows less than 36°.
 e Read it after 3 or 4 minutes.

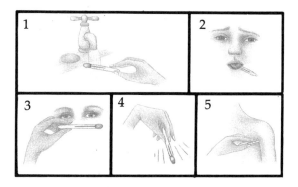

2 Read this thermometer. Is the patient ill?

3 Pair work – Temperature charts
 1 In your notebooks draw a vertical line 6 cm long. At right angles to the bottom of this line, draw a horizontal line 7 cm long. Mark the centimetres along the lines. Write the first letter of the days of the week along the horizontal line, starting with M for Monday. Write the numbers of degrees beside the vertical line, starting at the bottom with 36.
 2 Student A: close your book and ask Student B about Mrs Wilcox's temperature. Put the information on your graph.
 Student B: close your book and ask Student A about Mr Arthur's temperature. Put the information on your graph.

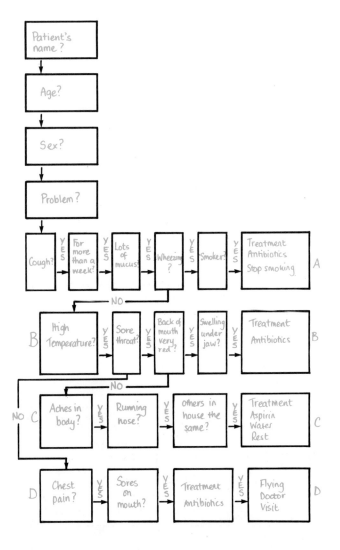

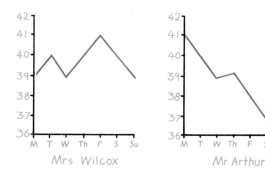

# CHECK YOUR ENGLISH

## Listen to THAT!

One day a very famous and brave explorer called Dr McGurk went out to the middle of Australia. He was looking for new places to explore. When he got there people told him not to be silly. They said (that) all the places in the middle of Australia had been explored already.

Dr McGurk said, 'But what about the Deadibone Desert? I bet that hasn't been explored!'

The people said (that) he was quite right. It hadn't been explored because it was so terrible, it was so hot in the day-time and so cold in the night-time. They said (that) it would never be explored.

'Hoots and toots', said Dr McGurk. 'That's exactly the sort of place I've been looking for.'

## English for talking to the doctor

She has a temperature of 39°.
She has a runny nose.
He has a sore throat.
He has had a bad cough for a week.
He is coughing badly at night.
I think he's got pneumonia.

## English for the classroom
Punctuation

.   a full stop
,   a comma
:   a colon
;   a semi-colon
?   a question mark
!   an exclamation mark
-   a hyphen (as in semi-colon)
' '   speech marks (or inverted commas)
ABC   capital letters
abc   small letters

## WORD WORK

1   *When we use tools or instruments to do a job, we usually use the preposition* with.

Complete these sentences.

a   He writes with . . . . . but I always write with . . . . . . .
b   Temperatures are taken with . . . . . . .
c   Do you do your hair with a brush or with . . . . .?
d   Knitting is done with . . . . . . .

2   **Opposites**

Use your dictionary to help you copy and complete this table.

| | verb, noun or adjective? | Opposites | |
|---|---|---|---|
| | | un- | dis- |
| able | adj. | unable | — |
| advantage | noun | — | disadvantage |
| afraid | adj. | | |
| agree | | | |
| appear | | | |
| attractive | | | |
| comfort | | | |
| comfortable | | | |

## KNOW YOUR GRAMMAR

### Reported speech

| Reporting verb | Present tense | Past tense | |
|---|---|---|---|
| Second verb | Does not change | Present → Past | Past → Past or Past Perfect |
| Example | 'I like him' → She says that she likes him.<br><br>'I liked him' → She says that she liked him. | 'I like him' → She said that she liked him. | 'I liked him' → She said that she liked him. OR → She said that she had liked him.<br><br>Note: these modal verbs do not change: *would, could, should* |

### The past passive

| Affirmative ⊕ | | | | Negative ⊖ | | | | Interrogative ? | | | | Short answers |
|---|---|---|---|---|---|---|---|---|---|---|---|---|
| I<br>He<br>She<br>It | was | | told. | I<br>He<br>She<br>It | was not | | told. | Was | I<br>he<br>she<br>it | | told? | Yes, I was.<br>No, I was not.<br>Yes, he/she was.<br>No, it was not. |
| We<br>You<br>They | were | | | We<br>You<br>They | were not | | | Were | we<br>you<br>they | | | Yes, you/we were.<br>No, they were not. |

**A** SCHOOLS OF THE AIR

**1** Read about the Schools of the Air

Because Australia is so big, a Flying Doctor Service is needed for people in the outback. Of course, they need education too. Children who live on cattle or sheep stations hundreds of kilometres from towns cannot travel daily to school. Sometimes they go to boarding schools but many of them stay at home and take correspondence courses and use the Schools of the Air.

The Schools of the Air were started as a result of the Royal Flying Doctor Service. The same radio stations could be used for both services. (If you want to find out how the Flying Doctor Service started, you will find some more information on page 64.) The Schools allow outback children to have daily contact with a qualified teacher and with one another. They also help the person at home who supervises them. In addition, they make the children feel that they belong to a group which is doing the same lessons and having the same problems.

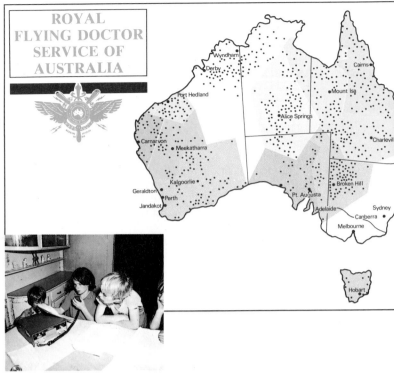

**B**  A SCHOOL OF THE AIR HISTORY LESSON

Listen to the School of the Air History Lesson and look at the worksheet.

---

**Worksheet – The Discovery of Australia and New Zealand**

**Revision**

Answer questions 1–4 as you listen.
Write letters or numbers for your answers.

1 Australia was first discovered by
   a the Dutch
   b the British
   c the Aborigines
   d the Spanish

2 The Aborigines lived in Australia for
   a 40,000 years
   b 40,000,000 years
   c 4,000 years

3 New Zealand was first discovered by
   a the British
   b the Dutch
   c the Maoris
   d the Aborigines

4 Write down the number of the map which shows us what was known about New Zealand in the early eighteenth century.

**New lesson**

Make notes so that you can answer Question 5. Answer Question 6 when you have finished listening.

5 Answer these questions from your notes.
   a In which year did Captain Cook take some scientists to Tahiti?
   b What nationality was Captain Cook?
   c Why did the scientists want to go to Tahiti?
   d What was in the envelope that Captain Cook opened?
   e Where did the *Endeavour* sail to first after leaving Tahiti?

6 Compare Maps 2 and 3 and decide whether the following statements are true or false.
   a Captain Cook thought that there was a small island to the east of the South Island.
   b He was correct about this.
   c Captain Cook thought that there was a small island to the east of the North Island.
   d He was correct about this.
   e Captain Cook thought that there was an island to the south of the South Island.

portable microphone
a record player
tape recorder

school and those in the distant farms and cattle stations.

The standard transceiver (radio set) that the children use at home is known as the Traeger Type 59 SA. It is a small unit, 16cm by 16cm, with a depth of 25 cm. It has only two controls on the front panel, a volume/on-off switch and a band switch. It is very easy for the children to use.

The classroom studios from which the School of the Air teachers broadcast are in the grounds of the local school in towns where the Royal Flying Doctor Service is based.

Each of these studios or classrooms is equipped with a tape recorder, a record player and a portable microphone. The microphone is often used by children from the local school. This helps to build up understanding between the children in the

2   True or false?

   a   The children cannot talk to other children by radio.

   b   The children can only use the School of the Air if their home is connected to the Flying Doctor Service.

   c   There are no boarding schools in Australia.

3   a   Draw a picture of the transceiver that the children use. Mark the measurements.

   b   Look quickly at p. 64 and find out why the transceiver is called a Traeger.

---

**C**   A SCHOOL OF THE AIR MATHS LESSON

Work out the following problems and then compare your answers with your partner's.

## MATHS WORKSHEET

1   30% of Class A are boys and 40% of Class B are girls. If there are 33 pupils in Class A and 35 in Class B, how many boys are there altogether?

2   A piece of string 3 metres long is cut into lengths of 25 centimetres. How many lengths are made? What fraction of the piece of string is each length?

3   A car travels 392 kilometres using 28 litres of petrol. About how many kilometres does the car travel using 1 litre of petrol?

4   The cows on Mr Hunter's farm give 43 gallons of milk each day. What is the total yield in the month of July?

5   368 children have tea at a school Christmas party. If 16 children sit at each table, how many tables are needed?

6   Bill spent ¼ of his money at the shop, and ½ of the remainder at the football match. He has 45p left. How much did he have at the start?

7   8 black balls are placed in a bag with 16 white balls and 3 pink balls. What is the probability of selecting:
   a   a black ball?
   b   a white ball?
   c   a white or pink ball?
   d   a black or pink ball?

8   There are 12 cards in a hat, each card has the name of a different month written on it. If one card is removed from the hat, what is the probability that:
   a   it is August?
   b   the first letter of the month is J?
   c   the last letter of the month is R?
   d   there are fewer than 7 letters on the card?

**D** FOR AND AGAINST

1 What are the advantages and disadvantages of learning by correspondence and by radio? Here are some ideas. Divide these ideas into two lists, one for **advantages** and one for **disadvantages**.

– You don't have to get up early in the morning.
– You don't have any friends to play with.
– You don't have to travel to school.
– You have to send your work in on time.
– You don't have to work in a classroom.
– You can be lazy sometimes.
– You can't play team games like football or volleyball.
– You never see your teacher.
– You can have friends in other parts of the country.
– Your parents know what you are doing all day.

2 Which would you prefer – to go to a normal school or to learn by correspondence and by radio? How many reasons can you give for your decision?
Find out about your partner's decision and make notes.

3 Work in groups of four. Tell the other two students about your partner's decision. Use language like this.

| . . . said that | she<br>he | would<br>wouldn't | like to live in the outback and learn by correspondence and by radio because . . . |
|---|---|---|---|

4 Take a class vote. What percentage of the class would prefer to learn by correspondence and by radio?

**E** A NEW RADIO STATION

1 Read the article quickly and find out
a when it was written
b where it was written
c the names of the two important people in the story.

2 Read your paragraph carefully and prepare three questions on it. Use three of these question words:

a Who? b When? c Where?
d Why? e What?

3 Turn to the next person in the chain and ask your questions.

**Queensland Times April 30th 1929**

# New Service will Save Lives

This has been an important week in the life of Cloncurry. On Monday Harry Kinzbrunner walked into Radio Station VJ1 in the church of this small town and began work. On the same day the first pedal radio was taken by Alfred Traeger to the cattle station at Augustus Downs, 250 kilometres to the north. These two events have made Augustus Downs a much safer place to live.

They are part of a programme to bring health and safety to people living in the Outback. The programme was first suggested by John Flynn. When he visited the Outback for his Church in 1912, he was horrified by the loneliness of the people, and the fact that if they were ill, there was no way of calling a doctor.

After the 1914-18 war, when aeroplanes had been improved and had radios, Flynn thought of starting a flying ambulance service. He wanted every cattle station to have a radio but there were two problems. Firstly radios cost a lot of money and secondly they were very heavy and difficult to work.

Fortunately, a few years ago at a meeting, Flynn met Alfred Traeger, who is a genius with radios. He has managed to invent a way of making electricity without using heavy batteries. This has made the radios cheaper and easier to work.

Cloncurry is a good place for a flying doctor base for several reasons. There is a hospital, a small airfield, and a telephone and telegraph service. It is also in the middle of an area of a quarter of a million square miles with very few doctors. Flynn and Traeger hope that within a few years there will be pedal radio sets near to every farm in that enormous area.

# PROJECT ENGLISH

## STARTING A CLASS LIBRARY

If you want to build a class library, it would be a good idea to find out what sort of books you all like reading. Do the Questionnaire with a partner.

---

**QUESTIONNAIRE**

1   What is your first language? . . . . .

2   What do you read in your first language? What do/would you like to read in English? Tick the correct box.

|  | First language | English |
|---|---|---|
| newspapers | | |
| magazines | | |
| comics | | |
| novels (i.e. stories) | | |
| factual books (i.e. books about true people and events) | | |

3   What do you like to read about in your first language? What would you like to read about in English?

|  | First language | English |
|---|---|---|
| crime | | |
| travel | | |
| politics | | |
| science | | |
| geography | | |
| food | | |
| famous people | | |
| history | | |
| science fiction | | |
| adventure | | |
| love | | |
| family life | | |
| animals | | |
| sport | | |

4   What do you think about your reading in English?
    Are you . . . . . a quick reader, or a slow reader?
               a careful reader, or a careless reader?
               an attentive reader, or a lazy reader?

---

**Radio caller 1**
Your 14-year-old daughter has a very bad cough. She has had it for three weeks now and you are worried because she cannot sleep at night. Call the Flying Doctor and ask for help. Give the doctor all the necessary details and answer the questions he or she asks.
    You live on a sheep farm, called Red Stone, 250 miles east of Charleville, the Flying Doctor Centre.
    Your daughter has not got a sore throat but she is coughing up a lot of mucus, is wheezing and is complaining that her chest feels tight.
    Your runway is two miles east of the farmhouse and runs in an east-west direction. It has good lights.

---

## MAKING A BOOK BORROWING SYSTEM

When you have decided on the books for your class library you will need a card index system so that students can borrow the books. On one side of the card you will need the details of the book. On the other side you will need the names of the students who have borrowed the book.

*Example*

Now make a card for one of the books on p.128 from Collins Level 3 Readers. Do not forget to mark whether it is fact or fiction. The description should help you to decide.

---

**Radio caller 2**
Your baby boy is 6 months old and has a bad cough. He has had a fever for the past three days and the cough for more than a week. His mouth looks very sore and his throat is swollen. His skin has suddenly become yellow. You are very worried. Call the Flying Doctor and ask for help. Give the doctor all the necessary details and answer the questions he or she asks.
    You live on a sheep farm 400 miles west of Charleville, the Flying Doctor Centre.
    Your runway is 4 miles south of the farmhouse and runs in a north-south direction. It has good lights.

---

**Radio caller 3**
An elderly aunt, Mrs Ella Wilson, is staying with you and is feeling ill. Call the Flying Doctor Service. Give the doctor all the necessary details and answer the questions he or she asks.
    Your aunt has a very bad cough. Her temperature is very high. She has aches in her body and she has a very sore throat. She also has sores on her mouth. You are very worried because of her age and because the other children in the house also have bad coughs.
    Your cattle station is called Blue Rock Station and it is 300 miles north of Charleville, the Flying Doctor Centre.
    Your runway is two miles north of the farmhouse. It runs north-south and has good lights.

# YOUTH ARTS

## CONTENTS

**Art Takes to the Streets**

**Getting Physical**

**Photography Corner – Competition**

**Behind the Camera**

## ART TAKES TO THE STREETS

## GETTING PHYSICAL

On Thursday of next week on *The Arts In New Zealand* you will have the opportunity to hear actress Michele Hine. Michele, who has just returned home after a long period in Europe, will be talking to Margaret Belich about her ideas on the theatre.

Michele had had an enormous variety of experience before she left for Europe. She had studied mime and dance, had been an actress and had trained teachers. (Some of you may remember an interview she gave us two years ago on drama studies in school.)

Now she has also had experience in Theatre in Education, working with children in schools, and has found a new interest in movement. It is this interest that she will be talking about on Thursday. If you are interested in modern theatre, don't miss it.

GETTING PHYSICAL will be on Channel 2 at 8.30 p.m.

Most paintings last for a long time. If you go into a museum or an art gallery you can find pictures that were painted five or six hundred years ago. David Humphries and Rodney Monk know that their paintings could disappear in a day but they say that it doesn't matter.

David and Rodney are 'muralists', that is, people who paint on to the walls of buildings, sometimes inside but often outside. Murals are very popular in Australia. Since the 1970s, 200 large community murals have been completed and there are about 20 important artists doing this sort of work.

One of the murals that David and Rodney painted was in front of the Sydney Opera House. The artists were asked to do the mural to celebrate the tenth anniversary of the Opera House in 1983. The mural was taken down again in 1984 but before that happened many people

had enjoyed both painting it and looking at it. When the artists were asked to do the mural they invited ordinary people to participate and they were delighted to find that many people wanted to help. 'We started with four people and ended up with a group of almost 30 who worked each day for six weeks,' Mr Humphreys says. 'We also had hundreds of children who came from schools around Sydney and used the mural as a learning experience.' Cleverly, the programme was planned so that it took place during the school holidays.

The finished mural celebrated the building of the Opera House and its architect, Joern Utzon, from Denmark. It also showed the many different types of people who have performed at the Opera House since it was officially opened in 1973.

## PHOTOGRAPHY CORNER  A competition

This week we are offering a prize of $15 to the person who sends in the first correct entry to our competition.
What you have to do:
Below, you will see three photographs that are not completely successful. You will also

see three explanations. All you have to do is match the explanations to the photographs. Send your answers on a postcard please to YOUTH ARTS, P.O. BOX, ADELAIDE, SA.
Please print your name and address clearly.

1

2

3

**a** The camera was not close enough to the subject; the composition is uninteresting because the subject (the girl) was put in the centre; she also looks awkward and unrelaxed.

**b** The photographer tried to take a moving subject with a shutter speed that was not fast enough to freeze the movement.

**c** This photo was taken with a strong light, such as direct sunlight or a very bright sky, on the camera lens.

# BEHIND THE CAMERA – A CAREER IN PHOTOGRAPHY

Lights, camera, and action! No matter what anyone says, the world of photography and cameras is a glamorous one... sharing the set with film stars, meeting models behind the scenes, photographing political leaders and famous people and going to places most of us would never get to see.

That's the glamorous part. The not-so-glamorous part is carrying camera equipment around, waiting for jobs to happen, photographing car accidents and chasing fire engines, dealing with people who are vain or difficult, and often working long days or nights.

Last year Michael was voted Young Photographer of the Year in the National Rothmans Photographer Awards and won a trip to Amsterdam as a prize – not a bad way to start a career! He won the award with a photograph of an equally successful young star, tennis player, Pat Cash.

Michael works mainly on the *Daily Mirror* and *Daily Telegraph* newspapers. He started his career four years ago as a copy person, after realising that he had a burning interest in photography and not much else. At school, he says, he was never very good at anything.

Through his job Michael meets many famous people who are often hard to work with.

'Some of them are very vain and will only be photographed from one particular side. But I guess that's only a superficial judgement – you only really talk to them for a couple of minutes so you never really get to know them.'

Michael prefers to work in stills photography because it enables him to be more of an individual.

Michele is a fashion photographer's assistant working mainly with Greg Barrett, a photographer who works from Sydney. Her job involves setting up the photographic equipment in Greg's studio or on location, running around to laboratories, making bookings, making coffee and anything else that helps to keep a business running smoothly. The day we met, Michele was preparing to go off with Greg to shoot in Fiji.

Michele's interest in photography started at school. Her parents gave her a camera for her 16th birthday and from then on she knew that she wanted to have a career in photography.

'I really admired Greg's work in magazines, so I rang him. He told me that he already had someone but to call back in a month. Well, I called back every month for a year until he finally asked me to go and see him. I did, and I started the following Monday!'

Four years later, Greg and Michele are still a team and

Michele Morrin, 21

Michele knows why. 'Well, every day is different – and I'm always attracted by a situation where I can wear jeans and a T-shirt. Plus, after four years, Greg and I are best friends and I think I'd find it really hard to work with anyone else.'

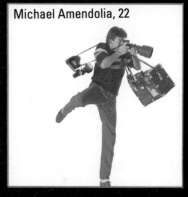

Michael Amendolia, 22

Deborah Kerr knows a lot about being a woman in a man's world. She's the only female camera assistant in the commercial television industry in Sydney, which she thinks is quite ridiculous.

Debbie, who comes from Perth, did a Film and Television course there before moving to Sydney to work as a news camera assistant at Channel Nine. Although Debbie wants to be a camera operator, as an assistant her job is mainly sound recording and she will continue with that until she earns a promotion to camera operator (which could be a few years away yet).

'Sometimes I feel frustrated. I want to be filming. I'm capable of doing it but I don't get many opportunities because the majority of my work is sound recording. But that's the way that things are done in this industry. Everyone has to come up through the ranks and you just have to accept it.'

Being involved in news, Debbie often sees human tragedy. 'At an accident scene the most upsetting part is that people abuse you for being there. You try to explain that you're just there to do your job but often they don't understand.'

Debbie says that the good things that her job offers are variety, excitement, the chance to meet lots of different people and unpredictability – you never know what will happen next.

'The bad things are that it can be deadly boring. You seem to spend half your time waiting for something to happen or for people to turn up! And the long hours. It's hard to organise your social life when

you never really know whether you'll be home in time for dinner or not.'

Despite the bad things, Debbie is surprised that there are so few women working as television camera assistants. 'Obviously the equipment is very heavy – I think that's one of the things that has kept a lot of women away. But if I can do it, a lot of women can, because I'm not particularly strong. It's a difficult industry to get into, male or female, and women seem to need more experience to get in than men. But, please, tell girls not to worry too much about that. If they're determined, they will get in.'

Deborah Kerr, 23

**A** ART TAKES TO THE STREETS

1 Read *Art Takes to the Streets* and find the word for a painting on a wall.
2 Copy and complete this entry on Sydney Opera House for the *Encyclopaedia of Australia*.

> Sydney Opera House _____ opened in _____. It _____ designed by a _____ architect, _____ _____. Since its opening many different people _____ performed there. To celebrate its _____ anniversary, a large _____ was _____ by _____ _____ and _____ _____. Because they believe in public participation, they _____ joined by many _____ and hundreds of _____ from _____ schools. The mural _____ now been taken down.

**B**  GETTING PHYSICAL

> 20.30 THE ARTS IN NEW ZEALAND
> In tonight's programme Margaret Belich talks to actress Michele Hine, who has recently returned home. Michele will explain what she means by 'getting physical'.

Listen to the interview and note down the answers to questions as you listen.

1 Michele comes from **a** Australia **b** New Zealand **c** Great Britain.
2 Michele is interested in **a** classical theatre **b** mime and movement **c** plot and costume.
3 Michele prefers **a** performing **b** directing.
4 Michele did a show in Britain called **a** *Women Alone* **b** *The Body Talk Show*.
5 Michele thinks that words in the British and New Zealand theatre are **a** very important **b** too important.
6 The word 'physical', as Michele uses it here, means **a** connected with the science of physics **b** connected with the body **c** connected with a doctor.

**C** BEHIND THE CAMERA

1 Read the introduction to the magazine article and make a list of the advantages and a list of the disadvantages of a career in photography.

2 Which do you think are the five most 'glamorous' careers on this list? Write them down and write at least one reason for each choice.

a journalist
an actor/actress
a film star
a television news reader
a pop star
a sportsman or woman
an airline pilot
a politician
an opera singer
a concert pianist

3 Compare your list with your partner's list. With your partner choose the three most 'glamorous' careers. You may have to persuade your partner by giving your reasons. Use language like this:

> I think that a ..... has the most glamorous career because ....
> Yes, I think you're right.
> Yes, but I think a ..... has a more glamorous career because ....
> Well, I'm sorry, I can't agree. I think....

When you have come to an agreement with your partner, make a group with two other people and decide upon the two most 'glamorous' careers.

**D** PHOTOGRAPHY CORNER

1 Write the answers to the competition on p. 66 together with your name and address, on a postcard. Address the postcard correctly.

2 Choose a solution for each problem.
1 The solution is to move the camera closer, compose more carefully, and place the person you want to photograph in a more comfortable position.
2 The solution is to use a faster shutter speed or, with a simple camera, to avoid pressing the button until the person has stopped moving.
3 The solution is to protect the lens with your hand or use a natural shadow, such as the branch of a tree.

3 Write three sets of instructions so that a beginner could avoid these mistakes. Begin the three paragraphs like this:
1 To avoid an uninteresting photo, follow these instructions.
2 To avoid a fuzzy photo, follow these instructions.
3 To avoid getting too much light in the camera, follow these instructions.

# CHECK YOUR ENGLISH

## Read it aloud

*This is the house that Jack built.*

*This is the corn*
*That lay in the house that Jack built.*

*This is the rat*
*That ate the corn*
*That lay in the house that Jack built.*

*This is the cat*
*That caught the rat*
*That ate the corn*
*That lay in the house that Jack built.*

## Inviting a friend to the cinema or theatre

**You:** Would you like to come out tonight?
**Friend:** Yes, where are you going?
**You:** Well, there's a good film on at the Odeon.
**Friend:** What's it called?
**You:** *Mad Max Beyond Thunderdome.*
**Friend:** What's it about?
**You:** Some children who survive a nuclear disaster.
**Friend:** That sounds a bit sad.
**You:** No, it's full of action.
**Friend:** Oh good, I like action films. What time does it start?
**You:** At eight. I'll see you at the cinema.
**Friend:** Fine, see you later.

## English for the cinema and theatre

*Example* I went to the <u>theatre</u> last night.
a I went to the cinema last night.
b Did you enjoy the film?
c Was it a good film?
d I saw a good play last night.
e What was it called?
f What was it about?
g Who was in it?
h Was the acting good?
i I like action films.
j I prefer romantic films.

## Word stress

Listen and put a mark (') over the syllable that is stressed.

photograph photographer photographic

photography theatre theatrical

### Sounds and spelling *ph* /f/

Look through Units 6–9 and make a list of all the words that have the letters *ph* with the sound /f/

---

## WORD WORK

### Nouns as adjectives (compound nouns)

In English, singular nouns are often used as adjectives in front of another noun.

*Example* Equipment for the kitchen is called kitchen equipment.

Make compound nouns for these things:

a shop that sells shoes
a theatre in Melbourne
a sandwich with egg in it
a store with lots of departments
a hall where concerts take place
a worker in an office
a station for buying petrol
a meal in the evening
a programme for the theatre

---

## KNOW YOUR GRAMMAR

### Relative clauses (defining)

| PEOPLE | | |
|---|---|---|
| Subject | | Verb |
| a boy<br>a girl<br>the man<br>the lady | who | likes carrots<br>likes maths<br>spoke to me<br>came last week |
| Object | | Verb |
| the boy<br>the woman | that<br>who(m) | you like<br>you saw |

| THINGS and ANIMALS | | |
|---|---|---|
| Subject | | Verb |
| a dress<br>a cup<br>the plane<br>the dog | that<br>which | is quite short<br>is broken<br>flew here<br>has a long tail |
| Object | | Verb |
| the dress<br>the dog | that<br>which | you like<br>you bought |

*Find these key phrases:*
a people who paint on to the walls of buildings
b people who are vain or difficult
c one of the things that has kept a lot of women away
d a boy who will do anything that Max does
e all the good things that they had left behind in Sydney
f exactly the colours that we needed
g the person you want to photograph

1 *In written English* which *is often used for things. In spoken English* that *is used more frequently.*

2 *We often omit* that *or* who *when we are talking about the object of the verb.*

### *Don't forget*

We **never** omit **that** or **who** when we are talking about the subject of the verb.

# MAD MAX
## BEYOND THUNDERDOME

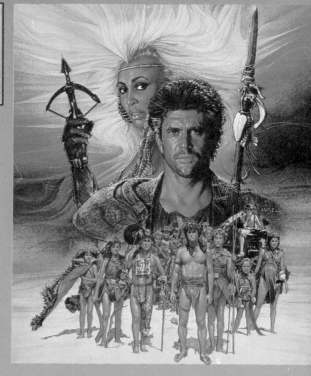

### A THINK ABOUT IT

1 How did people learn things in the past, when there were no books?

2 How would people learn things if all the books in the world were lost?

3 Which of these words could describe life after a nuclear war?
wonderful  horrible  empty  dark  beautiful

### B PRODUCTION NOTES

1 Read the notes and match them to the pictures.

---

#### THE WILD CHILDREN

**1** 'It's my turn to go and find Captain Walker,' says Savannah Nix. She is seventeen, strong and wild. She lives at Crack in the Earth, a deep canyon in the middle of the Australian desert with lots of other children. They were once on an aeroplane which crashed near to the canyon. Their parents had put them on Captain Walker's plane, hoping that they would escape the terrible results of nuclear war.

**2** For a while they lived there happily, and everything was new and wonderful and there was a lot to discover. Gradually, however, they began to think more and more about their parents and all the things that they had left behind in Sydney. So, one day Captain Walker left Crack in the Earth to find help. He had never come back. But the children had never given up hope.
'Yes, it's Savannah's turn,' the other wild children agree. So, she sets off into the desert, carrying three long spears and a heavy bag of food and water. She searches for days and days and finds nothing.
Then, one day, when her water bottle is almost empty and she has decided to turn back towards Crack in the Earth, she suddenly sees something strange under the sand. She stops to look more closely. Brushing away the sand, she realises that she is looking at the face of a man. She is sure that she has found Captain Walker.

---

(STOP) Do you think it is Captain Walker?

---

**3** Quickly she begins to dig his body out of the sand. She pours a little water over his face but he does not move. She decides that she will have to pull him back to Crack in the Earth. It takes her a long time because he is very heavy.
When she arrives at Crack in the Earth, the other children look in amazement. Some believe that it is Captain Walker, some do not. The children carry Walker down into the valley bottom.
**4**
The man wakes up, surprised to find a tribe of children all around him — children who are dressed in animal skins, and who are carrying strange pieces of metal. He is also surprised when the children call him Captain Walker. They tell him the story of the crash and he realises that they think he is going to be able to fly them away to a big city.
'But there are no cities,' he says, 'and I am not Captain Walker.'
Savannah is very angry. She does not believe him.

---

a

b

c

d

2 Pairwork
Choose one of the girls or boys in the picture. Do not tell your partner which one you have chosen.
Say

'I'm looking at the girl (or boy) who....'

Your partner must guess which one you are talking about.

## C CHILDREN IN FILMS

1 Read the article. Correct the chart below.

How did the organisers of the film, *Mad Max Beyond Thunderdome*, find the young people who play the roles of the wild children? Well, they spent several weeks searching schools for children who were physically fit and good at acting. 2,000 children wanted to take part in the film. Several hundred were chosen to try out the roles in front of the director. Finally a tribe of 60 children, who were between 20 months and 16 years, was chosen.

Then two months of workshops began. In these workshops the children learnt to know each other as a 'family'. They learnt to hunt together with primitive weapons, they climbed the kind of craggy peaks that they would meet on location and played improvisational games that were based on their screen roles. As well as the workshops the children had 20 hours weekly of traditional schooling with four full-time teachers.

2 Guess the meaning.

In this text, a workshop is
a   a shop where jobs are advertised
b   another name for a factory
c   a sort of lesson in which you can experiment with various skills, e.g. acting

3 Check your corrections with your partner. Use language like this.

> The table should say 'The number of children who ..... was ......'

| No.* of children who wanted to take part in the film | 300 |
|---|---|
| No. of children who tried out the roles in front of the director | 2,000 |
| No. of children who were chosen | 60 |
| Age of children who were chosen | between 16 months and 20 years |
| No. of teachers who gave them lessons | 20 |

*No.=Number

## D 🔲 EARLY CAREERS

In the film, Helen Buday plays the role of Savannah Nix, who thinks she has found Captain Walker. Margaret Belich interviewed Helen for the *New Zealand Youth Arts Magazine*.

1 Copy the table and complete Helen's column as you listen to the interview.

| Name of Actress/Actor | Helen Buday | Rod Zuanic |
|---|---|---|
| Role in *Thunderdome* | | |
| Date of Birth | | |
| Place of Birth | | |
| Place where she/he grew up | | |
| Studies | dancing, singing, playing the piano, ..... | |
| First important role | ..... in *Susannah's Dreaming* | |
| Other work | acted in a mini-series ..... *Mile Creek* | |

2 Read the article about Rod Zuanic and complete his column in the table above.

Rod Zuanic plays the role of ScrooLoose, the mute clown of the Crack in the Earth — a boy who will do anything that Max does, and thinks it is funny to mimic people. When Australian director, Ken Cameron, was looking for a rough teenager to star in his first film, *Fast Talking*, in 1983, he went to some of the roughest schools in Sydney and discovered Rod, who was 15 at the time. Although Rod had never thought of acting and had no training, he agreed to be tested for the role. He won it and the critics said that he was very good. As a result of this success, he has appeared in two television productions and now, at 17, he is in this very successful film.

3 Read this short biography of Helen Buday from the film programme and then write a similar one about Rod Zuanic.

Helen Buday, who plays Savannah in *Mad Max Beyond Thunderdome*, was born in 1963 in Melbourne and grew up there. She studied dancing, singing, playing the piano and acting. Her first important role was Susannah in *Susannah's Dreaming*. Since then she has acted in a television mini-series called *Five Mile Creek*.

4 Find out some facts about your favourite actor or actress and write a similar paragraph about him or her.

If you want to know more about this story look for the film called *Mad Max Beyond Thunderdome*.

71

**E**  MAKE-UP

1  Read about the children's make-up. First
answer this question. Is 'artificial' the opposite
of **a** man-made  **b** artistic  **c** natural?

2  True or false?

1  The production team could not find a
solution to the make-up problem.
2  Part of *Mad Max Beyond Thunderdome* was
filmed in Blackheath.
3  The children enjoyed being made up.
4  The make-up team had to hurry to get the
children ready in time.
5  Mud is wet earth.

**F**  HOW TO MAKE UP AS A WITCH

Actors and actresses usually use greasepaint for
their make-up. The greasepaint is made into sticks
and can be of many different colours.
Here are some examples:

| | |
|---|---|
| Light pink | Used for classical ballet dancers |
| Ivory | Almost white, used for cheekbones |
| Dark brown | Used for shadow on males and females |
| Yellow | Used to make people look older |
| Crimson lake | A sort of red, used for shadow and for the lips |
| Dark green | Used around the eyes |
| Blue | Used around the eyes or to make someone look frightening |
| Light olive | Used under all the other make-up – a base |

Read and match the colours to the numbers on the
drawing.

First of all cover your face and neck with a light
foundation; light olive would be suitable. Then use
dark brown for the lines on the forehead, for the
eyebrows, for the heavy shadows under the eyes
and for the shadows on the cheeks. Put crimson
lake on your eyelids and just under your eyes. The
space between your eyelids and your eyebrows
should be dark green. Your chin should be blue –
this will make it look very pointed. Use ivory on
your cheekbones to make them prominent. Lastly
put crimson lake on your lips. You should now
look very frightening.

**G**  HOW TO MAKE UP AS A CLOWN

1  Draw the clown in your notebook.

2  Decide which colours you would use for the
clown's face. (Do not colour the face)

3  Write instructions for your partner to colour
his/her clown with *your* colours.

4  Read your instructions to your partner. Your
partner will now colour his/her clown.

5  Listen to your partner's instructions and colour
your clown.

The production team had some problems
when the film was being made. One of
them was the children's make-up. The
director wanted them to look as if they had
lived in the desert for a long time.

We talked to Elizabeth Fardon, one of the
film's make-up artists, about her search for
the right colour. 'For several months we
tried various different artificial dyes but
none of them was quite right,' she
explained. 'And then we found the answer
almost by accident. There was a very slow
river running through the settlement of
Blackheath, which was one of the film's
remote sets. Its mud was an odd mixture of
red, yellow and burnt orange. These were
exactly the colours that we needed. So the
mud was made into a body paint and we
covered all 60 children with it, from head to
toe, each morning. To them it was a game.
For us, it was a constant panic to get them
on the set in time. In the end we could do it
in about 25 minutes – that's 25 minutes for
every child.'

# ENGLISH

**Now is the hour**

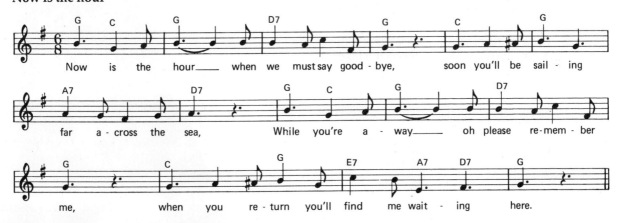

Now is the hour___ when we must say good-bye, soon you'll be sail - ing

far a - cross the sea, While you're a - way___ oh please re-mem - ber

me, when you re - turn you'll find me wait - ing here.

# J●ke sp●t

1 What four letters of the alphabet could you say to a person who just fell off a horse?

2 It was a very hot day, and two young students bought a beer. But they only had the price of one drink between them.
They filled the glass to the top. Then one of the students began to drink.
"It's OK," he said to his friend. "I'll stop when I've drunk exactly half."
And he did. But how did he know?

3 Why do firemen in some countries wear red trousers?

4 The steamship was in harbour at low tide. At midnight, just before the captain went to bed, he looked out of his window. He noticed that the water was 5 metres below his window.
That night, the sea level rose a metre every 2 hours. How long did the water take to reach the captain's window?

---

**Student B – Customs Official**

You are very busy, and get impatient with people who can't speak English properly. Ask your questions quickly – and in a different order. This is a good way to check the information on the Arrival Record.
Make sure that the passenger gives you the correct information.
Ask some extra questions if you can.
*Examples*   Why do you want to visit the USA?
             How long are you staying for?
             How much money have you got?

Can you think of any more questions?
Remember – if you don't believe the passenger, you can refuse to let him/her enter the country.

---

♀ 1
Your name is Kate Thomas. You come from Cardiff, Wales.
You are unmarried and you have no family left in Wales.
The bad weather is not good for your health.
You make very little money from your work. You are a dressmaker but nobody has any money to buy clothes.
You want to go and live with your brother and his family.
You don't have a job in the United States but you hope to continue dressmaking. You must work at home because you have trouble with your heart.
You have all your money with you, but it's not much.

♂ 2
Your name is Lucien Bourdet. You come from Douai, north France.
You're a young man with no family and you want a new life in a new country where the weather is good.
You hope to go to the south of the United States, where they speak French.
You don't know anyone in the United States, but you have the address of a relative of a friend of yours in New Orleans.
You worked in an office in Douai.
You are in very good health.
You know a little English.

# DISASTER IN THE OUTBACK

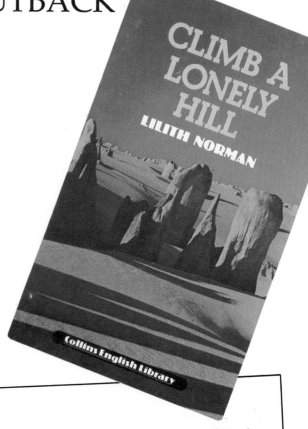

**A** READ A STORY

1 Look at the picture. Does it show **a** the seaside **b** the mountains **c** the desert **d** a lake?

2 From the picture do you think this story takes place in Australia or New Zealand?

3 Copy and complete the chart as you read.

| | Alive | Dead | Age |
|---|---|---|---|
| Jack | | | |
| Sue | | | |
| Uncle Bert | | | |
| Mother of Jack and Sue | | | |

## CLIMB A LONELY HILL
### Chapter One

Slowly Jack opened his eyes. His head hurt. His body felt strange, too: he couldn't move.

Someone was crying beside him. It must be Sue! Why was she crying? Where were they?

The car and Uncle Bert! They had been travelling with Uncle Bert. Then something had happened. An accident? There was broken glass all around.

With difficulty, Jack turned his head. His sister was lying on the back seat, crying quietly to herself.

'It's all right, Sue,' he said.

Sue lifted her head. She looked at him unbelievingly.

'I thought you were dead,' she said.

Her face was dirty, and wet from crying. There was dried blood under her nose. She sat up, and saw Uncle Bert. He was sitting in the driver's seat, his head was bent. He did not move. 'He looks really bad, Jack!' she said.

'All right, all right! He'll be OK in a minute. Just go and wash your face.'

Sue got out of the car and went to the back for some water.

Jack turned to look again at his uncle. He wouldn't tell Sue, but he was afraid. If his uncle was badly hurt, he didn't know what to do.

What could a boy of fourteen years and a girl of twelve do, alone in the Australian outback?

Jack put out his hand and touched his uncle's arm. The skin still felt warm and alive.

He shook his uncle gently, then harder. He didn't move. How could you be sure how badly hurt someone was?

'I'll have to get him out and lie him down,' he thought. Gently he started to lift his uncle's head. It was then that he saw it – the red-black blood where a broken piece of metal had gone through Uncle Bert's body – and ended his life. Jack got out of the car. He was suddenly very sick, again and again. Then, tired out, he fell to the ground.

'Jack! Jack!' He tried not to hear Sue's cries. 'Jack!' Now she was sitting beside him and shaking him. 'Jack! What's the matter?'

He opened his eyes. 'I'm all right now, Sue,' he said. 'It was just . . . Uncle Bert.'

'What about Uncle Bert? Can I help him?' Sue started to get up.

'No.' Jack's voice was high with fear. 'No! He's OK. No, he's not really.' He'd have to tell her. 'He's . . . he's dead, I think.'

Sue sat down again. Jack spoke quickly. 'I don't think that it hurt him. I'm sure it was very quick. But I don't want you to go back there, Sue.'

Suddenly he needed to think about death. This was the first time he had seen a dead person. Death wasn't new to him, of course. He often saw dead animals, dead birds. His mother was dead, too. But she had died many years ago, and in hospital, 250 kilometres away. Death was only something he had been told about – not something real, and close, like this.

**4** What did you feel about the story? Do you think that it is

a   frightening?   e   amusing?
b   interesting?   f   romantic?
c   boring?   g   tragic?
d   exciting?

Tell your partner about your feelings. Give your reasons. Use language like this:

> I think that the story is x because . . .

**5** Answer these questions. If you can't answer some of them, read Chapter 2.

a   Who is on the back seat of the car?
b   Where are Jack and Sue going?
c   Why are they in the outback?
d   How old is Sue?
e   Are Jack and Sue rich?
f   What happened to the car?
g   Have they got water with them?
h   Have they got food with them?
i   Have they got a radio with them?
j   Have they got a gun with them?
k   Where is Jack's father?
l   Has Jack seen a dead person before?
m   What time of year is it?

## B | FLASHBACK

**1** Read and find the answers to the questions that you could not answer.

## Chapter Two

Uncle Bert, Jack's father's brother, was a happy, friendly man. He spent much of his time travelling, alone. He had no children.

Jack sometimes wished he was Uncle Bert's son. His dad wasn't cruel, but he was weak, and drank much too much. Jack hated it when his father drank in the streets, and then slept in shop doorways. At first the children at school laughed at Jack. They copied the way his father walked when he drank too much. But they didn't do that so often now because Jack could copy his father's walk better than any of them. He did it to make them laugh. It didn't seem to hurt so much then.

During the Christmas holidays one year Uncle Bert came to see them.

'I've heard of some old gold-diggings that are near to the old Weilgumpie turn-off,' he said. 'I thought I'd try my luck for a week or two – see if I can get any gold there. How about you children coming along?'

Their father readily let them go. Jack and Sue were very happy. They were very poor, and had never been away for a holiday. Christmas Day had been nothing for them that year. Their father had drunk too much as usual and they had not received any presents.

It didn't take them long to get ready. Uncle Bert put a drum of petrol in the car, two drums of water, and a little food.

'We won't want to take much food. Mostly we'll live off the country. We'll shoot an animal and have all the fresh food that we need,' he said. He had his gun with him, and a box of bullets.

Before they started their journey on the Monday morning, they ate a big breakfast in the town cafe and Uncle Bert talked to the owner of the cafe about their journey.

'I've heard that the road out to Weilgumpie's very bad,' said the cafe-owner.

'Oh? Well, I think that my old car can get through most places. And if we do have trouble, we'll just camp beside the car and wait. Someone's sure to come along some day. We've got plenty of water. Enough for about two weeks. And they say there's a water-hole near the diggings. We'll be all right.'

When they left the town, they were soon in the open Australian bush. The road, which was very rough, went first through country that was flat, with a few small trees. The earth was a hard, red colour. There were often 25 or 30 kilometres between the houses, which were 15 kilometres or more off the road. This was the outback.

The people who lived here might not meet anyone else for months. It was a world that could not exist without the radio. News, school lessons, the doctor's care, conversation with friends – all this came only by radio.

The first night they camped by a river. They made a fire, and had a good supper: bread and sausages, with very strong tea. After supper they went for a swim in the river. Jack and Sue swam, and played, and laughed, and splashed each other. They felt freer than they had ever felt before.

Soon it was time to sleep and they lay on the ground, each in their own blanket. It was their first night sleeping in the open and they lay happily under the golden stars and the black night sky. This was going to be a holiday to remember.

2 Compare your answers with your partner's.

3 What do you think had happened between the happy start to the holiday and the moment Jack woke up in the car? (Chapter 1) Choose one of these possible reasons and tell your partner why you have chosen it.
 a A kangaroo had jumped into the road and caused an accident.
 b The brakes on the car had stopped working.
 c The steering on the car had stopped working.
 d Another car had crashed into them.
 e The car had hit a large stone.

4 Which of these things did they take with them in the car?
 a some oil
 b some petrol
 c some fresh meat
 d some water
 e a gun
 f some sausages
 g some fish
 h a box of bullets
 i a box of matches
 j some bread
 k some ice
 l some tea

## C   ANOTHER ACCIDENT

*Jack, Sue and Uncle Bert set off the next morning. After a while they turn off into the hills but suddenly the car goes wildly from one side of the road to the other. Uncle Bert can't control it and it crashes against a tree. When Jack and Sue wake they realise that Uncle Bert is dead.*

1 Read the next chapter and decide which of these pictures tells the story correctly.

Jack opened the back of the car, and found that everything was out of place. One of the water drums had fallen on its side, and water was running out. Food had fallen out of the broken bags. The bullets were everywhere except in their box.

'Let's move away from this hot place and camp near the river,' said Sue.

'All right,' said Jack, 'we'll have to move everything down there.'

It took them several journeys to carry all the things that they would need. At last nearly everything was in the new camp. Only one bag of food remained, the full drum of water, and the bullets. Jack took the bag of food. Sue stayed behind to put the bullets back in their box. She looked carefully to make sure that she had all the bullets, then she stood up. She was tired now. She felt very hot. She needed a drink badly.

She found Jack's cup, which was still lying by the car. She took it back to the water drum. She tried to move the drum towards her, but she couldn't quite reach it from the ground. So she climbed into the back of the car. Slowly, carefully, she moved the drum towards her. It was very heavy. She opened the top, and picked up the cup. Then, very carefully, she pulled the top down towards her, till a little water ran out into the cup. She held the drum against her body, to stop it falling right over.

At that moment she was bitten by a bull ant. Bull ants are very small, but dangerous. When they bite, they really hurt. Sue cried out, and jumped back, dropping the drum as she did so. It fell, and its edge landed right on her foot. That hurt even more than the ant's bite.

'Jack! Jack!' Sue cried.

Jack, who had taken the food to the camp, was just coming back. He ran, and was at her side in seconds. His first thought was the water. He quickly stood the drum up. But it was too late: there was almost no water in it now.

He turned to Sue. She was sitting on the ground, her legs held between her arms. Her foot was very badly hurt. Jack sat down beside her and looked at it. There was no blood, but already it was much bigger than the other one.

Carefully Jack tried to move Sue's toes up and down. But Sue cried out, and pulled her foot away.

'Did that hurt?'

'Yes.'

Jack sat back, and put his arm around Sue. 'If her foot is broken,' he thought, 'we're finished.' Even the loss of the water was forgotten in this new worry. He looked round, and realised suddenly that the sun was setting.

'Sue,' he said, 'we've got to get to the camp before dark. Come on, I'll help you.'

He helped her to stand. With Jack holding her, Sue tried to walk on one leg. It wasn't easy but very slowly they managed to reach the camp. When they got there Sue lay on a blanket and although her foot hurt badly, she fell asleep.

---

Jack went to see how much water was in the other drum. Only enough for about two days, he thought.

They must get water. But how? They would have to move. Where? The only water was in the hills. How far were they? And could Sue walk there? She would have to try? They couldn't stay where they were without water. He lay down, still thinking. What would they need? Tea . . . matches . . . Uncle Bert's gun? Jack fell asleep in the middle of his list.

---

## D THE SEARCH FOR WATER

*With great difficulty Jack and Sue walk slowly towards the hills. Jack has to carry everything and Sue is in great pain and can only walk very slowly with sticks. The journey takes two days. After a short rest, Jack decides to climb up to some trees half-way up a hill. He is sure that there is water there. He leaves Sue behind and climbs a very difficult path. Suddenly two enormous rocks appear in front of him.*

Now read on.

---

Jack felt hopeless. There *wasn't* any water. Only sand and rock and heat and death. Uncle Bert had been wrong. At that moment Jack hated his uncle. He was glad that he was dead. And he hated the rocks that stood in his way. He wanted to kick and bang his head against them.

He picked up a large stone and threw it as hard as he could at the rocky enemy. But he was too angry to throw straight. The stone went wide, and disappeared between the two rocks. He heard it fall on the rocks behind, then splash . . .

---

2 Write a list of the things Jack and Sue will need. Compare your list with your partner's. Persuade your partner to add things from your list. Give reasons. Use language like this:

> Why don't you put *x*? They will need it because …
> They will need it to …
> They will need it for …

3 When you have decided on the correct picture for the story, choose a caption from this list:

a 'Sue, you've spilt the water!'
b The bull ant bit her.
c 'Does it hurt?'
d She had dropped the water drum.

4 Some of your friends have missed some English lessons. Write a summary of the story so far so that they will understand the rest of the story when they return to class. Some of the summary has been done for you. Complete it.

> Jack and Sue are two _____ teenagers, aged fourteen and _____, who go off on _____ with their Uncle Bert. They go to find _____ in the _____. On the way the car crashes and Uncle Bert _____. Jack and Sue decide _____ _____ their things near to the _____ but Sue _____ bitten by a _____ _____ and she _____ so surprised that she _____ the water _____ on her _____. Her _____ is very badly _____. Jack _____ very worried _____ they have a long _____ in front of them.

Now read on.

1 What do you think happened next?

2 Use the verbs to complete the next part of the story.

> carried swam splashed had forgotten
> remembered jumped was angry
> ran back gave drank found

a Jack _____ into the water and _____ happily.
b Jack _____ Sue, below.
c Jack _____ _____ down the hill.
d Jack _____ Sue lying very still.
e Jack _____ _____ with himself because he _____ _____ Sue.
f Jack _____ Sue painfully up the hill.
g Jack _____ Sue with water.
h Jack _____ Sue some water in his shoe. Sue _____ it, thankfully.

If you want to find out what they did after that, you must read the book, *Climb a Lonely Hill* by Lilith Norman, in Collins English Library.

# SURVIVAL
## *a game for four players*

### Preparation
You need 52 **survival** cards, a dice or a spinner, some coloured buttons and a score card.
Here are 13 things. Cut 52 pieces of card or paper 8cm × 8cm. Copy each picture on to four **survival** cards.

a first-aid box

a gun

an umbrella

a drum of water

a knife

a bottle of insect-killer

a tent

a lifeboat

a parachute

a box of matches

a box of food

a spade

a rope

### Rules
Write the names of the four players on a piece of paper. One player is the scorer.
Shuffle the cards. Deal three cards to each player. Put the rest of the cards face downwards on the table.
Each player takes a different coloured button. Player 1 throws the dice and moves his or her button along the board. If the player lands on a 'disaster', he or she must try to use one of the **survival** cards in his or her hand to escape. Player 1 looks at his or her cards.

*Example*   If a player lands on No. 72, he or she needs to escape from the snake. If he or she has a GUN, he or she can say:

> I shot the snake with my gun.

If the other players agree that this is a good reason, Player 1 gets a point. The scorer marks this point on the Scorecard. The player puts the card at the bottom of the pack and takes another.
BUT, if the player does not give a good reason, for example:

> I poured the drum of water on the snake.

the other players will say that the reason is not acceptable. The player then loses a turn. (You can make the game even more difficult by insisting that the player gives the reason in correct English. If they make a mistake, they lose a turn!)
The player with the most points at the end of the game is the winner.

78

| 1 | 2 | 3 Boat sinking | 4 |
| 24 | 23 | 22 | 21 |
| 25 | 26 | 27 | 28 broken leg |
| 48 | 47 | 46 | 45 cut on the head |
| 49 | 50 killer ants | 51 | 52 |
| 72 | 71 plane on fire | 70 | 69 |
| 73 | 74 | 75 | 76 |
| 96 | 95 mosquitoes | 94 | 93 |
| 97 | 98 | 99 Perth | 100 |
| 120 | 119 | 118 | 117 a desert island |

| 6 Building collapses | 7 | 8 | 9 | 10 floods | 11 | 12 |
| 19 Down a well | 18 | 17 | 16 | 15 crocodile | 14 | 13 |
| 30 | 31 | 32 | 33 | 34 aircrash | 35 Great Barrier Reef | 36 |
| 43 | 42 | 41 • Cloncurry | 40 fire | 39 | 38 | 37 drowning in the sea |
| 54 desert thirst | 55 | 56 | 57 | 58 snowbound | 59 | 60 Brisbane • |
| 67 | 66 • Alice Springs | 65 | 64 | 63 | 62 | 61 fire on a ship |
| 78 bus crash | 79 Coober Pedy • | 80 | 81 | 82 | 83 fall from a rock | 84 • Sydney |
| 91 surfing accident | 90 | 89 Adelaide • | 88 | 87 | 86 bush fire Canberra | 85 |
| 102 shark attack | 103 | 104 | 105 | 106 Melbourne | 107 heatstroke | 108 |
| 115 | 114 | 113 | 112 | 111 | 110 drowning in a river | 109 |

r win

# New Zealand

## Passports

All visitors to New Zealand need passports except the following groups of travellers arriving direct from Australia:

**a** Australian citizens;
**b** Citizens of other Commonwealth countries who have been given permission to live in Australia.

Passports must be valid for a period of not less than six months beyond the date that the visitor will leave New Zealand.

## New Zealand money

New Zealand has a decimal money system:

| Notes | Coins |
|---|---|
| 1 dollar (100 cents) | 1 cent |
| 2 dollars | 2 cents |
| 5 dollars | 5 cents |
| 10 dollars | 10 cents |
| 20 dollars | 20 cents |
| 50 dollars | 50 cents |
| 100 dollars | |

## Banks, foreign exchange, travellers cheques

Banks are open from 10 a.m. until 4 p.m. from Monday to Friday. They are not open on Saturdays, Sundays, or on bank or public holidays (see 'Public Holidays' for dates). Travellers cheques can be changed at banks, large city hotels and many shops in the main cities and tourist centres.

## Public Holidays

New Year's Day
Waitangi Day (6 February)
Good Friday
Easter Monday
Anzac Day (25 April)
Queen's Birthday (first Monday, June)
Labour Day (fourth Monday, October)
Christmas Day
Boxing Day (26 December)

## Shopping

Stores and shops are usually open from 9 a.m. to 5.30 p.m. from Monday to Thursday, and until 9 p.m. on Friday nights. In some areas, particularly the suburbs, late night shopping occurs on Thursdays. Shops are also open on Saturday mornings in most areas. All shops, except small neighbourhood grocers', are closed on Sundays.

## Medical facilities

New Zealand's medical and hospital facilities, both public and private, provide a high standard of treatment and care. Hotels normally have a doctor who they can call if someone in the hotel is ill. There are no snakes or wild animals in New Zealand. There are sandflies in some areas and you should use an insect repellent if you are visiting such areas. The only poisonous creature in New Zealand is the very rare katipo spider.

Chemists are open during normal shopping hours and usually have other addresses on their doors for when they are closed.

Medical and hospital treatment is not free to visitors and you are recommended to have health insurance.

## Urgent help

Dial 111 for immediate contact with police, fire or ambulance services.

# Australia

## Passports

All visitors to Australia need passports except the following groups:

**a** New Zealand citizens;
**b** Citizens of other Commonwealth countries who have been given permission to settle in Australia.

## Australian money

Australia has a decimal money system:

| Notes | Coins |
|---|---|
| 2 dollars | 1 cent |
| 5 dollars | 2 cents |
| 10 dollars | 5 cents |
| 20 dollars | 10 cents |
| 50 dollars | 20 cents |
| 100 dollars | 50 cents |
| | 1 dollar |

## Business hours

Most Australian shops open at 9 a.m. and close at 5.30 p.m. from Monday to Friday and are open from 9 a.m. to noon on Saturday. Late shopping day (until 9 p.m.) is Thursday in Sydney and Canberra, and Friday in Melbourne and Darwin.

Banks are open from 10 a.m. to 3 p.m., Monday to Thursday, and until 5 p.m. on Friday. They are closed on Saturday.

Post Offices are open from 9 a.m. to 5 p.m., Monday to Friday.

Office hours are usually 9 a.m. to 5 p.m. Monday to Friday.

## Seasonal events

January: Ocean beach surf carnivals in all states. They include surf swimming competitions, races between life-savers' boats, surfboard races and rescue competitions.
February: Festival of Perth – a month-long festival of culture.
March: Canberra Festival – a week-long celebration of the founding of the national capital city. It includes popular entertainment: fairs, pop concerts and barbecues.
April: Barossa Valley Vintage Festival – a chance to taste some of the country's best wines.
May: Bangtail Muster, Alice Springs – a rodeo with plenty of horses and cattle.
June: Queensland Pacific Festival: Lasts three days and offers examples of the culture of South Pacific people.
July: Three important horse races, two in Brisbane and one in Melbourne.
August: Ballarat – singing competition.
September: Melbourne Royal Agricultural Show.
October: Australian Open Golf Tournament.
November: The Melbourne Cup – Australia's most important horse racing event.
December: Sydney to Hobart Yacht Race.
December – January: Australian Open Tennis Tournament.

# TEST YOUR ENGLISH

**A** Use the simple past or the past perfect to complete the passage.

### A bad start to the day

At 6 o'clock Sarah and Jo woke up. Most unusually the sheep dogs were barking. The girls looked out of their bedroom window and_____ (see) that some of the sheep_____ (escape). The two girls and their father_____ (get up) quickly and_____ (round up) the sheep before they_____ (have) their breakfast. After breakfast Sarah_____ (go) to take hay to the cattle. When she_____ (arrive) back at the farmhouse, she_____ (realize) that she_____ (lose) her keys. She_____ (go) back to the cattle shed and there they were! She_____ (drop) them in the mud. She_____ (hurry) back and_____ (get) into the car, where her sister and father were waiting for her. They_____ (set off) for school but after about five minutes Jo_____ (say) that she_____ (forget) her sandwich box. Her father_____ (look) very angry but he_____ (turn) the car around and_____ (go) back for it. They finally_____ (arrive) at school just after all the children_____ (go) inside.

**B**  SPOT DICTATION

Listen to Rosalind Ritchie talking about winemaking. Write down the missing words.

This is how the wine is made in our winery. After the grapes_____ _____in late summer, they _____ _____so that all the juice runs out. Then the juice_____ _____from the skins and pips and it_____ _____into large containers and_____ _____to ferment. Later, it_____ _____into smaller containers. Then it_____ _____for about a year when it_____ _____into bottles. If it is a good wine, the bottles_____ _____for several years but the cheaper wines_____ _____ immediately.

**C** Read this conversation and then complete the letter from Anna.

**Anna:** Did you go to the cinema last night?
**James:** Yes.
**Anna:** What did you see?
**James:** *Mad Max Beyond Thunderdome.*
**Anna:** Is it good?
**James:** Yes, it's fantastic! There are some very good fights in it.
**Anna:** Oh, I thought that it was quite a romantic film.
**James:** Well, there are some romantic scenes but I like the fighting and the photography. It's set in Australia and you see some very beautiful places.
**Anna:** Well, I think I'll ask Peter and Rosemary to come with me.

Dear Pete and Rosemary .....

**D** Write **who** or **that** where there is a missing word.

1 A surgeon is a doctor. ..... does operations, for example taking out an appendix.
2 A virus is a very small living thing ..... causes an infection.
3 A chemist is a person ..... makes and sells medicines.
4 An antibiotic is a medicine ..... is made from living things, for example penicillin.
5 A physician is a doctor ..... treats illnesses with medicines.
6 A prescription is a piece of paper ..... you give to the chemist so that you can get your medicines.
7 A nurse is a person ..... takes care of people when they are ill.
8 A pill is a medicine ..... is small and round, for example an aspirin.

**E** CLIMB A LONELY HILL CROSSWORD

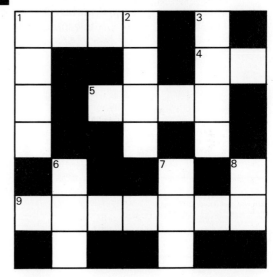

**Across**
1 When Jack tried to move his Uncle Bert he found that he was _____. (4 letters)
4 Jack and Sue could either try to find water __ they could wait and hope for someone to come along. (2)
5 The type of ant that bit Sue. (4)
9 The name for the large open parts of Australia. (7)

**Down**
1 Jack and Sue's mother did this before the story started. (4)
2 A large container for petrol or water. Sue dropped one on her foot. (4)
3 Jack thought that he would find water in one of these. He had to climb a rocky hill first. (4)
6 This is very hot. It made Jack and Sue very thirsty. (3)
7 Jack did this when he remembered Sue. (3)
8 Two letters that mean 'everything is all right'.

# AN INTERNATIONAL LANGUAGE

## A AMBITIONS FOR THE FUTURE

1 What would you like to be when you grow up? Do any of the jobs below interest you? Choose two or three.

I'd like to . . .

be a doctor

work in a bank

be an international sportsman/wom[an]

be an airline pilot

work in telecommunications

## B  INTERNATIONAL ENGLISH

1 Look at these examples of international English. They come from different worlds. Read them through and identify which world each example comes from.

| | |
|---|---|
| advertising | medicine |
| banking | air travel |
| business | telecommunications |

2 Discuss these questions for each example
Where could you find an example of this English?
Who was it written by?
Who was it written for?

3 Listen to these examples of international English. Write down the order in which you hear the examples.

Where would you hear these examples?

a air travel (pilot)  b air travel (steward/ess)

c sport  d tourism  e sea travel

So you can see that nowadays English is not just the language of English-speaking countries like Britain, the United States, Australia and New Zealand. It is the language that people in many countries use to communicate with each other. English is also used as a means of communication between different parts of a country, when the people of that country speak several different languages. (India is a good example.) As a result you will now find English spoken and written all over the world. English no longer belongs to the English!

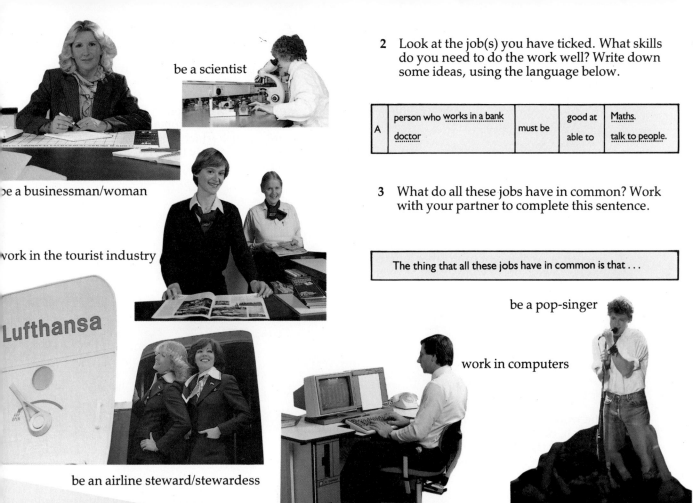

be a scientist

be a businessman/woman

work in the tourist industry

**Lufthansa**

be an airline steward/stewardess

work in computers

be a pop-singer

**2** Look at the job(s) you have ticked. What skills do you need to do the work well? Write down some ideas, using the language below.

| A | person who works in a bank / doctor | must be | good at / able to | Maths. / talk to people. |
|---|---|---|---|---|

**3** What do all these jobs have in common? Work with your partner to complete this sentence.

> The thing that all these jobs have in common is that . . .

---

C JOB INTERVIEWS

For this role play, work in groups of five. There are two interviewers and three applicants for the job advertised on the right. The interviewers will interview each applicant individually and choose the best person for the job.

> **TOURS INTERNATIONAL**
> Tour guide needed to conduct international groups of tourists round the principal sights of the country. Knowledge of two foreign languages, including English, essential. Previous experience not necessary as full training given.
> Contact 730 2812

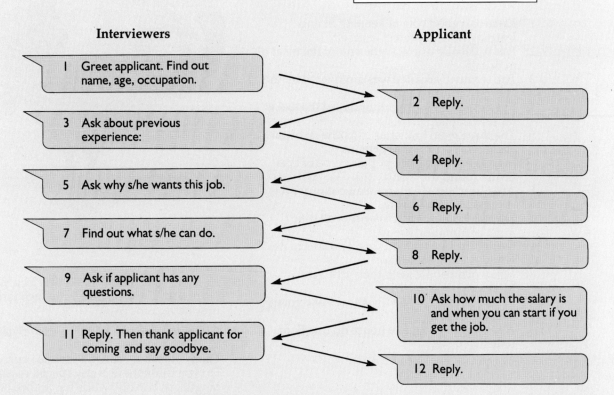

**Interviewers**

1 Greet applicant. Find out name, age, occupation.

3 Ask about previous experience:

5 Ask why s/he wants this job.

7 Find out what s/he can do.

9 Ask if applicant has any questions.

11 Reply. Then thank applicant for coming and say goodbye.

**Applicant**

2 Reply.

4 Reply.

6 Reply.

8 Reply.

10 Ask how much the salary is and when you can start if you get the job.

12 Reply.

1 Languages frequently borrow words from other languages. Do you know any words in your language that have come from English? How many can you find in five minutes? Make a list with your partner.

*Example* computer popstar taxi

Next make a class list. Do you know if the words on your list have exactly the same meaning as in your language?

2 English is no different from other languages: it has borrowed lots of words from all over the world. Some famous examples are the words that we use for the meat we eat:

| Animal | Meat |
|--------|--------|
| cow | beef |
| pig | pork |
| sheep | mutton |

The words for the animals come from old English, but the words for the meat come from French (at the time of the French domination of England): beef-*boeuf*, pork-*porc*, mutton-*mouton*.

Here are some examples of English words which have come from other languages. Which languages have they come from? Choose the correct language from the box.

| Arabic | Dutch | French | German |
|--------|--------|------------|---------|
| Greek | Hebrew | Hindi | Italian |
| Japanese | Polish | Portuguese | Spanish |

1 *Karate* is a good way of keeping fit and learning how to protect yourself.
2 *Port* is usually drunk at the end of the meal in Britain.
3 The element *polonium* was discovered by the scientist, Marie Curie.
4 The *Sabbath* is an important day of the week for Jewish people.
5 The three main branches of mathematics are arithmetic, *algebra* and geometry.
6 *Lager* is now the most popular type of beer drunk round the world.
7 After lunch in Mediterranean countries it is common to take a *siesta*.
8 The most famous *psychologist* of all time must be Sigmund Freud.
9 One of the most famous *opera* houses in the world is La Scala, Milan.
10 Many rich people keep their *yachts* in Monaco.
11 Young people on holiday always like going to *disco(theque)s*.
12 A *bungalow* is a type of house on one floor only.

3 In English this is *an orange*. But it used to be called *a norange* which comes from the Spanish word *naranja* which comes from the Arabic word *naranj* which comes from the Persian word *narang* which comes from the Sanskrit word *naranga* which comes from . . . who knows? The funny thing is – the Persians now call the fruit a *portugal!*

Put the travel stickers of this particular traveller in the correct order.

4 In English this bird is called a *turkey*. The Portuguese word for it is *peru*. What is it in Turkish, I wonder?

5 Here are some more words that English has borrowed. Can you find out which language they have come from?

**Clothes:** anorak bikini jeans pyjamas sandals
**Food:** alcohol banana coffee curry tea
Do you think there is any special reason why languages borrow words for clothes and food?

# CHECK YOUR ENGLISH

ENGLISH SPOKEN HERE

## Social English: going for an interview

*(Practise this conversation in groups of three.)*

**Interviewer 1:** Come in. You must be . . . . .
**Applicant:** Yes, that's right.
**Interviewer 1:** My name's . . . . . and this is my colleague, . . . . .
**Applicant:** How do you do?
**Interviewer 2:** How do you do? Please sit down.
**Applicant:** Thank you.
**Interviewer 1:** So you've come about the job. Have you ever done work like this before?
**Applicant:** . . . . .
**Interviewer 2:** Why do you want the job?
**Applicant:** . . . . .
**Interviewer 1:** What can you do – are you good at working with people for example?
**Applicant:** . . . . .
**Interviewer 2:** And are you able to type?
**Applicant:** . . . . .
**Interviewer 1:** Have you any questions?
**Applicant:** . . . . .
**Interviewer 2:** Well, thank you for coming. We'll telephone you later. Goodbye.
**Applicant:** . . . . .

## Word stress

1 *Listen and mark the stressed syllables in these words from Unit 11:*

mathematics   information   international
calculator   domination   electronic
telecommunications   instruction   calculation
competition   technology   synthesiser
psychologist   Mediterranean

2 *Sort the words above into three groups:*

A words with the stress on the second last syllable
B words with the stress on the third last syllable
C words with the stress on the fourth last syllable

3 *Can you work out two rules for the words in Group A?*

## Spelling test

1 *You are going to be tested on seven words from Unit 11. Write down each word.*

*Example*
You hear: *psychologist* – The most famous psychologist of all time must be Sigmund Freud – *psychologist*
You write: *psychologist*

2 *All the words have one or two silent letters. What are they?*

*Example* ⓟsychologist

---

## WORD WORK

1 *Add -er, -or, -ist, -man/woman to the words below to make nouns describing people at work.*
bank   business   design   edit
interview   psychology   publish
sports

2 *Sort the words below into three lists and give each group a title.*
beef   calculator   computer
digital watch   mutton   pilot
pop singer   pork   stewardess
synthesiser   tour guide   turkey

---

## KNOW YOUR GRAMMAR

### Defining people and things (1)

1 *Study these ways of defining people and things from Unit 11:*

a A person who works in a bank must be good at maths. (p.82)
b Do you know any words in your language that have come from English? (p.84)
c Here are some examples of English words which have come from other languages. (p.84)
d Some famous examples are the words that we use for the meat we eat. (p.84)

2 *Study the box below and match a–d with 1–6.*

|  | PEOPLE | THINGS |
|---|---|---|
| Subject | ① who | ② which |
|  | ③ . . . that . . . . . . . |  |
| Object | ④ who(m) | which |
|  | ⑤ . . . . . | ⑥ |

3 *Look for ways of defining people and things in the article* Catching The Bug *on p.88.*

Find: five examples of ①   three examples of ④
one example of ②   one example of ⑤
one example of ③

# ENGLISH FOR COMPUTERS

**A** 📼 COMPUTERS IN THE WORLD TODAY

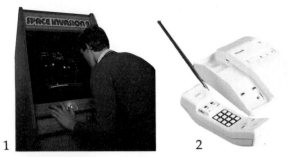

3

1

2

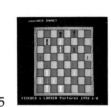
4

5

6

7

8

1 Look at pictures 1–8. What are they called? Match the names (a–h) to the objects.

**a** calculator **b** synthesiser **c** digital watch
**d** cordless phone **e** factory robot
**f** cash dispenser **g** electronic game
**h** arcade game

Listen and check your ideas.

2 How many of these things 1–8 have you got? How many have you used or seen? Make two lists and prepare to tell your partner.

> I've got a.....

> I've never used a.....

Conduct a quick class survey with your teacher's help.

3 What do all these things have in common? Work with your partner.

> The thing that all these things have in common is.....

4 In two minutes, how many other things can you think of which use a microchip? Work with your partner.

**B** COMPUTERS AND WORK

1 Computers are widely used in many professions today to help people work faster, more easily and more efficiently. For example, the computers which the police use today help them to solve crimes more efficiently.

Write four similar sentences from the box below about computers and work.

| The computers | which that | secretaries travel agents postmen businesspeople | use today help them to | understand the market better. sort letters faster. write letters more easily. book tickets more efficiently. |
|---|---|---|---|---|

2 Here are three examples of computers which are used regularly at work today. What help is the computer giving?

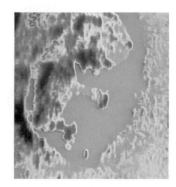

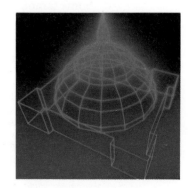

Write sentences about the help the computer is giving. Use the model in **1** above to help you, and the words in brackets.

(pilot/land and take off in bad weather)
(doctor/check the condition of the unborn baby)
(architect/design building)

## C  SETTING UP A HOME COMPUTER

1   Look at this picture of a home computer. Listen to this extract from a school talk on home computers and label the picture correctly. Use the words in the box.

| | |
|---|---|
| a  2 floppy disks | d  the monitor |
| b  the instruction manual | e  the printer |
| c  the keyboard | |

2   What do these five parts of the home computer do? Listen again and match the definition to the part.

   a   the book which tells you how to operate your computer
   b   the machine which prints everything you want
   c   the screen where you see everything you have typed in
   d   the part which contains the computer and which you use to type in your material and instructions
   e   the parts which store your material

3   Check your ideas with your partner. Ask and answer questions like this:

> What's a monitor?

> A monitor is the thing which.....

4   Here are the instructions for the first stages of setting up a home computer system. The pictures are in order but the instructions are not. Put them in the correct order.

1   Switch on the monitor.

2   Connect the printer to the monitor using the 34-pin plug on the end of the printer cable.

3   Connect the keyboard to the monitor using the 4-pin plug on the end of the keyboard cable.

4   Connect the disc drive to the keyboard.

5   Fit a plug to the mains lead on the monitor. Make sure you use the correct fuse. DO NOT PLUG YOUR COMPUTER INTO THE MAINS SUPPLY YET.

6   Plug the monitor into the mains supply.

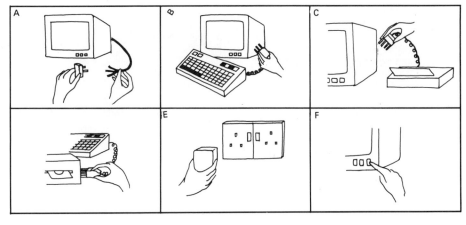

## D A COMPUTER PROGRAM

You can use a computer to do many different jobs – store information, do calculations, play games and even draw pictures. For each job the computer needs instructions to tell it what to do. A set of instructions for a computer is called a *program*.

Programs are written in special computer languages. One of the most common computer languages is BASIC. BASIC uses both symbols and English words. All computer languages work in the same way. If you want to work with computers, you must be able to read and understand English.

Look at this simple program in BASIC.

1   What is this program used for?
   a   for identifying a person's name
   b   for calculating your age in seconds
   c   for finding out the date of your birthday

2   Look at 3Ø and 4Ø. What do you think D, M and Y refer to? Check your ideas in 5Ø and 6Ø.

3   Look at 19Ø and 2ØØ. Can you explain the numbers? What do they refer to?

```
10  CLS:DIM N(12)
20  FOR K=1 TO 12:READ N(K):NEXT K
30  PRINT "WHAT DATE IS IT?"
40  INPUT D1,M1,Y1
50  PRINT "WHEN WERE YOU BORN?"
60  INPUT D2,M2,Y2: LET D=D1-D2
70  LET M=M1-M2:LET Y=Y1-Y2
80  IF D>=0 THEN GOTO 100
90  LET D=D+N(M1):LET M=M-1
100 IF M>=0 THEN GOTO 120
110 LET M=M+12:LET Y=Y-1
120 IF Y/4<>INT(Y/4) THEN GOTO 140
130 IF M1=3 AND M2=2 THEN LET D=D+1
140 LET D=365.25*Y+30.24*M+D
150 LET S=D*24*60*60
160 PRINT "YOU ARE NOW ABOUT"
170 PRINT INT(S/1000000)
180 PRINT "MILLION SECONDS OLD."
190 DATA 31,31,28,31,30,31
200 DATA 30,31,31,30,31,30
```

1 Read the article and find the answers to these
questions.

Who are they?
How old are they?
Where do they live?
What is the magazine called?
How many readers does it have?
What does it contain?

# Catching The Bug

If you like computer games and
are bored with the computer
magazines you buy, become a
publisher and write your own. All
over the country, small groups of
people are now producing
computer game magazines which
they print cheaply and sell to their
friends.

Among the best is one which is
produced in North London – *The
Bug*. Since its simple beginning in
1984 *The Bug* has got better and
better. It appears every month
and now has a readership of over
200. It provides reviews, articles,
competitions and cartoons – all
for 25p.

What makes *The Bug*
surprising is its editorial team:
Jaron Lewis who is 15, his brother
Kelsey who is 13, Jeffrey Davy
who is 14 and Genia Davy who is
10. They control every stage of
the magazine, from writing to
editing, design to printing.

Jaron explains why they started
*The Bug*. 'We all had computers
and we were fed up with the
articles in the main magazines.
We didn't agree with their
opinions on the games. For
example, they might give a good
review of a game that we all
thought was rubbish. So we
decided to write our own reviews
of games that we already had.'

Now they are in touch with 45
companies all over the country
who regularly send their games to
*The Bug* for reviewing. They try
to be independent, but this can
have its problems, as Jaron

explains. 'One company didn't
like it when Jeffrey said that his
ten-year-old sister could draw
better graphics than the ones in
their game. They didn't send us
any more games.'

The team also send their
articles to famous people for their
comments. For example, they
recently sent an article that was
called *Women and Computers* to
Anita Dobson, one of the stars of

the popular television
programme, *EastEnders*. She
wrote back saying she did not
know anything about computers,
but she wished them the best of
luck.

The team are hoping that *The
Bug*'s second birthday issue will
be the best yet.

Contact *The Bug* at 28 Leaside
Avenue, London N10.

2 List all the jobs the children have to do to
produce the magazine.

3 Role play – work in groups of four. Each
member of the group should be one of the
editorial team of *The Bug*. So first decide who is
who. Each member of the team should think of
two interesting ideas for articles about

computers to include in the second birthday
issue. When you are ready, hold an editorial
meeting. You only have room for five ideas, so
you must decide which are the best. Choose a
secretary who will report your five ideas to the
rest of the class. Which group will produce the
best magazine?

# PROJECT ENGLISH

### PRODUCE A CLASS NEWSPAPER

**A  CLASS DISCUSSION: THE CONTENTS**

1  **Name** Choose a name for your newspaper.

2  **Size** Agree on the size of your newspaper. (About 4 pages will be plenty.)

3  **Topics** Choose eight topics for your newspaper. For example:
   a Why don't I smoke. Choose the best composition from the class. (See unit 11 lesson 2)
   b Family remedies. Collect all the reports. (See unit 11 lesson 1)
   c Advertisements in English
   d A sports report.

4  **Election** Elect an Editor, a Publisher and a Business manager.

**B  GROUPWORK: TOPICS**

1  Divide the class into eight groups, each group to be responsible for one topic.

2  Elect a group sub-editor and a secretary.

3  Discuss your topic and decide what will go into your article.

4  The secretary will write a first version of the article.

5  Discuss this version.

6  Agree on a final version. It should be not more than 300 words.

6  If possible, type the article. Remember to write in the names of the group at the end.

**C  EDITORIAL BOARD**

The Editorial Board consists of the Editor, the Publisher, the Business manager and the eight sub-editors.

1  Discuss the articles and decide where each article will be placed.

2  Discuss how the newspaper will be printed. Probably the best way to print the paper is by photocopying. The Business manager will need to find out how much this will cost per copy.

3  Decide how many copies will be printed and how much each copy will cost.

4  Decide when the newspaper will be published.

**D  SALE AND DISTRIBUTION**

1  The Business manager will take orders for the newspaper. It is a good idea to collect the money with the orders. This will determine how many copies are printed.

2  When the newspapers are printed the Business manager will deliver copies to those who have ordered them and collect the money.

3  The Business manager will pay for the printing.

Here is some information about photocopiers and the kind of pens you should use.

## Photocopies

Most photocopiers produce copies the same size as the original. Many printing/copying shops and some offices now have photocopiers that enlarge or reduce.

They usually enlarge or reduce in one stage from one 'A' size down to the next; A4 reduced to A5, A4 enlarged to A3. You can occasionally find a photocopier that does not go from an 'A' size to another 'A' size, some work by percentages – ask them for details.

Therefore, on many photocopiers you can enlarge or reduce an image again and again until it is much bigger or smaller. Always squeeze as many things as you can on the original piece of paper so as to get more done for your money. Do shop around for copying as prices vary enormously.

Very few photocopiers enlarge above A3. Any places that do, may charge far more than the price for doing each half of a image up to A3 then joining them together.

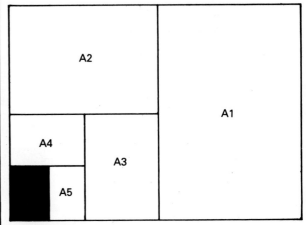

'A' sizes
| | |
|---|---|
| A1 | 594mm×841mm |
| A2 | 420mm×594mm |
| A3 | 297mm×420mm |
| A4 | 210mm×297mm |
| A5 | 148mm×210mm |

## Headings

Fat felt-tip pens are the easiest medium for hand lettered headings.

# EASY+BOLD

# CURES, OLD AND NEW

## A VACCINATION

The cartoon shows a famous English doctor called Edward Jenner. He is on the left giving the fat lady an injection in the arm. Jenner had been looking for a cure for smallpox, a disease which in those days caused half of all blindness in Europe and killed thousands of people every year. One day, he learned from a woman living in the country that people who caught the disease cowpox from their cows never seemed to catch smallpox. Jenner thought about this and then had an idea. He made a vaccine* containing serum** from a cow which had the disease, then he injected this into the arm of a young boy. The boy never caught smallpox. And that's how the practice of vaccination started. Of course, at the time many people thought Jenner was mad, and some people actually formed an Anti-Vaccine Society.

*  vaccine – comes from the Latin word for 'cow'.
** serum – the part of the blood which is watery and colourless.

Think about these questions, and discuss them in your own language.

1   What happened to people who caught smallpox?

2   Why did people think Jenner was mad?
3   People in the cartoon have cows coming out of their bodies. Why?

## B  HOME MEDICINE

1   These are all cures for the common cold.

a foot bath containing mustard

a hot drink containing honey and lemon

a steam bath made with herbs

tea made from Eucalyptus leaf

garlic

tea made from red pepper

Discuss these questions in groups of four.
   Have you tried any of them? If yes, tell your group.
   Do you think they could work?
   Do you know any other cures for the common cold?

2   What cures, old or new, does your family have for:

|   | cuts | black eye | stomach ache | headache | cough | burns |
|---|---|---|---|---|---|---|
| 1 |  |  |  |  |  |  |
| 2 |  |  |  |  |  |  |
| 3 |  |  |  |  |  |  |
| 4 |  |  |  |  |  |  |

Copy and complete the chart with your teacher's help.
Fill in 1 for yourself.
Fill in 2–4 for the others in your group.

3   Write a report about your family cures. Start like this:

   My family's cure for burns is ice cold water.
   Our cure for ................. is ...................
   We use ..................... for .....................

Read each other's reports.

## C ACCIDENTS AND ILLNESSES

1 Have you ever had an accident or been ill?
What was the worst thing about it? What was
the best thing about it?

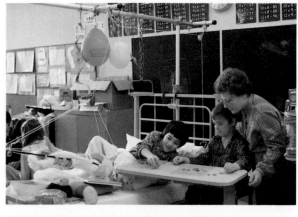

Name ................................................................

What was wrong?

When did this happen?

Did you stay at home?

      go to hospital?

What medicine did you have?

What other treatment did you have?

How many doctors asked you questions?

How did you feel about the accident/illness?

2 Copy this questionnaire and interview your
partner.

3 Write a report about your partner's experience.
Give it to your partner to check.

## D 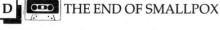 THE END OF SMALLPOX

1 Look at this newspaper extract.

2 Look at the map and these photographs from a
book about the last case of smallpox.

New York Times 14 November 1975

### THE END OF SMALLPOX
The World Health Organisation said
today that there were no more cases
of smallpox in the world. Twenty
years ago 2,000,000 people a year
died from this disease. The last case
of smallpox was reported from
Bangladesh six weeks ago.

Bilkisunessa led the
health workers to the
last case on Bhola
Island.

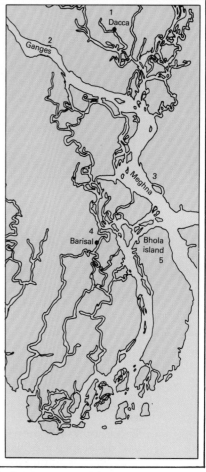

The 'Speedy Rocket'
leaves for Bhola Island.

Rahima Banu, the last case
of smallpox in the world.

Every house had to be
checked for smallpox.

3 Listen to the radio interview with Dr Stan Foster of the World Health Organisation. Then
choose the correct answer to each question.

| | | a doctor | a health worker | a policeman |
|---|---|---|---|---|
| 1 | Who was Shahabudim? | a doctor | a health worker | a policeman |
| 2 | How old was Bilkisunessa? | 8 | 11 | 14 |
| 3 | How old was Rahima Banu? | 3 | 11 | 14 |
| 4 | How many health workers came to the island? | 200 | 800 | 1,400 |
| 5 | How many people did they vaccinate? | 16,150 | 16,295 | 18,150 |
| 6 | How long does it take for smallpox to appear? | 3 weeks | 6 weeks | 2 months |
| 7 | How long did they wait? | 6 weeks | 2 months | 10 weeks |
| 8 | When was the last case of smallpox in the world? | 1975 | 1976 | 1978 |

**E** A TOWN CALLED MATHARE

1 Look at this photograph of Mathare, a shanty town near Nairobi, the capital of Kenya.

What are the houses made of?
Where do you think the people get their drinking water from?
What sort of illnesses could people catch?
What are the dangers of living in a place like this?

2 Kaari Kisuke and her friend, Toro, live in Mathare. They are 'health scouts'. That means they have learnt how to treat common diseases. They also know what to do if there is an accident, and how to make their homes safe. Kaari decided to keep a diary of her job as a health scout. Read what happened to Kaari and Toro one day.

> Toro and I were ......¹ home from school. It was about 4 o'clock. Suddenly we heard ......² and saw flames leaping into the sky. One of the houses made of cardboard was on ......³ so we ran to have a look.
>
> Many people were standing in a long line passing buckets of ......⁴ from the tap to the house. Others were getting their own drinking water and throwing it on to their roofs to stop them ......⁵ fire too.
>
> Our neighbour Mrs Kidera was very worried. I knew she had a daughter about eight ......⁶ old who was disabled and couldn't walk properly. But where was she? I went around to get a closer look and saw
>
> someone pull her out of the house. She was burned.
>
> I told Toro to run very quickly to the church about a mile away where someone had a car. I thought the owner might take the girl to hospital if Toro told him about the fire. I ran into my own home and found a ......⁷ sheet. I asked Mrs Kidera if she would wrap the child in my sheet to keep her warm and stop the burns getting dirty. The child looked very pale, and I knew that it was ......⁸ to get her to a hospital quickly.
>
> It seemed ages until Toro returned with the man in his car, but it was only about 30 minutes. He took the child and her mother straight to the ......⁹

3 Kaari's diary got wet. The missing words are given below. Match them to the numbers.

catching   hospital   walking   fire   shouts
clean   years   water   important

4 Facts about Mathare. True, false or don't know?
a The houses are very close together.
b Every house has a bathroom.
c The streets are dirty and dusty.
d Only one family lives in each house.
e The houses are all made of brick.
f All houses have running water.
g The houses are made of expensive materials.
h All houses have electricity.

5 What can people do to make Mathare a safer place? Make a list of five ideas.

**F** AMBULANCE

This photograph shows a bicycle ambulance which was developed in Malawi. It is designed to provide cheap transport for patients who live in the rural areas of developing countries. In a country like Malawi, where there are not many roads, transporting ill or injured people to hospital has always been a problem. Motor ambulances cannot reach many areas, and people who live in the country do not have their own means of transport. The bicycle ambulance is light, can be attached to any kind of bicycle, and can be made very easily.

Think of three reasons why bicycle ambulances are a good idea.

92

# CHECK YOUR ENGLISH

ENGLISH SPOKEN HERE

**Social English: joining a sports club**

| | |
|---|---|
| Instructor: | How are you? |
| You: | ................................................................ |
| Instructor: | What sports do you play? |
| You: | ................................................................ |
| Instructor: | How much exercise do you take every day? |
| You: | ................................................................ |
| Instructor: | How much do you weigh? |
| You: | ................................................................ |
| Instructor: | Do you smoke? |
| You: | ................................................................ |
| Instructor: | When were you last ill? |
| You: | ................................................................ |
| Instructor: | What was wrong with you? (OR What was the matter?) |
| You: | ................................................................ |
| Instructor: | Do you have to take any special medicines? |
| You: | ................................................................ |
| Instructor: | Are you careful about what you eat? |
| You: | ................................................................ |

**Unstressed syllables**

1 Mark the stressed syllables in these words from Unit 12.
   a ability   around
   b decided   destroy   expensive   returned
   c beginning   developed   report
   d discussion   important   injected   kilometre
   e complete   containing   opinion   policeman

2 What can you say about the position of the stressed syllables?

3 Sort the words into two groups.
   a words with the first syllable pronounced /ə/
   b words with the first syllable pronounced /ɪ/

**Spelling test**

1 You are going to be tested on fifteen words from Unit 12. Write down each word.

2 All these words, except one, have one or two silent letters. What are they? Sort the words into two groups. Which word is the exception?

## WORD WORK

1 *Add* -ion, -ity, -ment, -ness *to the words below to make nouns. Be careful – sometimes you have to make spelling changes.*

active blind decide discuss electric except fit ill inject move treat vaccinate

2 *Sort the words below into these three categories.*

Good Health   Bad Health   Medicine

cure disease dizzy fit healthy ill injection pale sick slim strong tired treatment vaccination well

## KNOW YOUR GRAMMAR

**Defining people and things (2)**

1 Study these ways of defining people and things from Unit 12.
   – a famous English doctor <u>called</u> Edward Jenner (p.90)
   – one of the houses <u>made</u> of cardboard (p.92)
   – a woman <u>living</u> in the country (p.90)
   – a vaccine <u>containing</u> serum from a cow (p.90)

   You can also say
   A   a famous English doctor *who was called* Edward Jenner
       one of the houses *which was made* of cardboard

   B   a woman *who lived* in the country
       a vaccine *which contained* serum from a cow

2 Look at the six cures for the common cold on page 90. Write out the six captions in full as in A and B above.

3 Look at the story from Malawi on page 92. Find two examples of A and two of B and rewrite them as in **1** above.

93

# KEEPING FIT

## A  HOW FIT ARE YOU?

True physical fitness is something more than simply being fit to cope with the stresses and strains of everyday life. It consists of three important ingredients — stamina, suppleness and strength — *the S–Factors*.

### S Stamina

First and most important is stamina. This is the ability to keep going without being short of breath. For stamina you need a strong heart and muscles.

### S Suppleness

Next is suppleness. This is the ability to move easily. You need a lot of movement in your neck, spine and joints.

### S Strength

Finally strength. This is the ability to lift heavy weights. You need strong shoulder, back and leg muscles. The muscles in your stomach help too.

1  Look at the S–Factor table. Make your own personal S–Factor table by copying out the sports or activities you do *regularly* (i.e. two or three times a week). Put the scores in each of the three columns for your sports or activities.

2  Compare and contrast each of your sports or activities. Write a sentence for each.

   e.g.  Football is better for suppleness and strength than jogging, but not as good for stamina.

   Compare your sentences with your partner's.

3  Work out a simple total S–Factor score for each of your sports or activities by adding the three scores together. Put your list in order with the highest score first.
   Note: You can also do this ordering for *each* of the three S–Factors.

4  Conduct a class survey on the top three sports or activities for the class.

### S-FACTOR SCORE

|  | Stamina | Suppleness | Strength |
|---|---|---|---|
| Badminton | ★★ | ★★★ | ★★ |
| Canoeing | ★★★ | ★★ | ★★★ |
| Climbing Stairs | ★★★ | ★ | ★★ |
| Cycling (hard) | ★★★★ | ★★ | ★★★ |
| Dancing (disco) | ★★★ | ★★★★ | ★ |
| Football | ★★★ | ★★★ | ★★★ |
| Gymnastics | ★★ | ★★★★ | ★★★ |
| Housework (moderate) | ★ | ★★ | ★ |
| Jogging | ★★★★ | ★★ | ★★ |
| Karate | ★★ | ★★★★ | ★★ |
| Rowing | ★★★★ | ★★ | ★★★★ |
| Sailing | ★ | ★★ | ★★ |
| Squash | ★★★ | ★★★ | ★★ |
| Swimming (hard) | ★★★★ | ★★★★ | ★★★★ |
| Tennis | ★★ | ★★★ | ★★ |
| Walking (briskly) | ★★ | · ★ | ★ |
| Weightlifting | ★ | ★ | ★★★★ |
| Yoga | ★ | ★★★★ | ★ |

| ★ No real effect | ★★★ Very good effect |
|---|---|
| ★★ Good effect | ★★★★ Excellent effect |

## B  STAMINA

1  Read these four stamina tests. Match the pictures to the texts.

**Stamina Test 1**
Try walking up and down a flight of stairs (about 15 steps) *three* times, fairly quickly. You should be able to hold an ordinary conversation without being at all out of breath.

**Stamina Test 2**
Run on the spot. Lift your feet at least 15cm off the floor. Keep going until you start to feel a bit short of breath or tired, then stop. Young people should find three minutes quite easy.

**Stamina Test 3**
Using either the second step of the stairs or a strong chair, step up and down quickly, alternating your leading foot. Stop as soon as you feel a bit short of breath or tired. A fit young person should be able to hold a conversation without being too short of breath after three minutes of this exercise.

**Stamina Test 4**
Don't try this until you are fit enough to do Test 3 comfortably. Jog gently and easily for one kilometre. You should be able to do it in six and a half minutes. (Girls are allowed two minutes extra.) You should be able to hold an ordinary conversation without being too short of breath during the test and immediately afterwards.

A  B

C  D

2  Do the tests after school and copy and complete the chart when you have done them.

|  | Date done | Passed | Failed |
|---|---|---|---|
| STAMINA TEST 1 | ........................ | ☐ | ☐ |
| STAMINA TEST 2 | ........................ | ☐ | ☐ |
| STAMINA TEST 3 | ........................ | ☐ | ☐ |
| STAMINA TEST 4 | ........................ | ☐ | ☐ |

**Remember:**  start gently, build up gradually, and don't keep going if you feel uncomfortable.

## C SMOKING: THE FACTS

1 Read this extract from a Health Education booklet. The sentences in the fourth paragraph are in the wrong order. Put them back in the correct order. Use the words in italics to help you.

---

**WHAT DOES SMOKING DO TO YOUR BODY?**

**A closer look at our lungs**

If you are a non-smoker and you take a few puffs of a cigarette you may *cough, feel sick* or *feel dizzy*.

This is not surprising: you are breathing in hot smoke containing many chemicals. Did you know that the tip of a cigarette, burning at 880°C, is nearly nine times as hot as the temperature of boiling water?

Look at the pictures. They are enlarged many thousands of times. They show the inside of your lungs, covered with millions of tiny hairs.

*Here* the mucus is swallowed so that the germs are killed. Germs and dirt are trapped in a layer of jelly-like mucus on the inside of the lungs. *These* hairs keep the lungs clean. The hairs sweep *this* dirty mucus upwards to the throat.

---

3 With your partner
   a describe in your own words how the lungs are kept clean.
   b explain why smokers often have more coughs and chest infections than non-smokers.

 ## D SMOKING: FOR OR AGAINST

1 Listen to these six people a-f giving their opinions about smoking. In what order do they speak? Match the voice and the opinion 1-6 to the photos. *Example* 1c.

2 Listen again and write down if the speaker is for or against smoking, or if s/he has no strong feelings about it.

3 Who do you agree with most? Work in groups of four and explain your ideas.

4 Role play: *Smoking in school*

   *Student* has been caught smoking several times by *Teacher*. A meeting has been arranged with *Headmaster, Teacher, Student* and *Parent* to discuss the problem.
   Work in groups of four. Choose a role and read the correct role-card. Take a few minutes to prepare your ideas.

2 Write captions for these pictures of the insides of lungs. Put the verbs into the correct form, *-ing* or *-ed*.

a
Lungs of a non-smoker. Here you can see healthy lungs (CONTAIN) clean hairs to move and sweep the dirty mucus up out of the lungs.

b
Lungs of a smoker (1). Here you can see the hairs (DAMAGE) by cigarette smoke.

c
Lungs of a smoker (2). Here you can see most of the hairs (DESTROY) by cigarette smoke.

d
Lungs of a smoker (3). Here you can see the hairs completely (DESTROY) by cigarette smoke.

---

*Teacher*
Explain the problem: you have caught *Student* several times smoking in the classroom. At first you told *Student* to stop, but *Student* continued, so you reported this to *Headmaster*. The school rule is no smoking anywhere in school and you have taught lessons about the health dangers of smoking. You're a non-smoker.

---

*Student*
Defend yourself: your friends all smoke, it's your body, your parents smoke and they know you smoke and do nothing about it.

---

*Parent*
You don't want your child to smoke but you smoke yourself so it's difficult to stop your child. Try to persuade the headmaster not to send your child home.

---

*Headmaster*
The school rule is: any student caught smoking can be sent home for up to two weeks. You must support your teachers and the school rules. You are a non-smoker yourself. At this meeting you must come to a decision.

---

Use this plan to control the meeting.
1 Open the meeting by introducing everyone. Ask *Teacher* to explain the problem.
2 Ask *Student* to reply.
3 Ask *Parent* for his/her opinion.
4 General discussion.
5 Organise a decision about the problem.

After your group has finished, report this decision to the rest of the class. How does it compare to the other decisions?

95

1   What did you eat yesterday? Make a list of *everything* that you ate. Think of breakfast, lunch and dinner. Don't forget all the snacks you had between meals.

2   Look at this extract from a school text book.

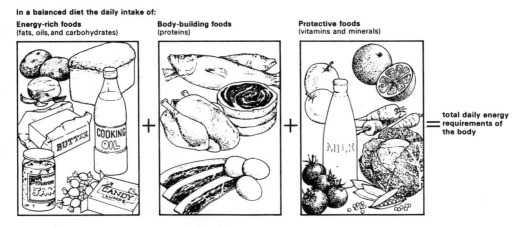

**In a balanced diet the daily intake of:**

Energy-rich foods
(fats, oils, and carbohydrates)

Body-building foods
(proteins)

Protective foods
(vitamins and minerals)

total daily energy
requirements of
the body

Divide the food you ate yesterday into the same three columns.

Do you think *you* have a balanced diet?

3   How much do you weigh? Is this a good weight for your height? Look at the chart.

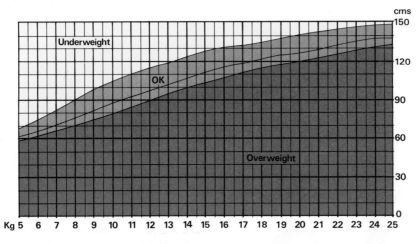

4   Some people have a problem keeping slim. Here is a very simple way to choose the foods that'll keep you slim and feeling well. And you don't have to count calories.

All the main sorts of food are divided into three groups according to their calorie concentration – ranging from RED (high in calories) through AMBER (medium in calories) to GREEN (low in calories).

Obviously, how much you eat is as important as what you eat. But even small quantities of RED-group foods contain as many calories as quite large helpings of GREEN-group foods.

Use the three groups to discover a sensible balance which suits you.

Organise what you ate yesterday into three groups – one for red, one for amber and one for green. Are you eating sensibly?

**RED – stop and think**
Sugar, sweet desserts, chocolate, cakes, pies, biscuits, heavy puddings, honey, jam, marmalade, fruit tinned in syrup, cream, butter, margarine, cooking oil, fat on meat, salad dressing, salad cream or mayonnaise, chips, crisps, peanuts, pastry.

**AMBER – go carefully**
Fatty meats (like bacon or salami), sausages, liver pâté, eggs, milk, oily fish (like herring, mackerel, sardines, tuna, salmon), cheese (except cottage cheese), thick creamy soups, nuts, white bread, rice pasta (like spaghetti and macaroni), savouries, wines, beer and cider.

**GREEN – go right ahead**
Fresh fruit, salads, green and root vegetables including potatoes (not fried), beans and peas, whitefish, seafood, poultry, kidneys, cottage cheese, yoghurt (natural), skimmed milk, wholemeal bread, bran, wholegrain cereals, clear soups, low-calorie soft drinks, coffee and tea (without sugar), water.

# ENJOY YOUR ENGLISH

**She'll be coming round the mountain**

She'll be com - ing round the moun-tain when she comes, she'll be
com - ing round the moun - tain when she comes, she'll be
com - ing round the moun-tain, com - ing round the moun - tain,
com - ing round the moun - tain when she comes.

**Crossword**

**Across**
2. It's very easy to catch a ____.
5. Houses in Mathare don't have running ____.
6. A small boy got an ____ in his arm.
7. They kept the child warm in a ____.
8. The child in the fire was very ____.

**Down**
1. If you're very ill, you should go to ____.
3. Jenner made a ____ from cow serum.
4. Diseases are dangerous if there is no ____.

# J●ke sp●t

1 How long should a horse's legs be?
  *Long enough to reach the ground.*

2 When you heat iron, it gets bigger.
  Martin heated an iron ring until it was
  red-hot. Did the hole in the middle get
  bigger or smaller?

# UNITED WORLD COLLEGES

**A** STEP ONE: LOOKING AT THE BROCHURE

These photographs are all of the same school.

1 What kind of school do you think it is?
2 What countries do the pupils come from?
3 Have you any idea where the school is?

Discuss your ideas with the class.

**B** STEP TWO: GETTING GENERAL INFORMATION

1 Raquel Marin from Madrid wrote to United World Colleges' office in London to find out about them. Here is their reply. What did Raquel write in her letter?

## What are the United World Colleges?

The United World Colleges (UWC) are an international movement whose aim is to promote peace and understanding through education. The movement consists of six Colleges, UWC Committees in over fifty countries around the world, an active association of former students, and an International Office in London which coordinates and executes the policies laid down by the UWC International Board.

The Colleges are international communities where young people of all races, creeds and backgrounds are given the opportunity of living and studying together; through their own experiences they learn about each other's cultures and societies, and in the process increase their understanding of their common humanity.

Two of the Colleges – in Singapore and Swaziland – provide full secondary education for students aged 11 to 19. The Colleges in Canada, Italy, the UK and USA offer two-year upper secondary courses to students aged 16-19. In all the Colleges the programme combines academic study of a high standard, leading to the International Baccalaureate Diploma, with service to the local community and challenging activities that encourage in students a sense of responsibility and interdependence. At the upper secondary level around 1,000 young people from all over the world attend the Colleges on UWC scholarships, including all the students at the two-year Colleges.

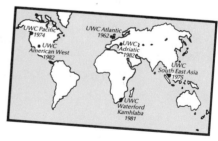

### UNITED WORLD COLLEGES

PRESIDENT OF THE INTERNATIONAL COUNCIL:
H.R.H. THE PRINCE OF WALES

Chairman, International Board: THE HON. KINGMAN BREWSTER
Director General: SIR IAN GOURLAY

25 March 1987

Ms Raquel Marin
c. Lope de Vega 123-4
Madrid
SPAIN

Dear Ms Marin

Thank you for your letter of 18 March. I am enclosing a leaflet about United World Colleges, which I hope answers your questions, and an application form. However, if you wish to know more, please do not hesitate to write to me again.

Yours sincerely

*Robert Creighton*

Robert Creighton
International Secretary

LONDON HOUSE, MECKLENBURGH SQUARE, LONDON WC1N 2AB.    Tel: 01-633-2626.    Cables: UNIWORLDCOL LONDONWC1
United World Colleges (International) Limited: UK Registered Charity, No 313690.    Telex: 296459 UWCLON G

2 Read this page from the information leaflet and then answer these questions.

1 How many colleges are there?
2 What countries are the colleges in?
3 What do you think the dates on the map mean?
4 Would you like to go to a school like this? Why or why not?

**C** STEP THREE: FINDING OUT ABOUT THE COLLEGES

**1** Look at the information from the leaflet about the six colleges.

### Waterford Kamhlaba United World College of Southern Africa

Waterford Kamhlaba was founded in 1963, the first school in Southern Africa open to all races and religions. This has given it a special focus on and concern for the social and political issues of Southern Africa. More than half of the student body of 360 students come from Southern Africa, though 40 different nationalities are represented. The College (with students from age 11 through to 18) with its strikingly designed buildings is located on a hill overlooking Mbabane, the capital of Swaziland. The College has a very strong community service programme. The academic year runs from January to November.

### The United World College of South East Asia

This, the largest of the Colleges with over 1,300 students aged 11 to 19, is located in Singapore, one of the world's great cultural meeting places, in a region of increasing international significance. Its student population, largely day pupils, reflects the College's balance between East and West, at all levels the College offers Asian languages and themes of study, and there is a strong tradition of expeditions in South East Asia. Within Singapore the College is famous for its annual festival of the arts and vigorous social service programme.

### The United World College of the Atlantic

Founded in 1962, this is the first of the United World Colleges and one of the pioneer schools of the International Baccalaureate (IB). It has 350 students, and is situated in a medieval castle on the coast of South Wales. The College has been the centre for the development of a number of innovative courses within the IB, and its coastal rescue services (in-shore lifeboats, beach rescue and cliff rescue) are credited with having saved over 190 lives. In addition to running a substantial programme of social services, it has its own estate which is farmed with the help of the students. Its Arts Centre serves the local community.

### The United World College of the Adriatic

The area of north-eastern Italy, around Trieste, is an especially appropriate location for a United World College, because for many centuries it has been a meeting-place for the Latin, Germanic and Slav cultures. The UWC of the Adriatic gives expression to these varied influences through its close connections not only with the local Italian population and government authorities, but also with Austria and Yugoslavia. The College is closely integrated into the village of Duino; the main teaching buildings are located within the village, and arrangements are made for some of the students to live in local guest houses or with families. While teaching is in English, all students are expected to learn Italian to a good standard. The College is developing a strong social service programme and a special interest in environmental work on land and sea.

### The Lester B. Pearson United World College of the Pacific

Founded in 1974, this College was built as the Canadian national memorial to Lester B. Pearson, the Canadian Prime Minister and winner of the 1957 Nobel Peace Prize. It is situated among fir trees on the rocky shores of an inlet on Vancouver Island, British Columbia, Canada, and its buildings are made entirely from local wood. The warm, friendly, informal atmosphere for which the College is renowned is fostered by the way the College has been designed to function as a small village. Most of the faculty live on campus and they, along with the students, experience the family feeling of a close community.

### The Armand Hammer United World College of the American West

The site for this College is the 100-year-old former Montezuma hotel complex in north-eastern New Mexico: in one direction lie broad plains dotted with cattle ranches, while on the other rise rugged mountains. The College is thus well situated for a variety of challenging outdoor pursuits and environmental programmes. Social service is undertaken in the neighbourhood and there is ready access to the cultural centre of Santa Fé. The College seeks to introduce students to the cultures of the three ethnic groups which give such diversity to the state – the native Indians, the Hispanics and the Americans of European origin.

Raquel wanted to compare the colleges. Copy and complete her table. You will need to look at page 1 of the leaflet for some things. Write DK (for 'don't know') if you can't find the information.

| name of college | country | opened in | type of building | special activities | main language |
|---|---|---|---|---|---|
| Adriatic | | | | | |
| Armand Hammer | | | | | |
| Atlantic | | | | | |
| Pacific | | | | | |
| South East Asia | | | | | |

Which college is shown in the photographs in A?

**2** You read about Atlantic College in Book 2, Unit 11. What can you remember about it?

**D**  STEP FOUR: GETTING SPECIFIC INFORMATION

After Raquel had finished her table there were still one or two things she wanted to know. She mentioned these to an English friend, Julian Harris, and asked him to telephone UWC offices and ask some questions for her.
Work in pairs.

**1** Listen to Julian's call. Student A: note down his first question. Student B: note down his second question.

**2** Listen again and take brief notes of the answers to your question.

**3** Use your notes to write down Julian's questions, in order, and the answers he received.

**4** Julian phoned Raquel that evening to give her the information. Sit back to back with your partner and practise their phone call.

1 Raquel intends to apply to the College of the Atlantic. This is the first part of her completed application form.

**PART 1**

1. Name: *RAQUEL MARIN*

2. Date of Birth: *23RD AUGUST 1969*

3. Sex: *FEMALE*

4. Nationality: *SPANISH*

5. Address: *LOPE DE VEGA 123-4, MADRID, SPAIN.*

6. Choice of College:

(Please give your order of preference)

UWC of the Adriatic, Italy *FIFTH*

Atlantic College, United Kingdom *FIRST*

UWC of South East Asia, Singapore *FOURTH*

UWC of the American West, USA *SECOND*

Pearson College, Canada *THIRD*

2 Here is the second part of an application form for UWC. Complete it in your notebook with information about yourself.

**Application Form Part 2**

1. List the subjects you are studying at school this year. .....

2. Do you regularly take part in sports? Give details. ..........

3. Do you have musical or artistic interests? ....................

4. Do you have any experience of working with people outside school? ........

5. Which organisations do you belong to? .................

6. Describe any special achievements you would like the Selection Committee to know about. ..................

3 Which college do you prefer? Choose one, and imagine you are applying for a place at it. Write a letter to go with your application, saying why you think the college you have chosen is most suitable for you. (Use the frame below.)

............................ ← your address

............................ ← today's date

United World Colleges
London House
Mecklenburgh Square
London WC1N 2AB
Great Britain

Dear Sir or Madam

I am applying for a place at .................................... ← give name of chosen college

.................................... I have chosen this

give reasons for choice of college → college..................................

....................................

My interests are .................................... ← state interests and say why chosen college is suitable

.................................... so ........................

....................................

....................................

say why you and your achievements would be good for the school → I think that I would be a suitable student ................................

....................................

....................................

....................................

I look forward to hearing from you.

Yours faithfully

your full name → ....................................

If you are interested in applying for a place at a United World College, write to this address:

United World Colleges, London House, Mecklenburgh Square, LONDON WC1N 2AB, Great Britain.

# CHECK YOUR ENGLISH

## Social English: talking on the telephone

**Julian:** Hello?
**Raquel:** Hello, is that you, Julian?
**Julian:** Yes. How are you?
**Raquel:** ..... And you?
**Julian:** ..... Well, I phoned UWC today and got some more information for you.
**Raquel:** Oh good. What did they tell you?
**Julian:** ...................................................
**Raquel:** That's great – just what I wanted to know. Thanks a lot for calling for me.
**Julian:** Oh that's all right. And if there's anything else I can do, just call me. OK?
**Raquel:** ..... Thanks very much, and – bye for now.
**Julian:** Bye.

## Intonation and stress

You are going to hear the reply to *one* of the three questions in each group. Decide which is the correct question for the reply you hear.

1  a  How are you?
   b  Are you well?
   c  Who is it?
2  a  Are you from Italy?
   b  Where do you come from?
   c  You're from Italy, aren't you?
3  a  Who's been to England?
   b  Have you been to England?
   c  Where have you been?
4  a  Is her name Julia?
   b  What's her name?
   c  Which one is Julia?
5  a  Coffee?
   b  Do you want some tea?
   c  What would you like to drink?
6  a  Shall we get married?
   b  When can we get married?
   c  Will you marry me?

## Spelling test

You're going to hear a list of words beginning with the sound /w/ from Unit 13. Write down only the words which begin with *wh-*.

## Adjective word order

1  Study the table and notice the order of adjectives.

| DETERMINER | ADJECTIVE(S) | | | | | | | | NOUN |
| | VALUE | SIZE | TEMPERATURE | AGE | SHAPE | COLOUR | NATIONALITY | MATERIAL | NOUN | NOUN |
|---|---|---|---|---|---|---|---|---|---|---|
| the<br>this<br>my<br>some<br>two<br>very<br>a | dirty<br>interesting<br>beautiful | small<br>big | cold<br>hot | young<br>old | round<br>circular | red<br>brown | French<br>African | glass<br>plastic | egg<br>dining<br>shoe | table<br>shop<br>sandwich<br>box<br>painting<br>student<br>car |

2  Add as many words as you can to each adjective list.

3  Describe some of the nouns. Use a maximum of three adjectives for each description.

   *Examples*  This beautiful old African box.
   Two dirty old dining tables.

---

## KNOW YOUR GRAMMAR

### Describing people and things

1  Study these ways of describing people and things from the story of the Young Werewolf on p.102.

   ... she was collecting <u>interesting</u> information for her latest book
   The arrival of the Young Werewolf had a <u>surprising</u> effect on the Professor
   When she saw her grandson she was <u>delighted</u>
   This made him even more <u>frightened</u>

   These *-ing* and *-ed* words all come from verbs:

   |  | -ing | -ed |
   |---|---|---|
   | delight | – | delighted |
   | frighten | frightening | frightened |
   | interest | interesting | interested |
   | surprise | surprising | surprised |

   We can use *-ing* and *-ed* words to describe people and things. These words go in the same position as adjectives.

2  Look at the two diary extracts on page 103. Find examples of *-ing* and *-ed* words used to describe people and things.

3  **Exercise:**
   Put the words in a–d in order to make four correct sentences.
   a  amusing/folk/performance/the/an/second/was/tale
   b  detailed/students/two/created/the/stories
   c  exciting/story/an/performance/detective/the/was/first
   d  impressed/students'/the/were/their/with/teachers/work

101

# CREATIVE THEATRE

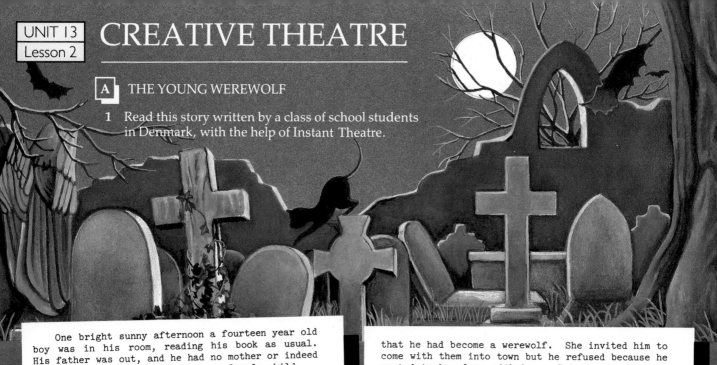

**A** THE YOUNG WEREWOLF

**1** Read this story written by a class of school students in Denmark, with the help of Instant Theatre.

One bright sunny afternoon a fourteen year old boy was in his room, reading his book as usual. His father was out, and he had no mother or indeed any other relation. He was a very lonely child.

Suddenly his father flew in through the window: some time earlier he had been bitten by a werewolf and he was now a werewolf himself. He comforted his son, telling him not to be afraid. Then he bit him and the boy changed into a werewolf too. This made him even more frightened and shy than he had been before.

His father flew off with another werewolf to attack the sun. They began to eat it when suddenly it burst into flames and the two werewolves were burned up. Earth was covered in darkness and slowly, in the opposite side of the sky, a strange full moon rose.

The Young Werewolf mourned for his father. Then he thought of the only person he had ever really loved, his grandmother, who had died a year before. He went to the graveyard to visit her, for he was desperate for company but he could not bear to see any living thing.

But when he reached the graveyard he found that, after the death of the sun, all the dead bodies had come out of their graves. The graveyard was full of dancing and celebration. Sitting in a tree was an older woman: she was a Professor of Werewolves and she was collecting interesting information for her latest book. She was in love with the dead.

The dead decided to take a coach into town to continue their celebrations. Among them was the Young Werewolf's grand-mother. When she saw her grandson she was delighted, although she was sad

that he had become a werewolf. She invited him to come with them into town but he refused because he wanted to be alone with her. But she didn't want to leave her friends; so she joined them in the coach and told him she would see him later.

The arrival of the Young Werewolf had a surprising effect on the Professor. She was so moved by his looks that she immediately fell in love with him and she left the tree and came and sat beside him. When he saw her and realised that she understood him, he responded to her love with his own, and they were both so happy that they agreed to get married as soon as possible. They decided to go to Hawaii for their honeymoon. The Professor went into town to arrange the tickets as quickly as possible and left the Young Werewolf behind, waiting for her in the graveyard.

The strange full moon shone down on the graveyard and the young Werewolf sat in silence waiting for the Professor to return.

However, across the fields surrounding the graveyard a huntress appeared. She was dressed in silver and was hunting for any animal she could find. When she saw the Young Werewolf sitting by the graves, she drew a silver arrow, strung it to her bow and fired. The arrow passed right through his heart and he was killed instantly. He returned to the form of a young boy, and the huntress, very upset by what she had done, faded away guiltily into the moonlight. And when the Professor returned found the dead boy shot through the heart with a silver arrow, she realised at once what had happened and she too ended her life, overcome with despair.

**2** Make a list of all the words for feelings that you can find in this story.
*Example* lonely afraid

**3** Copy these sentences about the story, and complete them with a suitable word from the box.

delighted comforting exciting horrified frightening interested shocked surprised

1 It was very .... for the Young Werewolf to see his father again.
2 The grandmother was .... to see her grandson again.
3 The dead were having an .... time after the death of the sun.
4 The Young Werewolf wasn't .... in joining the dead in town.
5 The huntress was .... when she saw what she had done.
6 The Professor was .... when she returned and saw the young boy dead with an arrow through his heart.

**4** How did the characters in the story feel?
With your partner, act out each situation 1-6 above.

**5** How did they behave?
With your partner, mime the actions and feelings of:
a the boy when his father died.
b the huntress when she shot the Young Werewolf.
c the Professor when she returned and found the dead boy.

**6** What did they say?
With your partner, create the scene when:
a the father returns to comfort his son, then bites him.
b the grandmother and the Young Werewolf meet again.
c the Professor and the Young Werewolf meet for the first time.

## B INSTANT THEATRE

1 If, after reading that story, you wanted to know more about Instant Theatre, these are some of the questions you might ask.

    1 How was this story of the Young Werewolf created?

    2 What is Instant Theatre?

    3 Who are the performances for?

    4 Where does Instant Theatre travel to?

    5 How does Instant Theatre work?

    6 What is necessary for a performance?

Below you can find the answers A-F to these questions. Match the correct answers to the questions 1-6 above.

2 Answer these questions, using the texts to help you.

    1 Could Instant Theatre visit your school?

    2 Which theme would your class choose as a starting point?

    3 Which of these spaces is best for an Instant Theatre performance?

    1    2    3

• = performers
— = audience

---

**A**

*Word And Action (Dorset)* started in December 1972 as a language-arts organisation, concerned with the creative use of language, through speech, writing and acting. Instant Theatre is the form of theatre most used by the organisation in performance.

**D**

A story is created (through a question and answer routine) by the audience which is then invited to join the actors in the performance of their play.

There are many themes used as a starting point for Instant Theatre, including:

| | |
|---|---|
| Voyage | Ghost Stories |
| Fear | Prejudice |
| Detectives | Horror Stories |
| The Road | Science Fiction |
| The Island | Time Machine |
| Folk Tales | The Window |

**B**

They are for students and teachers either in language schools in England or in schools and institutions abroad who are concerned with the use of English as a second or foreign language.

**E**

*Word And Action (Dorset)* started touring overseas regularly in January 1980. Since then it has set up 17 tours abroad, covering 92 weeks, and containing over 1,000 performances and many teachers' courses. In 1985 it visited nine countries on tours lasting 24 weeks, giving over 350 performances of Instant Theatre and over 20 teachers' courses. Countries visited include: Belgium, Denmark, Finland, France, Italy, the Netherlands, Norway, Portugal, Spain, Sweden and West Germany.

**C**

All performances to be 'in the round': that is, the audience to sit on all four sides of a rectangular acting area, with four corner entrances.

Space requirements: small hall or large room with flat floor. No special lighting required.

There must be a chair or desk for each member of the audience to sit on.

Audiences not to exceed 100 in number, except by previous agreement with Word And Action.

**F**

It was created during one of Instant Theatre's performances at a school in Denmark. Working with three members of Instant Theatre, the students created the story together, acted it and then wrote it down.

---

## C ON TOUR

1 In May 1986 *Word And Action (Dorset)* took Instant Theatre to four European countries. Look at their itinerary and find the names of the four countries.

    1 How long did Instant Theatre spend in each country?

    2 Which place did they spend longest in?

    3 Where did they do the most performances?

2 One of the members of the group kept a diary of the tour. Read the two extracts below and decide from what day in her diary each extract comes.

a
We managed to get two quite detailed stories from the audience accompanied by a great deal of laughter. The first was a Folk Tale about a Frog, a Dwarf and a Princess and the second was a Detective Story.
Talking to the teachers afterwards, they seemed quite impressed with the fact that some individuals who came out to act were the ones who tended to be less active in class.
Unfortunately, we were unable to stay and talk with the teachers as long as we would have liked to, but time was pressing and we had to be in Brussels by the early evening.

b
The first performance was an interesting Folk Tale with a Friar, a king, and a unicorn. The audience really appreciated and enjoyed the performance, as did Dr Lopes. We were given lunch by the school. After lunch we were taken on a swift tour of Lisbon.

```
ITINERARY

Monday 19 May       Travel down into Portugal
Tuesday 20 May      Santarem, 2 performances

Wednesday 21 May    Povoa de Varzim, 1 performance
Thursday 22—
Sunday 25 May       Festival Internacional Jovem Teatro, 1
                    performance
Monday 26 May       Lisboa, 4 performances
Tuesday 27 May      Porto, 3 performances
                    Travel to Spain through night

Wednesday 28 May    Madrid, International House, 2
                    performances
Thursday 29 May     Madrid, British Council/School,
                    1 performance
Friday 30 May       Madrid, 1 performance
Saturday 31 May—
Sunday 1 June       Travel to the Netherlands through France
                    and Belgium
Monday 2 June:      Venlo, 1 performance

Tuesday 3 June:     Brussels, European School, 1 performance

Wednesday 4 June    Return to England
```

D  INTRODUCTION TO A PERFORMANCE

You are going to hear the beginning of the introduction to a performance made at a school in Portugal. The actor covers the nine points below. In what order does he cover them? Listen and order the sentences a-i.

a He introduces the actors.
b He explains how the performance space is organised.
c He explains how Instant Theatre works and how it is different from other forms of theatre.
d He explains the name *Word And Action*.
e He explains that the audience creates the play.
f He explains that Instant Theatre works with anybody anywhere in Europe.
g He explains what *Word And Action (Dorset)* is and where they come from.
h He says that no one has to take part if s/he doesn't want to.
i He talks about this trip to Portugal and Spain.

E A FAIRY STORY

1 Look at the pictures of typical elements from a fairy story a-h. Write a caption for each picture using two adjectives. Use the language frame to help you.

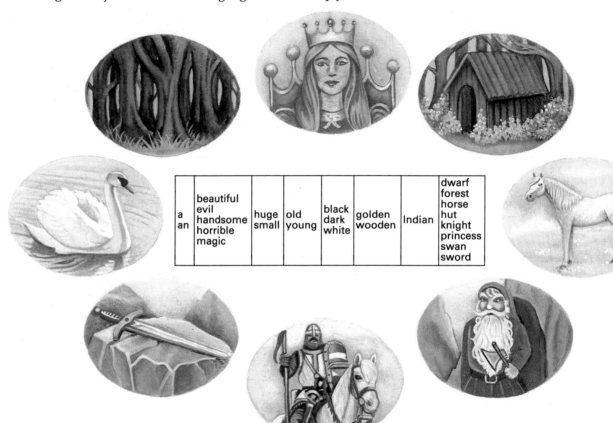

| a an | beautiful evil handsome horrible magic | huge small | old young | black dark white | golden wooden | Indian | dwarf forest horse hut knight princess swan sword |
|------|----------|----|----|----|----|----|----|

2 a The word *when* is used six times in the story on p.102. Find the six examples and study how to use *when* in a story.

b Which of these two sentences is correct for the story?

> The sun burst into flames when the two werewolves were burnt up.
> When the sun burst into flames the two werewolves were burnt up.

Note: you can put the *when* part of the sentence first or second:
*Example* The Young Werewolf mourned for his father when he died.
*or* When the Young Werewolf's father died, he mourned for him.

The meaning is the same.

b Join these ideas with *when* in the correct way for the story. Make any other changes to the sentences which are necessary.

1 The boy's father bit him.
The boy turned into a werewolf.
2 The dead bodies came out of their graves.
The sun died.

3 The Professor saw the Young Werewolf.
The Professor fell in love with the Young Werewolf.
4 The Young Werewolf stayed in the graveyard.
The Professor went into town to buy the tickets.

3 Find these joining words in the story and study the way they are used.

| And/and | But/but However, | ;  so, | Suddenly Then |
|---------|------------------|--------|---------------|

4 Look at these ways of beginning a fairy story.
- One sunny day,
- One dark night,
- One day, a long, long time ago, *and, most popular of all,*
- Once upon a time,

5 Can *you* write a fairy story in English? Working in groups of four, use any of the elements in 1 above to create an imaginative story. When your story is ready and checked, give it to the class newspaper.

# ENJOY YOUR ENGLISH

**My way**

# J●ke sp●t

1   There's a place where a railway passes through a tunnel. It's a narrow tunnel, so there's only room for a single railway track inside it. Outside the tunnel at each end, the single track separates into two again.

One afternoon, a train went into the tunnel at one end, and another train went into the tunnel at the other end. Both trains entered the tunnel at top speed, and they didn't slow down or stop.

But there was no crash, and both trains came out safely and went on their way.

How?

2   It takes Dave 3½ minutes to boil an egg. How long does he take to boil seven eggs?

Student B

1   New Zealand is made of two main islands and one small one.
2   New Zealand has a small island to the south.
3   New Zealand is about the same size as Great Britain.
4   New Zealand is very mountainous.
5   In New Zealand over 75 per cent of the land is very high.
6   The mountains in New Zealand are all over the South Island.
7   No-one in New Zealand lives more than 110 kilometres from the sea.
8   New Zealand has some interesting geographical features.
9   The highest mountain in New Zealand is 3,764 metres high.
10  New Zealand has volcanoes, hot springs and fjords.

# WE ARE THE WORLD

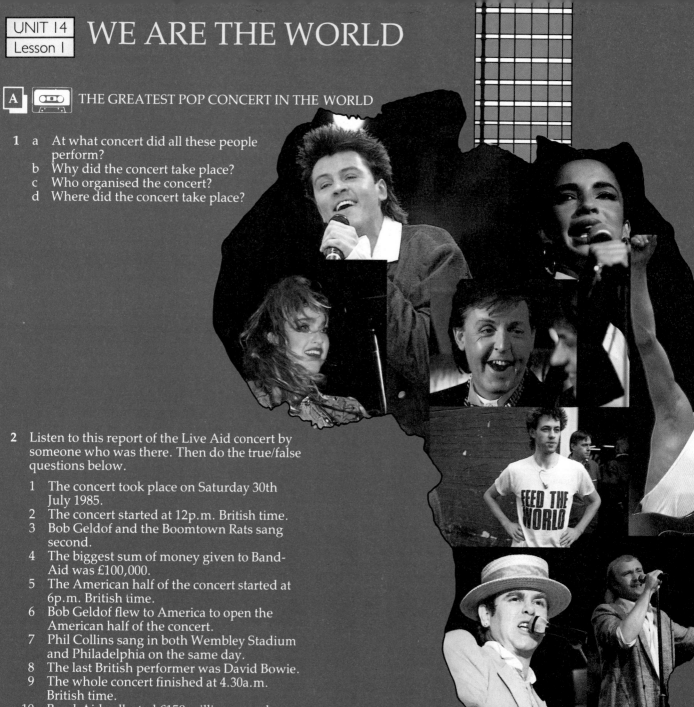

**A** 🔲 THE GREATEST POP CONCERT IN THE WORLD

1 a At what concert did all these people
    perform?
  b Why did the concert take place?
  c Who organised the concert?
  d Where did the concert take place?

2 Listen to this report of the Live Aid concert by
  someone who was there. Then do the true/false
  questions below.

  1 The concert took place on Saturday 30th
    July 1985.
  2 The concert started at 12p.m. British time.
  3 Bob Geldof and the Boomtown Rats sang
    second.
  4 The biggest sum of money given to Band-
    Aid was £100,000.
  5 The American half of the concert started at
    6p.m. British time.
  6 Bob Geldof flew to America to open the
    American half of the concert.
  7 Phil Collins sang in both Wembley Stadium
    and Philadelphia on the same day.
  8 The last British performer was David Bowie.
  9 The whole concert finished at 4.30a.m.
    British time.
  10 Band-Aid collected £150 million pounds
    from the concert.

**B** WHY THE CONCERT HAPPENED

Michael Buerke is a BBC reporter. Read what he said about starving
people in Ethiopia on the BBC news on Tuesday 14th October 1984.

..... There are 10,000 people in this camp.
There is food for only 300. So this nurse has
to choose. Only a small wall separates those
chosen to live and those condemned to die.
The people picked to be fed stand ashamed
of their good fortune on one side of the wall,
turning their backs in shame on the others.
The ones left behind, condemned to die,
stand and watch with a beautiful dignity.....

1 How do you feel about this story?
2 What can we do to help?

1  Bob Geldof is a pop singer with a group called the Boomtown Rats. Read what he did after he saw Michael Buerke's report on television.

'What could I do? I could send some money. Of course I could send some money. But that didn't seem enough. A horror like this could not happen without our consent. I would send some money, I would send more money. But that was not enough. What else could I do? I was only a pop singer. And by now not a very successful pop singer. I could not help the nurse or the man running without hope behind the food truck. All I could do was make records. But I would do that, I would give all the profits from the next Rats' record to charity. But what good would that do? It would be a pitiful amount. But it would be more than I could give from by bank account.

Next morning I spoke to my girlfriend, Paula, on the telephone. "I've been thinking about doing a record to raise money for Ethiopia," I said. "The only thing is, if the Rats do it, it won't sell very well. So I thought I might ask a few other people to come in on it."

First I spoke to Midge Ure of Ultravox. He agreed at once. "Have you got a song?" he asked. "No, I've got a bit of a thing…" "I'll try and think of something. We'll work out something." Then I rang Sting. "Did you see the thing about Ethiopia on the news last night?"

"Yes, it was terrible, wasn't it?"

"I think we should do something. I'm thinking of getting a few people together to get a quick record out before Christmas to raise a bit of money."

"OK, I'll be there."

I started to telephone everyone I could. Some could not help because they would not be in the country but most of the singers and groups I telephoned said 'yes'. I soon had a list of forty of the top singers and musicians in the country. They all agreed to perform for nothing. "If only the record makers, the record companies and the shops do the same we will make a lot more for Ethiopia." And they agreed to make and sell the record for nothing too.

Meanwhile Midge and I worked on the song. Slowly it came together. When it started the song was called *It's My World*. The words came easily – some of them in a taxi. Then when I wrote the words *Do They Know It's Christmas Time?* I knew we had the right title.

We needed lots of publicity for the record because there were only three weeks before Christmas. I didn't think people would buy it after that. "If I can get a picture of the recording on the front page of a national newspaper everyone will know about it." So I spoke to the owner of the *Daily Mirror*, Robert Maxwell, and he promised me the front page.

Then on November 25 we made the recording. I saw Sting come in with a newspaper under his arm. Soon the room held most of the stars of British pop music. Duran Duran had come back early from Germany to do it, Spandau Ballet were just back from Japan, U2 had given up one of their free days in their world tour and flown over from Dublin, Culture Club had flown back from New York.

Except for Boy George. "Where's Boy George?"

"Maybe he's still in New York."

"Which hotel is he in?" I dialled the number and asked for the room. "George, it's Geldof. Where are you?"

"I'm in… er… New York."

"What are you doing in New York?"

"Er…"

"You're meant to be here."

"Who's there?"

"Everyone. Sting, Paul Young, the Spandaus, the Durans, Marilyn, Bono, Bananarama, Kool and the Gang, George Michael, Paul Weller, Heaven 17. Everybody is here. Everybody except you. There's a Concorde leaving at 9am. Get up and come." And come he did – a little late, but he came.

We worked through the night so that the completed tape could be taken to the factory the next morning. I left the studio and went straight to the BBC with the tape and a videotape of the recording. "If I can get them to play it it will be great." And they did.

"If we are lucky," I thought, "we will make £70,000 or maybe £100,000 for Ethiopia." But all the world had seen the terrible pictures on TV and the song was a good one. Within one hour of its release it had made £100,000. It became the best-selling single of all time in the United Kingdom. It raised £8 million worldwide.'

'Do They Know It's Christmas?'

2  How did these people help Bob Geldof do what he wanted to do?
a  Sting
b  Midge Ure
c  Robert Maxwell
d  Members of the public
e  Top singers and musicians
f  Boy George
g  Record makers and sellers

3  Who do you think helped Bob Geldof most? Why?

4  Who do you think was the most difficult to persuade? Why?

5  Write the dialogue between Bob Geldof and the newspaper owner.

**D** WHAT BAND-AID DID

1 In pairs, think of ways to spend the money to help the people in Ethiopia. Write down ten uses for the money, in order of importance.

2 Tell the class what you have decided. Start like this.

> If we can get enough money, we'll ..... , then we'll ..... and we'll also ..... .

3 These pictures show what charities like Band-Aid do. Match each picture to the words in the box.

| | |
|---|---|
| a | collect/money |
| b | count/money |
| c | plan/distribution |
| d | transport/food |
| e | unload/ships |
| f | feed/people |
| g | vaccinate/children |
| h | clothe/people |

1

2

4

3

6

7

5

8

4 Write a description of what Band-Aid did with the money people gave. Use these words to join your sentences.

| |
|---|
| First |
| Then |
| And then |
| Afterwards |
| Later |
| Finally |

**E** WHAT CAN YOU DO?

After Band-Aid, people all over the world continued to collect money to help others in need. There was Air-Aid, Bear-Aid and Sport-Aid. School-Aid collected food and clothes through pupils in schools.

1 In groups of five or six, think of a charity and ways that you could raise money for it.

2 Then: a Choose a chairperson and a secretary.
  b Make plans for what to do and when to do it.
  c Make a list of responsibilities.
  d Decide how much money you want to raise.
  e Make plans for publicity (e.g. posters, advertisements).
  f Decide how long you are going to spend on the project.

3 The secretary of each group reports to the class.

4 Class votes for the best proposal.

# CHECK YOUR ENGLISH

## ENGLISH SPOKEN HERE

### Social English: talking about English

**Friend:** Let's talk about your English. How good do you think your English is?
**You:** ...........................................................
**Friend:** How many years have you studied English for?
**You:** ...........................................................
**Friend:** What did you like best about your English course?
**You:** ...........................................................
**Friend:** And what did you *not* like very much?
**You:** ...........................................................
**Friend:** Why was that?
**You:** ...........................................................
**Friend:** Do you think it's useful to be able to speak English?
**You:** ...........................................................
**Friend:** Are you going to continue learning English?
**You:** ...........................................................
**Friend:** Have you ever been to an English-speaking country?
**You:** ...........................................................

### Pronunciation and word stress

It is common not to hear every word in a sentence, but still to understand everything. The meaning of the rest of the sentence helps you. Listen to the following sentences on the cassette. In each case which of the three words did you hear?

1   a sing   b single   c singer
2   a record   b recording   c record
3   a musicians   b musical   c music
4   a could   b should   c would
5   a Indian   b India   c indeed
6   a communication   b community   c committee
7   a office   b official   c officer
8   a right   b light   c might

### Spelling test

You are going to hear fifteen words which contain either the unstressed syllable /ə/ or /ɪ/ (see Unit 12). Write down the words.

## WORD WORK

**1**   *Look at these examples of nouns used as adjectives.*

member states – two separate words
Secretary-General – two words joined by a hyphen
spacecraft – one word

*There are lots of examples of all three types in Unit 14, Lesson 2. How many can you find?*

**2**   *Which nouns do these adjectives used in Unit 14 come from?*

educational   global   industrial   legal   national   official   political   beautiful   successful   useful economic   historic   scientific   distant   important

**3**   *Which verbs do these nouns used in Unit 14 come from?*

communication   entertainment   expression invasion   organisation   performance   visitor

## KNOW YOUR GRAMMAR

### Expressing conditions

**1**   '. . . if the Rats do it, it won't sell very well.'
'If I can get them to play it it will be great.'

In the second example above, Bob Geldof is not sure that the BBC will play the videotape of the recording and so give his record lots of publicity. The publicity $\boxed{B}$ depends on the BBC playing the videotape $\boxed{A}$. But Bob can imagine the result if the BBC plays it – lots of publicity.

*Put the correct verbs in the gaps in the examples below.*

**2**   *Imagine you are Bob Geldof. Using the words below, make sentences for him. Then check your ideas on page 107.*

   1   A   I must get a picture of the recording on the front page of a national newspaper.
       B   Everyone will know about the record.

      If I . . .

   2   A   The record makers, the record companies and the shops must work for nothing.
       B   We will make a lot more money for Ethiopia.

      If the . . .

   3   If/we/be/lucky,/we/make/£70,000 for Ethiopia.

$\boxed{A}$                     $\boxed{B}$

| | Present simple | Future simple |
|---|---|---|
| IF | I ☐ get them to play it, | it ☐ great. ⊕ |
| | the Rats ☐ it, | it ☐ very well. ⊖ |

## A  A MESSAGE FOR THE PEOPLE OF OUTER SPACE

**'As the Secretary-General of the United Nations, an organisation of 147 member states who represent almost all of the human inhabitants of the planet Earth, I send greetings on behalf of the people of our planet...'**

On 5th September 1977 the American spacecraft Voyager One was started on its historic journey to the planet Jupiter – and beyond. Voyager One will travel on and on, past Jupiter, past Saturn, into distant star-systems. Inside the spacecraft, on a gold-plated disc, there are messages for the people of outer space from the people of planet Earth. There are short messages in 55 languages of the world. But first come the greetings from all the people of Earth (above) – in English, the most common international language on the planet.

Today English is used by at least 750 million people (some estimates calculate nearly a billion). No more than half of these speak it as a first language. At the end of the twentieth century English has become the first really *global* language: no language has ever been more widely spoken or written. It can truly be said that English is *the* language of our planet.

1  Translate the Secretary-General's message into your language for a relative or friend who can't speak English.

2  Prepare a short message in your language for the people of outer space. Translate this into English for the rest of the people of planet Earth.

## B  A GLOBAL LANGUAGE

English is still used as a second language in most of those countries which were once British colonies. In Nigeria, for example, it is an official language; in Zambia it is one of the state languages; in Singapore it is the major language of government, the legal system and education; in India it is an 'associate' official language. This may not always be comfortable politically for the country, but it makes life easier. For instance, in India nearly 200 languages are spoken: English is a very useful language to unify the country.
An Indian professor has said of his country of 750 million inhabitants, 'More Indians speak English and write English than in England.' And a famous English writer has said, 'The last Englishman left will be an Indian.'

1  What other languages are still used in countries which were once colonies? Make a list.
    *Example*
    Portugal/Portuguese

2  Imagine that you come from a country which is an English colony and which is becoming independent. Many people want to stop using English as an official language. Can you think of arguments against this? You can find ideas in the texts on this page. Make sentences like the model.

> If we stop using English, what language will we make our official language?
> It will be easier for our businessmen if we keep English as an official language.

English has become the first foreign language that much of the world wants to learn. The need to communicate internationally is one basic reason for this: the more English is spoken around the world, the more people want to learn it. There are many communities and institutions where a knowledge of English is important. How many can you think of?

## TELEVISION AND FILMS

The first worldwide TV audience was for the Coronation of Queen Elizabeth II in Westminster Abbey on 2nd June, 1953. The age of television communications had arrived. In the 1950s American television and movies took American English and the American way of life (seen through Hollywood's eyes) round the world. Many immigrants to the USA say that they first learned English in the cinemas of Europe.

1  What is the most recent film or television programme, made in English, that you have seen?
   Was it subtitled or dubbed?
2  With your partner make a list of the advantages and disadvantages of:
   a  subtitling  b  dubbing

## COMPUTERS

Silicon Valley, half an hour's drive south from San Francisco, is the heart of America's electronics industry. The valley is the home of the video game, the VDU, the word processor, the silicon chip and 'computerese' – computer language. Words like *input, software, high-tech* and *interface* are already in the dictionary. Streets in Silicon Valley have names like *Semiconductor* Drive. If you can use these, and other, computer words then you are *computer-literate*. American 'computerese' has invaded other languages too: French now has digitaliser, semi-conductor, interface; German has *repeat funktion*. Through high technology, American English is travelling across the world and into other languages.

Have any American 'computerese' words come into your language? Make a list. Do you know what they all mean?

## POP

The Swedish pop group Abba, who won the Eurovision Song Contest in 1974 with a song in English, recorded their songs in English but since 1975 singers in the Eurovision Song Contest have had to sing their songs in their own language. Before that time some countries used English and many people thought that this was unfair. So it was decided that each country should use its native language.

1  How many songs in English are there in your Top Ten at the moment?
2  How many groups or singers in your country have released hit songs in English?
3  Imagine you are a singer: will you record in your language or in English? Make a list of arguments FOR and AGAINST. Working in small groups, say what you think. With your teacher's help conduct a class survey.

## SINGALONG

In the bars and clubs of Japan there is a new kind of entertainment – KARAOKE (pronounced Kara-okay). People stand up and sing. They have a microphone and behind them a large TV screen. They choose a song on a video disc and the music starts to play. They sing along with the music.

In some bars there are songs in English to sing. In case you do not know much English the words appear on the TV screen along with the group. With a little English you can be a David Bowie or a Bruce Springsteen.

To practise their English some people afterwards go into the street and sing their songs in English as loud as they can.

Learn the song on page 105 and sing it in the playground today.

## OLYMPICS
Seoul    May 1986

President Chun said last night in an interview that all Koreans must learn English. 'We cannot learn all the languages of the world but most people who will be coming can speak English – if only a little.' He called on all Koreans to start learning now. In particular he said those in direct contact with visitors must learn English, hotel staff, police, bus drivers and taxi drivers . . . .

Imagine you are a South Korean taxi driver. What six English expressions will you need to learn first? Make a list and then compare your ideas with your partner's.

Recently experts have realised that English is no longer dependent on either its British or American parents. It is now a global language and is developing a life of its own. English is now everyone's second language, and it can live in totally non-English situations. A Brazilian businessman might learn English to do business in Japan. A Russian might learn English to do research in Berlin. An Arab doctor might learn English to practise in Amsterdam. And when an Italian pilot learns English, it could be to talk to ground control in Spain or Kuwait.

Why are *you* learning English? What will you be able to do with English? How many ways can you find to finish this sentence?

If I can speak English well, I will be able to .........

**C** ENGLISH – FRIEND OR ENEMY?

Computerese is not the only type of English which has invaded other languages. In Hong Kong a disco (originally of course a French word!) is called a *dixie-go*. In Germany teenagers wear *die Jeans*, in Sweden they have *tajt jeans* (tight jeans). In Russia you can drink ¹*visky* or ²*dzhin-in-tonic* and go to a ³*dzhazz-saission*. The French talk of *le weekend, le hit parade, le playboy*, ⁴*le snacque-barr* and ⁵*le bifteck*.

Can you translate the numbered words into English?

Look back at your lists on page 84. Can you think of any other English words that have invaded your language?

Sometimes so many words are taken into a language from English that it is almost possible to talk of a new language, for example *Japlish* or *Franglais*.

### JAPLISH

Since the Second World War, contact with the worlds of American technology and finance has introduced, it is estimated, up to 20,000 new words into the Japanese vocabulary. Can we call these words examples of 'Japlish'?

For example, the word for an apartment is *man-shon*, from the English *mansion* (originally from the French *maison*); there is *mai-town* for *my town* and *mai-com* for *my computer*.

What do you think these 'Japlish' words mean in English?
*mai-kaa   mai-homu   aisu-kurimu*

### FRANGLAIS

In the mid 1970s President Pompidou wanted people to know that English was not the only possible language for industrial, economic and scientific communication. He started an attack on the English words used in French – he called this language *la langue du Coca-Cola* (the Coca-Cola language). Expressions like *jumbo jet* or *fast food* were forbidden and French expressions were invented. The fight continues today, but it is estimated that one word in 166 in the French newspaper *Le Monde* is English, and that about one word in 20 of day-to-day French vocabulary comes from English.

Has anything like this happened in your country? Is there an Academy that is fighting against the English invasion?

**D** WHERE DO I GO FROM HERE?

There are several things you could do to keep up your English when this course is finished.

a You could listen to the BBC World Service on your radio.
b You could correspond with an English-speaking penfriend.
c With your teacher's help you could organise an educational exchange with a British school.
d You could even visit Britain to take a language course!

Which would you like to do most? Put these four suggestions in order of personal preference and read about your favourite in the information sheets below. Which address can you write to for more information?

Working with a partner, write a letter to one of the organisations asking for more information.

DON'T FORGET TO SEND YOUR LETTER.

## BBC WORLD SERVICE

BBC World Service is the BBC's 24 hour service in English to all parts of the world. It contains:

**News:**
Broadcast on the hour, every hour (with occasional exceptions) in *World News, Newsdesk, Radio Newsreel* and one-minute summaries.

**Features and Talks:**
Important subjects, both topical and historical, are examined by journalists, historians, philosophers, scientists and other experts.

**Science and Industry:**
A full service of information and education provided in specialised weekly programmes, including *Science in Action, Discovery, Business and Industry, New Ideas* and *Stock Market Report.*

**Drama:**
Presenting the heritage of British and world literature and drama. *Play of the Week* and *Radio Theatre* offer the finest works, both classical and contemporary, performed by leading actors and actresses.

**Music:**
Many hours a week of serious music, with particular emphasis on leading orchestras and distinguished conductors and soloists. Also a full range of pop, folk, jazz and light music.

**Sport:**
A comprehensive sports service with daily reports, weekly reviews and live coverage of important events.

**London Calling:**
Full details of BBC World Service programmes and how to hear them, plus timings and frequencies of other language services, can be found each month in the magazine London Calling. For a free sample and subscription form write to:
London Calling (Distribution), P.O. Box 76, Bush House, London WC2B 4PH, England.

*Continuity studio, the focal point of World Service programmes.*

INFORMA        SHEET

SPEAK ENGLISH!

Short and long-term English language courses are offered by local education authorities, universities and private schools. There are holiday courses during Christmas, Easter and summer for children aged 7-16 and for adults. Some courses are residential, while others provide the opportunity of living with an English family. Leisure and social activities are usually provided; centres offering children's courses normally include comprehensive programmes of supervised sports, cultural and social activities.

ARELS/FELCO, the Association of Recognised English Language Teaching Establishments in Britain, has a membership of private schools and course organisers which have been recognised as efficient by the British Council. The schools offer courses of varying lengths throughout the year; a few are residential, the remainder help their students to find accommodation, usually with families. A brochure giving details of schools and courses is available from ARELS/FELCO, 125 High Holborn, London WC1V 6QD, and from British Council offices, British Tourist Authority offices or British diplomatic missions.

**Central Bureau for Educational Visits & Exchanges**
Seymour Mews House, Seymour Mews
London W1H 9PE
Tel 01-486 5101
3 Bruntsfield Crescent, Edinburgh EH10 4HD
Tel 031-447 8024
16 Malone Road, Belfast BT9 5BN
Tel 0232-664418/9

*Central Bureau for Educational Visits & Exchanges*
16 Malone Road, Belfast BT9 1BN        telephone 0232-664418/9

### SCHOOL LINKS

The Central Bureau can help teachers to link their schools with their counterparts abroad. Such links provide a framework for contact in several subject areas and at different levels. Especially popular are links with countries whose language is taught in British schools, eg Austria, Belgium, France, the Federal Republic of Germany, Italy and Spain.

### CLASS LINKS

Under the guidance of the teacher, a group can exchange individual letters, tapes and cassettes, joint project work, photographs and all types of educational material with classes in schools abroad. Correspondence and exchange projects with schools in many parts of the world are valuable on a purely cultural level and can be used to enrich the curriculum for subjects such as European and world studies, history and geography as well as in the teaching of modern languages.

### PENFRIEND LINKS

The Central Bureau can help to find penfriends in France, the Federal Republic of Germany, Italy, Spain and many other countries in the developing world for school pupils aged 11 to 18.

Teachers wishing to receive further information on the schemes listed should contact the Central Bureau at the above address as soon as possible.

ment of Education for Northern Ireland        Department of Education and Science        Scottish Education Department

# PROJECT ENGLISH

POSTERS

In lesson one of this unit you discussed collecting money for a charity. If you want to make a success of your collection you will need good advertising. A very good way of advertising is a poster.

You can put posters up in your school to tell other pupils about your plans. If you put one poster in each classroom everyone will know about your collection. So you will need a lot of posters! Each person in your class can make one poster.

If you are making a poster, here are two important things to remember:

1 KEEP THE MESSAGE SIMPLE
2 COMBINE THE VISUAL WITH THE WRITING

Here are some ideas you might find useful.

## How to use the illustrations from printed material you have

If you want to use illustrations from the printed material you have, but need them larger or smaller, you can enlarge or reduce them by:
1 using a photocopier (see Project English page 89)
2 drawing it larger or smaller freehand
3 the squares method

● If the original image cannot be damaged –

Trace the original picture on to greaseproof paper, and then treat as an original that can be damaged.

● If the original image can be damaged –

Cut out the picture and cut a similar shaped piece of paper to the size you want the finished image to be.

Fold each an equal number of times (at least three).

Copy the image square by square.

Finally transfer the image on to whatever you want by scribbling on the back with a pencil, by using a carbon paper or tracing through.

When tilting letters, tilt up not down and similarly when arching words.

SLANT WORDS UP NOT DOWN

ALSO TRY TO ARCH WORDS ESPECIALLY THE FIRST WORDS

TO START BY GOING DOWN MAKES IT HARD TO READ!

KEEP FIT

## Guidelines for making headings

### Size
The words must be large enough to be read but can be larger than necessary for impact.

EEEEEEEEE

### Weight
The weight of the letters usually depends on their colour. Simply by changing this, you can alter the emphasis of some words.

a a a=a

These posters will give you ideas for *your* posters.

Buy a Ticket! Win A Prize
Help Mother Teresa ~ of Calcutta ~

Save the Children
DISCO
TUESDAY 13 NOVEMBER
Class 1°H

SPONSORED Fun Run RED CROSS
Saturday 22 January
Entry Forms From Maria — Class 3B —

BUY A 'T' SHIRT!
LIVE AID
Feed the World
Class 2B

---

♀ 1

Your name is Helena Theodopoulos. You come from Patras, Greece.

You have left Greece because your brothers want you to marry. They have chosen a husband for you but you hate the man.

You're going to your uncle's family in San Francisco.

Your father was a greengrocer and you helped him in the shop. But he died two months ago.

Your uncle owns a restaurant in San Francisco and you hope to work in the kitchen there.

You have just enough money to get to San Francisco.

You sometimes get high fevers: nobody knows why. Otherwise, your health is good.

You speak very little English.

---

♂ 2

Your name is James Collins. You come from Halifax, north England.

Your brother (the writer of letter 5) is a farmer and you are going to join him. You are a successful physician, but you are bored with your life in England.

You have brought a lot of money with you and you have left a large house in England where your mother and young wife still live.

If things go well, you will send for your wife.

You had a good salary in England, but you hope to make even more money in the United States.

Your health is all right, but you have had one or two problems with your heart – nothing serious, but you have to be careful.

# GROWING UP

**A** THE TWO STORIES

Look at the book covers and the information about the writers.

Camara Laye
Born: Guinea, 1924
Died: 1980
Wrote stories, mostly about life in Africa.

Charles Dickens
Born: England, 1812
Died: 1870
Wrote novels, mostly about life in industrial England.

Discuss the answers to these questions with the class.

How old do you think the boys on the covers are?
Where do you think the boys come from?
When do you think the stories take place?
Have you ever heard of Charles Dickens?
If yes, have you read any of his stories?
Did you read them in English or in your own language?

*David Copperfield* was written in 1849, and is one of the most famous novels in English. It is fiction, but some of the events are based on Charles Dickens' life as a child. *The African Child* was written originally in French in 1954. It is an autobiography of Camara Laye's early life.

Although the stories take place at different times, they are both about young boys growing up. By reading the books, and by finding out something about the characters, you can explore your own feelings and compare other people's lives with yours.

**B** FIRST LESSONS

1   Read these two passages carefully.

---

**The African Child**

I was a little boy playing in the yard at home. How old? Five, maybe six. I could just hear my father and mother in the workshop.

Suddenly I stopped playing to watch a snake near the workshop. After a moment I went over to him. I had a long piece of grass in my hand. I pushed this into the snake's mouth. He did not try to get away. He was enjoying our little game. He was slowly eating the grass, his mouth coming nearer and nearer to my hand.

I was laughing. I had no fear. I did not know that the snake was dangerous. Suddenly I felt myself lifted off my feet. I was safe in my father's arms. Everybody was shouting, my mother louder than anyone else. She hit me several times. But it was .the sudden noise more than her blows that made me cry.

Later, when it was quiet, my mother warned me never to play such a game again. I promised, but I could not see why it was dangerous.

---

**David Copperfield**

'Clara! Don't help the boy,' cried Mr Murdstone. 'He either knows his lesson or he does not.'

'He does *not* know it!' said Miss Murdstone.

I tried again. I made more mistakes – many more. Mr Murdstone threw the book at me.

My lessons took this form for about six months. Then one morning Mr Murdstone was waiting for me with a stick. 'Now, David,' he said. 'If you are not careful, I'll beat you.'

Everything went out of my mind – words, lines and whole pages. I began badly and got worse.

My mother cried.

'Clara, be quiet!' said Miss Murdstone.

Mr Murdstone picked up his stick and took me to my bedroom.

'Mr Murdstone! Sir!' I cried. 'Please don't beat me. I try to learn, but I can't learn when you are in the room.'

Mr Murdstone held my head under his arm and beat me. But I caught his hand in my mouth – and bit it. Mr Murdstone, wild with anger, then beat me harder. He threw me to the floor and left the room, and I heard the key in the door.

I was locked in that room like a prisoner for five days.

---

2   Write your answers to these questions.
   a   Both boys were beaten. Did they deserve to be punished? Give reasons for your answer.
   b   What was the difference between the attitude of Mr Murdstone and Camara's mother?
   c   What frightened David and Camara most?
   d   Did the beating the two boys received really teach them a lesson?

Compare your answers with your partner.

3   Discuss these questions in small groups.
   a   Have you ever been beaten?
   b   What were your reactions?
   c   Do you think that beating young children teaches them anything?

Take a class vote.

## C  SCHOOL

1  Read these two passages carefully.

Once in school, we went straight to our seats. Boys and girls sat side by side, our quarrels over. And as soon as we sat down, we were all ears and sat quite still. The teacher gave his lessons in complete silence.

Our teacher was here, there and everywhere. He talked so fast that if we didn't listen very hard we couldn't follow what he said. But we did listen very hard. For us, school work was something deadly serious. Everything we learned was strange, as if we were learning about life on another planet. We never grew tired of listening.

Even if we weren't interested, the silence would have been complete. Our teacher was so quick to punish. Most of all, we lived in fear of being sent out to the blackboard. Here the tiniest detail was important. If we wrote one letter not quite the same height as the others, we would receive an unforgettable beating.

Next day lessons began. I shall never forget that day. The boys were playing about in the school-room, making a great noise. Suddenly the room became silent. Mr Creakle entered. He stood in the doorway, with a stick in his hand, and looked at us.

Mr Creakle came to my desk. 'You're famous for *biting*. Well, I'm famous for *beating*!' he said – and beat me on my back. I cried.

I was not the only boy who felt his stick. Many were crying before lessons began.

Mr Creakle was the worst teacher who ever lived: he *enjoyed* beating boys. He never beat Steerforth, because his parents were rich.

Traddles was the most unlucky boy in the school. Poor Traddles was beaten every day of the week. He never cried; he laughed to hide his feelings.

2  Discuss answers to these questions with your partner.
   a  What was the same about both schools?
   b  What was different about the schools?
   c  Who was the better teacher?
   d  How was the attitude of the pupils different?

3  Discuss these questions in small groups.
   a  Both lessons were held in silence except for the talk of the teacher.
      Why was this so?
   b  Have you ever had lessons like these?
   c  Are lessons like these good or bad? Give your reasons.

Report on your discussion to the class.

## D  SCHOOL BULLIES

1  Read these two passages carefully.

The next day, as soon as Kouyaté entered the school yard, he went over to Himourana, the big boy who had beaten him so hard the day before.

'My father wishes to meet the boy who has been kindest to me. I thought of you at once. Can you come and share our dinner this evening?'

'Of course I can!' Himourana was as unintelligent as he was cruel – and he liked eating.

That evening Himourana arrived at Kouyaté's house. As soon as he was inside the yard, Kouyaté's father carefully locked the gate. Himourana, noticing nothing, sat down with Kouyaté's family. He could hardly wait to start eating. But Kouyaté stood up and pointed at him.

'My father,' he said, 'that is the big boy who never stops beating me, and who takes my food and money!'

'Well, young man,' Kouyaté's father said to Himourana, 'What have you to say for yourself?'

For a moment, Himourana was too surprised to speak or move. Then his one thought was to get away. But there was no way out of the yard. He had only run a few steps before he was caught.

'Now listen carefully,' said Kouyaté's father. 'I do not send my son to school to be beaten by boys like you!'

I was welcomed to the school by J. Steerforth. He was about six years older than myself, very good-looking, and clever. I thought Steerforth was a fine fellow.

'How much money have you got, Copperfield?' Steerforth asked.

I told him 'seven shillings'. He offered to take care of my money. I accepted his kind offer and gave it to him.

'Perhaps you'd like to spend a shilling or two on some drinks – a bottle of wine for the bedroom?' said Steerforth, 'And you'll want to buy some cakes, I dare say?'

I smiled because he smiled.

Steerforth spent all my money. He bought enough food and wine for all the boys in the bedroom. That night we had a grand supper.

2  Write your answers to these questions.
   a  In what way were Steerforth and Himourana bullies?
   b  How were their characters different?
   c  If you were David, would you like Steerforth as a friend? Give reasons.

3  Discuss these questions with your partner.
   a  Do you know any bullies?
   b  Do bullies always bully people who are smaller and weaker than them?
   c  If you were bullied, what would you do?

Make a class list of how to deal with bullies.

OUT OF SCHOOL

Write about one of these things:  my first class
my worst class
a school bully

**E** WELCOMES

1 Read these two passages carefully.

> Before we reached even the edge of Tindican, I saw my grandmother coming to meet us. I ran shouting towards her and she lifted me high in the air. I held her as hard as I could, throwing my arms about her, I was so happy.
> 'How are you, my little man?' she said.
> 'I'm fine.'
> 'Now, is that so?' And she looked me over and felt me to see if I was fat enough. Her fingers felt only skin and bone (I grew very fast, and this made me thin), so she said,
> 'Look at that! Don't they give you anything to eat in town? You're not going back to Kouroussa until you've put some fat on these bones. Do you hear me?'
> 'Yes, Grandmamma.'
> 'And how are your mother and father and everybody at your place?'
> She didn't put me down until I'd told her all the news about everybody at home. Then she took my hand and we walked to the village. As soon as we reached the first huts, my grandmother would shout:
> 'Here's my little man just arrived.'

> Almost black with dirt, and afraid, I waited to meet my aunt.
> A lady wearing a mob-cap came out of the house. 'Go away!' cried Miss Betsy. 'No boys here!'
> 'Please, Miss Trotwood, you are my aunt,' I said.
> 'Oh, God!' cried my aunt.
> 'I am David Copperfield,' I said. 'My dear mama has died – and I am very unhappy. I have walked all the way to Dover. I haven't slept in a bed since I began my journey.' I broke down and cried.
> My aunt caught hold of my neck and took me quickly into the house. She got a bottle and emptied some medicine into my mouth.
> 'Janet!' she called to her servant. 'Heat the bath.'
> The bath comforted me. After my bath, my aunt tied me up in some great blankets. I expect I was a funny sight. Feeling very hot, I lay on a chair and fell asleep.
> When I woke, we had dinner – a hot chicken, followed by fruit cake.

2 Discuss these questions in small groups.
   a How did the two boys feel when they met their relations?
   b How did the relations feel about meeting the boys?
   c What did each of the women do first?

Write a group report of your answer and tell the class.

3 Discuss these questions with your partner.
   a Would you like to meet either of these women? Give reasons.
   b Do you know anyone like Betsy Trotwood or Camara's grandmother?
   c What makes you feel welcome when you visit a friend or relative?

4 Write about a warm welcome you have had and then show your story to your neighbour.

**F** WORK

1 Read these two passages carefully.

> When they arrived at the first field, the young men would line up at the edge, knives ready. Then my Uncle Lansana would invite them to begin work. At once the black backs would bend over the great golden field, and the cutting would begin.
> The knives rose and fell fast and regularly. The men had to cut the rice very carefully, so that only the bottom leaf was left behind. They hardly ever missed.
> My young uncle was the best of all the rice cutters. I would follow happily behind him, ready to take each handful as he cut it. Then I would take the leaves off and cut all the pieces to an equal length. I would always do this very gently. If the rice is roughly handled, the best part may be lost.

> So, at the age of ten, I began to work for my living.
> Murdstone and Grinby's storehouse stood by the river. The building was very old and almost falling down. The rooms were blackened with the dirt of a hundred years, I dare say.
> I worked with four other boys. We had to wash empty bottles; label them for new wine; and put them in wooden cases. The other boys were very rough, and I hated them. I cried as I washed the bottles on my first morning.

3 Discuss these questions in small groups.
   a Have you ever worked? Who for, and what did you do?
   b What did you like or dislike about this work?
   c What is the minimum working age in your country? Do you think this is the right age? Take a class vote.

2 Write your answers to these questions.
   a What was different about David and Camara's work?
   b What was different about the places where they worked?
   c Did David and Camara enjoy their work? Give reasons.

116

**1** Read these two passages carefully.

---

During that year I became friendly with Marie. Whenever I think about our love – and I often think about it, dream about it – it seems to me that nothing in all those years meant more to me.

Marie was a pupil at the Girls' High School. Her father and my Uncle Mamadou had been close friends since school days, and Marie spent all her Sundays in my uncle's house. We both found there the warmth of a family home.

My aunts always cooked something special on Sundays. They would have liked me to eat with Marie. But how could I? We both felt shy about eating at the same table: it was not our custom. Our aunts could not understand our shyness. But Marie and I never even discussed it. We would never think of meeting again until after the meal.

Then we usually went to my Uncle Sekou's rooms. Being unmarried, he was often out, and we were left alone there.

My uncle would leave his gramophone and records for us, and Marie and I would dance. It is not the custom in our land, of course, to dance in one another's arms. We dance opposite each other, not touching, or at the most holding hands. In our shyness we desired nothing better.

---

Mr Spenlow led me into a bright and very comfortable sitting-room. I heard him say: 'Mr Copperfield, this is my daughter, Dora.'

I looked at Dora with wondering eyes – and fell deeply in love with her. It happened in a moment.

Dora seemed to me the most beautiful girl in the world – everything that every man wanted. She had a pretty little voice, a happy little laugh, and the sweetest little ways.

I spent the rest of the day in a dream.

In the morning, I rose early and walked in the garden. I tried to picture my happiness if I could marry this dear beauty. I turned a corner – and met her.

'You are out early, Miss Spenlow,' I said.

'It's not a good idea to stay indoors on a fine morning,' she replied. 'This is the brightest time of the day, don't you think?'

I said slowly: '*You* brighten the day for me!'

She reddened and turned her face away.

---

**2** Discuss these questions in small groups.

  a  How were Dora and Marie alike?

  b  How did David and Camara behave with their girlfriends? Compare the behaviour.

  c  Give a title for these two passages. Compare your idea with the rest of the class.

**3** Discuss these questions in small groups.

  a  At what age do young people have boyfriends or girlfriends in your country?

  b  Have you ever felt shy with someone of the opposite sex?

  c  What would your ideal boyfriend or girlfriend be like? Make a list of words like these: friendly  beautiful.

Choose the three most important words from your group. With your teacher's help, take a class vote for the most popular words.

 OUT OF SCHOOL

**1** True or false?

  a  David marries Dora.

  b  David becomes a doctor.

  c  Steerforth dies horribly.

  d  Camara marries Marie.

  e  Camara becomes a farmer.

  f  Camara beats up Himourana.

If you want to find out, read the two stories.

**2** Write a composition about yourself called 'Growing up'. Write three paragraphs of 50 words each.

  a  life at home

  b  life at school

  c  friends

TIME for
Q

# A

## Partner A

Read these questions to your partner.
record the answers.

## How to Play

1 Toss a coin to decide who is **A** and who is
   **B**.
2 While **A** asks the first block of 8 questions,
   **B**'s book is closed.
3 Change over. Now **A** closes his or her book
   and **B** asks the questions.

**UNIT 1 Lesson 1**
**UNIT 1 Lesson 2**
**UNIT 2 Lesson 1**
**UNIT 2 Lesson 2**

1 Who was the first President of the USA?
2 What did the American colonists call the British soldiers?
3 There have been people in the USA since 20,000 BC. True or false?
4 What country do the most recent immigrants to the USA come from?
5 What time does school normally start in the USA?
6 Is there a national health programme in the USA?
7 The Samaritans is a group of people who raise money for charity. True or false?
8 What word is used in English for bright red hair?

**UNIT 3 Lesson 1**
**UNIT 3 Lesson 2**
**UNIT 4 Lesson 1**
**UNIT 4 Lesson 2**

9 In which state is Miami?
10 How many people visit Sea World, Orlando each year?
   3 million   4 million   6 million
11 There are 100 cents in a dollar. How many cents are there in a quarter?
12 'Bathroom' in American English. What is it in British English?
13 What colour is the flower called a poppy?
14 Approximately how many shades of green can the human eye see?
   80,000   800,000   8,000,000
15 What country did the pop group Menudo start in?
16 Which city in the USA has the largest population?

**UNIT 6 Lesson 1**
**UNIT 6 Lesson 2**
**UNIT 7 Lesson 1**
**UNIT 7 Lesson 2**

17 When it's spring in Europe, what season is it in New Zealand?
18 What is the name for a mountain that sometimes pours out hot melted rock?
19 What sort of boats did the Maoris travel to New Zealand in?
20 In the 18th century, how long did the trip from England to Australia take?
   3 months   8 months   15 months
21 Do the majority of Australians live in urban or rural areas?
22 What is the Australian word for land that is not cultivated?
23 Sport is not very popular in Australia and New Zealand. True or false?
24 What destroyed the city of Darwin in 1974?

**UNIT 8 Lesson 1**
**UNIT 8 Lesson 2**
**UNIT 9 Lesson 1**
**UNIT 9 Lesson 2**

25 There are special doctors in Australia who visit sick people living far away from towns. What are these doctors called?
26 What part of the body do pneumonia and influenza attack?
27 Is New Zealand a Spanish name, an English name or a Dutch name?
28 How long have Aboriginal people been in Australia?
   over 4,000 years   over 40,000 years
   over 400,000 years
29 What are murals painted on?
   large sheets of paper   walls of buildings
   roads and footpaths
30 There are many women working as television camera assistants in Australia. True or false?
31 2,000 children wanted to take part in *Mad Max Beyond Thunderdome*. How many were finally chosen?
   60   90   200
32 What is the opposite of 'artificial'?

**UNIT 11 Lesson 1**
**UNIT 11 Lesson 2**
**UNIT 12 Lesson 1**
**UNIT 12 Lesson 2**

33 The English language is used in India as a means of communication between different parts of the country. True or false?
34 'Karate' is a word used in English. What language was it borrowed from?
35 What is the book which tells you how to operate a computer called?
   a monitor   an instruction manual
   a printer
36 What is 'The Bug'?
   an insect   a disease
   a computer magazine
37 What important medical practice did Dr Edward Jenner discover?
38 Garlic, red pepper tea and hot lemon drinks are all home cures for what common illness?
39 What temperature does the tip of a cigarette burn at?
   80°C   180°C   880°C
40 Name two foods that are high in calories.

**UNIT 13 Lesson 1**
**UNIT 13 Lesson 2**
**UNIT 14 Lesson 1**
**UNIT 14 Lesson 2**

41 What country is the United World College of the Atlantic in?
42 Students at The United World Colleges are between 16 and 19 years old. True or false?
43 The instant theatre group, Word And Action, works in many different languages. True or false?
44 What words are most commonly used to start a fairy story?
45 What continent is Ethiopia in?
46 What does Bob Geldof do for a living?
47 The American spacecraft, Voyager I, carries messages in how many earth languages?
   55   105   155
48 The first worldwide television event took place on 2nd June, 1953. What was it?

# B

4  Check back to the appropriate lessons to
   see if your partner's answers are right.
5  Score 1 mark for each correct answer.
6  **A** asks the next block of 8 questions.

Continue like this until all the questions have
been asked. Add up the scores to find the
winner.

## Partner B

Read these questions to your partner.
Record the answers.

**UNIT 1 / Lesson 1**
1  How many states are there in the USA?
2  July 4th is a special day in the USA? What
   is it called?

**UNIT 1 / Lesson 2**
3  All new immigrants to the USA still pass
   through Ellis Island. True or false?
4  San Francisco had a terrible disaster in
   1906. What was it?

**UNIT 2 / Lesson 1**
5  Children must go to school for thirteen
   years in the USA? True or false?
6  What do Americans spend most of their
   money on?

**UNIT 2 / Lesson 2**
7  At what age can you become a Samaritan
   volunteer?
8  What word is used in English for a special
   group of friends?

**UNIT 3 / Lesson 1**
9  Florida is called 'The Golden State'. True
   or false?
10 What is the name of the big fish you can
   see in Sea World, Orlando?

**UNIT 3 / Lesson 2**
11 American paper money is all the same
   colour. True or false?
12 'Elevator' in American English. What is it
   in British English?

**UNIT 4 / Lesson 1**
13 What word for food means *ready to eat*?
14 More men than women are colour blind.
   True or false?

**UNIT 4 / Lesson 2**
15 No performers in Menudo can be more
   than 14 years old. True or false?
16 What's the capital city of the USA?

**UNIT 6 / Lesson 1**
17 Can emus fly?
18 What is the name for a piece of land with
   water all around it?

**UNIT 6 / Lesson 2**
19 When did the first convict ships arrive in
   Botany Bay?
   1698   1768   1788
20 Most people could read and write in the
   18th century. True or false?

**UNIT 7 / Lesson 1**
21 What is the name for a baby sheep?
22 Dogs are a great help on sheep farms.
   True or false?

**UNIT 7 / Lesson 2**
23 The Opera House is one of the most
   famous buildings in Australia. What city
   is it in?
24 Australian lifesavers don't get paid for
   saving people's lives. True or false?

**UNIT 8 / Lesson 1**
25 What is the name of the instrument used
   to measure body temperature?
26 Flying doctors lead very comfortable
   lives. True or false?

**UNIT 8 / Lesson 2**
27 Over the radio on Schools of the Air,
   pupils can talk to their teacher but not to
   other pupils. True or false?
28 How long have Maoris been in New
   Zealand for?
   1,000 years   10,000 years   100,000 years

**UNIT 9 / Lesson 1**
29 When was the Sydney Opera House
   opened?
   1873   1953   1973
30 On a camera, what do you press if you
   want to take a photo?
   the film advance lever   the view finder
   the shutter release button

**UNIT 9 / Lesson 2**
31 A boomerang is used by Aboriginals for
   hunting. True or false?
32 In *Mad Max Beyond Thunderdome*, what
   were the children's bodies covered in?

**UNIT 11 / Lesson 1**
33 A good knowledge of English is needed
   for many jobs these days. True or false?
34 'Disco' is a word used in English. What
   language was it borrowed from?

**UNIT 11 / Lesson 2**
35 What is the screen on a computer called?
   a monitor   an instruction manual
   a printer
36 What is BASIC?
   a computer language   a guitar
   the first step

**UNIT 12 / Lesson 1**
37 What disease did Dr Edward Jenner's
   vaccination prevent?
38 What year was the last case of smallpox
   in the world?

**UNIT 12 / Lesson 2**
39 The insides of your lungs are covered
   with millions of tiny hairs. True or false?
40 Name two foods that are low in calories.

**UNIT 13 / Lesson 1**
41 What country is the Lester B Pearson
   United World College of the Pacific in?
42 The International Baccalaureate is a
   secondary school entrance examination.
   True or false?

**UNIT 13 / Lesson 2**
43 The instant theatre group, Word And
   Action, invite the audience to act in their
   plays. True or false?
44 What does the word 'abroad' mean?
   overseas   very wide   a street

**UNIT 14 / Lesson 1**
45 What was Live Aid?
46 How much money did the Live Aid
   concert raise around the world?
47 How many people use English in the
   world today?
   at least 550 million   at least 650 million
   at least 750 million

**UNIT 14 / Lesson 2**
48 What town in America is famous for film
   making?

# FACTS ABOUT ENGLISH

## DID YOU KNOW?

More than 400 million people in the world use English as a second language. About 350 million people use English as their mother tongue. The complete Oxford English Dictionary lists 500,000 words. There are another 500,000 scientific and technical words in English.

Shakespeare had an English vocabulary of about 25,000 words.
Winston Churchill knew 80,000 words.
A well-educated English speaker knows 36,000 words.

An average English speaker uses 3–4,000 words. A five-year old child knows about 3,000 words. When you finish *Time For English* you will have met about 3000

This diagram shows the 20,000 words in an average English vocabulary. All the most important words are printed. Words that occur most often are in large print. Words that occur less often are in smaller print.
You should know the words printed here. Test yourself and other students in your class.

a and he
I in is
it of that
the to was

all as at be but are for had have him his not on one said so they we with you 20

about an back been before big by call came can come could did do down first from get go has her here if into just like little look made make me more much must my no new now off only or our other out over right see she some their them then there this two when up want well went were what where which who will your old. 68

After Again Always Am Ask Another Any Away Bad Because Best Bird Black Blue Boy Bring Day Dog Don't Eat Every Fast Father Fell Find Five Fly Four Found Gave Girl Give Going Good Got Green Hand Head Help Home House How Jump Keep Know Last Left Let Live Long Man Many May Men Mother Mr. Never Nest Once Open Own Play Put Ran Read Red Room Round Run Sat Saw Say School Should Sing Sit Soon Stop Take Tell Than These Thing Think Three Time Too Tree Under Us Very Walk White Why Wish Work Woman Would Yes Year Bus Apple Baby Bag Ball Bed Book Box Car Cat Children Cow Cup Dinner Doll Door Egg End Farm Fish Fun Hat Hill Horse Jam Letter Milk Money Morning Mrs. Name Night Nothing Picture Pig Place Rabbit Road Sea Shop Sister Street Sun Table Tea Today Top Toy Train Water 150

This area represents 19,750 more words. Space does not permit the printing of these words.

---

ANSWERS TO JOKES

**Page 17**

3   John had nine girl-friends.

5   None. You can't dig half a hole.

**Page 33**

1   Anything you want. He can't hear you.

2   Because not many graduate from high school.

**Page 57**

1   Patsy lived in England but was born in Australia.

2   Dora hit the ball straight up in the air.

3   119.

4   day, dictionary, dirt, do, Dr, dry, I, in, into, iron, it, can, car, card, cat, city, coat, coin, cry, to, today, train, try, on, or, nation, no, not, a, act, action, actor, air, an, and, art, at, radio, rain, road, yard.

**Page 73**

1   R.U.O.K.?

2

3   To keep their legs warm (the colour doesn't matter!).

4   The water will never reach the captain's window. The ship rises with the tide.

**Page 97  'CROSSWORDS**

| Across | Down |
|--------|------|
| 2   cold | 1   hospital |
| 5   water | 3   vaccine |
| 6   injection | 4   cure |
| 7   blanket | |
| 8   pale | |

1   Long enough to reach the ground.

2   Smaller.

**Page 105**

1   One train went through the tunnel at 2 pm. And the other went through at 3 pm.

2   The same!

# TEST YOUR ENGLISH

## A  FILL IN THE GAPS

The rise of English is a remarkable success story. When Julius Caesar landed in Britain nearly two thousand years ago, English did not exist. Five hundred years later, *Englisc* – which we could not understand today – was not spoken by many people and was not important. Nearly a thousand years after that, at the end of the sixteenth century, when William Shakespeare was writing, English was the native language of between five and seven million Englishmen.

Four hundred years later the contrast is extraordinary. Between 1600 and the present, speakers of English travelled to every corner of the globe, carrying their language and culture with them. Today, English is used by at least 750 million people. (Less than half of those speak it as a mother tongue.) Some estimates have put that figure closer to one billion. Now, at the end of the twentieth century, English is more widely spoken and written that any other language has ever been. It has become *the* language of the planet, the first truly global language.

The statistics of English are incredible. Of all the world's languages (which now number 2,700) it is probably the richest in vocabulary. The *Oxford English Dictionary* lists about 500,000 words; and there are a further half million technical and scientific terms not in the dictionary. German has a vocabulary of about 185,000 words and French fewer than 100,000, including such Franglais as *le snacque-barre* and *le hit-parade*. About 350 million people use English as a mother tongue: about one-tenth of the world's population. Only Chinese speakers are more numerous.

Fill in the gaps with the information taken from the box.

1  . . . . . Julius Caesar landed in Britain.
2  . . . . . not many people spoke *Englisc*.
3  . . . . . English was spoken by between 5 and 7 million people.
4  . . . . . English is used by at least 750 million people.
5  Today . . . . . use English as a mother tongue.
6  Today . . . . . use English as an international language.
7  German has about . . . . . more words than French.

> 90,000
> 1 in 10 people
> In 400 AD
> 400 years later
> In 54 BC
> At least 450 million people
> In 1600 AD

## B  COMPLETE THE STORY

Finish this famous fairy-story in your own words.

### The Princess and the Pea

. . . there lived a . . . Prince who wanted to marry a Princess.
  'She must be a real Princess,' he thought. 'The woman I marry must . . .'
But he could never find the right Princess for him: there was always something wrong. One Princess . . . , and another . . . so finally he returned home to his castle alone.

. . . there was a terrible storm: the sky was . . . and it rained and rained for hours. Suddenly there was a noise at the door. Knock knock! Knock knock!
  'There's someone . . .' said the King and he went to open the door. There stood a young woman. She was . . . .
  'Please can I . . . ?' she asked. 'I'm a real Princess.'
The King said, ' . . .'
But the Queen thought: 'A real Princess? Hmmm, we'll see.' So she prepared a bed for the Princess. She put twenty feather-beds on the bed and under the twenty feather-beds one pea. Then the Princess went to bed.

. . . the Queen asked the Princess: ' . . . ?'
  'Oh no,' replied the Princess. 'I couldn't . . . . It was terrible. There was something . . . in my bed.'
Then they all knew that . . . and the next day the Prince . . . .

## C  SPOT DICTATION

Listen to this talk on computers and fill each gap with one word.

There are [1]. . . . . basic parts to your [2]. . . . . computer system: the keyboard, the monitor, the disk drive and the [3]. . . . . . The keyboard is like a typewriter and the computer is [4]. . . . . the keyboard. You use the keys both to print [5]. . . . . and numbers – just like on a normal typewriter, and also to print [6]. . . . . to the computer. You see what you [7]. . . . .  . . . . . on the monitor. When you are [8]. . . . . with everything on the monitor [9]. . . . . you instruct the computer to print it out. The disk drive contains the floppy disks: one floppy disk contains the program, and the [10]. . . . . your input.

## D  TRUE OR FALSE?

1  Acupuncture is an old Japanese form of treatment.
2  Flu can be treated by acupuncture.
3  The acupuncturist only puts the needle into the part of the body that is sick.
4  It doesn't hurt when the acupuncturist puts in the needles.
5  Modern scientists don't understand how and why acupuncture works.

# WORD LIST

This is a complete list of the words you have met in TIME FOR ENGLISH Books 1, 2 and 3. Now you can read all the books in Collins English Library levels 1, 2 and 3. Happy reading!

## A

a
able
about
above
abroad
absent
accept
accident
ache
across
act (v n)
action
active
actor
actress
add
address (n v)
adult
adventure
aeroplane
afraid
after
afternoon
afterwards
again
against
age
agent
ago
agree
ah
air
aircraft
airline
airmail
airport
airhostess
alight
alike
alive
all
allow
all right
almost
alone
along
already
also
always
ambulance
among
amount
amuse
an
and
anger
angry
animal
another

answer
any
anybody
anyone
anything
anywhere
apartment
apologise
appear
apple
appointment
aquarium
argue
arithmetic
arm
armchair
army
around
arrival
arrive
art
artist
asleep
at
attack
aunt
autumn
awake
away

## B

baby
back
backwards
bacon
bad
bag
baggage
bake
baker
balcony
bald
ball
ballet
banana
bandage
bang (n v)
bank
bar
basement
bath
bathroom
battle
be
beach
beans
beautiful
beauty
because
become

bed
bedroom
beef
beer
before
begin
beginning
behind
being
believe
bell
belong
below
bend
beside
best
better
between
beyond
bicycle
big
bike
bill
bird
birth
birthday
bit (n)
bite
black
blackboard
blanket
blood
blouse
blow (v)
blue
beat
board
boarding pass
boat
body
boil
bone
book
bookshop
born
borrow
both
bottle
bottom
box (n)
boy
brain (n)
brake
branch
brave
bread
break
breakfast
breath
breathe

bridge
briefcase
bright
bring
broad
broadcast
brother
brown
brush
build
building
bullet
burn
bus
business
bus-stop
busy
but
butcher
butter
button
buy
by
bye-bye

## C

cabbage
café
cake
call
be called
call-box
came
camera
camp
camping-site
can (modal v)
canal
cancel
canteen
capital (city)
captain
car
car park
card
care (v n)
careful
careless
carpet
carry
case
cash
castle
cat
catch
cathedral
cattle
cause (n v)
cellar
cent

centimetre
central-heating
centre
century
certain
certainly
certificate
chair
chalk
chance
change
chapter
charge
charter-flight
cheap
cheat
check
check in
cheerio
cheese
chemist
cheque
chicken
child
chips
chocolate
choose
Christian name
Christmas
church
cigarette
cinema
circle
circus
city
class
classical
clean
clear
clerk
clever
climate
climb
clock
close
clothes
cloud
club
coach
coast
coat
coffee
coin
cold
collect
collection
college
colour
comb
come

comfort
comfortable
command
company
complete
concert
condition
congratulations
connection
contain
continue
conversation
cook
cool
copy
corner
correct
cost
cotton
could
count
country
course
cover
cow
crash
cream
crime
criminal
cross
crossing
crossroads
crossword
crowd
crown
cry
cup
cupboard
currency
curtain
customs
cut

## D

dad
daily
dance
danger
dangerous
dare
dark
date
daughter
day
daylight
daytime
daily
daybreak
dead
dear

death
decide
declare
deep
degree
delay
delighted
dentist
department
   store
departure
describe
desert (n)
desire
desk
dessert
detective
dial
dictionary
did
die
difference
different
difficult
dig
dining room
dinner
direction
dirt
dirty
disappear
discount
discover
disease
dish
distance
do
doctor
document
dog
dollar
door
doorway
double
down
downhill
downstairs
downward
Dr
draw
dream
dress
drink
drive
drop
dry
during
dust
duty

**E**
each
ear
early
earn

earth
east
easy
eat
edge
education
effect
egg
either
electric
electricity
elephant
else
emergency
empty
end
enemy
engine
enjoy
enough
enquiries
enter
entrance
envelope
equal
escape
even (adv)
evening
ever
every
everybody
everyone
everything
everywhere
exact
examination
example
excellent
except
exciting
excursion
excuse
excuse me
exhibition
exist
exit
expect
expensive
explain
explode
eye

**F**
face (n)
fact
factory
fail
fair
fall
false
family
famous
fan
fancy
far

fare
farm
farmer
farmland
fashion
fashionable
fast
fasten
fat
father
fear
feed
feel
fellow
female
ferry
fever
few
field (n)
figure
fill
film
finally
find
fine (adj)
finger
finish
fire
first
fish
fit (v)
fix
flag
flat
flight
floor
flower
fly
fog
follow
food
foot
football
for
foreign
force
forest
forget
fork
form
formerly
forwards
free
freeze
fresh
friend
from
front
frontier
frost
fruit
fry
full
fun
funny

furnished
furniture
future

**G**
gallery
gallon
game
garage
garden
gas
gate
gentle
gentlemen
geography
get
girl
give
glad
glass
glasses
goal
God
god
goddess
golf
gold
good
good-bye
good day
good evening
good morning
good night
govern
gramme
grand
grandfather
grandmother
grand-son
grass
grateful
great
green
grey
grill
grocer
ground
group
grow
grown-up
guest
guide
guitar
gun

**H**
had
hair
half
hall
hallo
ham
hand
happen
happy

harbour
hard
hardly
hat
hate
have
he
him
himself
his
head
health
hear
heart
heat
heating (n)
heavy
hello
help
her
hers
herself
here
hi
hide
high
hill
history
hobby
hold
hole
holiday/s
home
homework
hope
horse
hospital
host
hostess
hot
hotel
hour
house
housewife
how
hungry
hunt
hurray
hurry up
hurt
husband

**I**
I
ice
ice-cream
idea
if
ill
illness
immigration
import
important
impossible
in

inch
included
income
incorrect
indeed
indoors
industry
information
initials
injury
ink
insect
inside
instead (of)
intend
interest
interesting
interval
interview
into
introduce
invitation
invite
iron
island
it
its
itself

**J**
jacket
jam
jazz
jet
jewel
job
join (v)
joke
journey
jump
just

**K**
keep (v)
key
kick
kill
kilo
kilometre
kind
king
kingdom
kiss (v n)
kitchen
knife
know

**L**
label
lady
lake
lamb
lamp
land
language

large
last
late
laugh
law
lazy
lead
leader
leaf
learn
least
leather
leave (v)
left
leg
lend
less
lesson
let
letter
library
lie
life
lift (v)
light
lightning
like
line
lion
lioness
lip
list
listen
litre
little
live (v)
living
living-room
lonely
long
look
lorry
lose
loss
lost
lot
loud
lounge
love
lovely
low
luck
lucky
luggage
lunch

**M**
machine
madam
magazine
mail
make
male
man
manage
manager
many

map
march
mark
market
marriage
marry
master
match
material
mathematics
may
me
might
mine
meal
mean (v)
meat
medicine
meet (v)
member
mend
mention
don't mention it
menu
message
metal
metre
midday
middle
midnight
might
mild
mile
milk
million
millionaire
mind
minister
mist
minute (n)
Miss
miss
mistake
modern
moment
money
month
monthly
moon
more
morning
mother
motor
mountain/s
mouth
move
movies
Mr
Mrs
much
mum
murder
museum
mushrooms
music
must
mustard

my
myself
mystery

**N**
name
narrow
nation
nature
near
nearly
necessary
neck
need
neighbour
neighbourhood
neither... nor...
never
new
news
newspaper
next
nice
night
no
nothing
nobody
no-one
nowhere
noise
none
normal
north
nose
not
note (n)
nothing
notice
now
number
nurse
nut

**O**
occupation
ocean
o'clock
of
off
offer
office
often
oh
oil
OK
old
on
once
only
open
opera
operate
opinion
opposite
or
orange
order

ordinary
origin
other
ought
our/s
ourselves
out
outdoors
outside
outwards
over
ow!
own
oz.

**P**
page
pain
paint
pair
palace
pan
paper
parcel
pardon
parent
park
part (n)
party
pass (v)
passenger
passport
half-past
pastry
path
patient
pay
peace
pear
peas
pedestrian
pence
pencil
penny
people
pepper
per
performance
perhaps
person
pet
petrol
phone
photo
photograph
pick (v)
picnic
picture
piece
pig
pill
pilot
pink
pint
pipe
pity
place (n)

plan (n v)
plane
plant
plastic
plate
platform
play
please
pleasure
plenty
p.m.
pocket
point
police
policeman
political
politics
poor
pop
popular
pork
port
possible
post
pot
potato
pound (=£)
pound (=lb)
power
prefer
prescription
present
president
press (v)
pretty
price
prince
princess
prison
probably
profession
programme
promise
pronounce
prove
pub
pull
pupil
purple
purpose
purse
push
put (v)

**Q**
quality
quarter (=¼)
queen
question
quick
quiet
quite

**R**
race
radio
rail

railway
rain
rarely
rather
reach
read
ready
real
realise
really
reason
receive
recently
reception
recognise
recommend
record (=disc)
red
referee
refreshments
refuse (v)
register
regulations
religion
remain
remember
rent
repair
repeat
report
request
reservation
reserve
rest
restaurant
result
return
rise
rich
ride
right
ring
rise
river
road
roast
rock (n)
roll
roof
room
root
rose
rough
round
row
rubber
rubbish
rugby
rule
run (v)

**S**
sad
safe
safety
sail
salad

salary
sale
salt
same
sand
sandwich
saucer
sausage
save
say
school
science
scientist
scissors
scooter
sculpture
sea
seaside
season
search
seat
second
secret
secretary
see
seed
sell
send
sense
sentence
serve
service
set
several
sex
shade
shadow
shake
shall
shape
she
sheep
sheet
shelf
shine
sunshine
ship
shirt
shoe
shoot (v)
shop
short
shot (n)
should
show (v n)
shut
sick
side (n)
sight (n)
sight-seeing
sign
signature
silence
silent
silver
simple
since

sing
single
sir
sister
sit
size
skiing
skin (n)
skirt
sky
sleep
sleepy
slow
small
smell
smile
smoke
smooth
snackbar
snow
so
soap
socks
soft
soldier
some
somebody
somehow
someone
something
sometimes
somewhere
son
song
soon
sorry
sort (of) (n)
sound
soup
south
space
spaghetti
speak
specialist
speed
spell
spend
splash
spoon
sport
spring
spy
square
stadium
stage
stage
stair/s
stamp
stand
star
start
state
station
stay
steak
steal
steel

step
stewardess
stick (n)
still (adv)
stockings
stomach
stone
stop
store
storm
story
straight (n)
strange
stranger
strawberry
street
string
strong
student
studies
study
subject
succeed
success
successful
such
sudden
suddenly
sugar
suit
suitcase
summer
sun
supermarket
supper
suppose
sure
surgeon
surname
surprise
surprising
sweet
swim
sword

**T**

table (n)
tablet
take
talk
tall
tape
taste
tax
taxes
taxi
tea
teach
team
telegram
telegraph
telephone
television
tell
temperature
tennis
tent

term
terminal
test
than
thank/s
that
the
theatre
their/s
them
themselves
then
there
therefore
these
they
thick
thief
thin
thing
think
thirst
this
those
thought (n)
through
throw
thumb
ticket
tie
tiger
till (until)
time
tip
tired
to
tobacco
today
toe
together
toilet
tomato
tomorrow
tongue
tonight
too
tooth
top
torch
touch
tour
tourist
towards
towel
town
traffic
train (n)
training
translate
travel
traveller
treasure
tree
trip
trouble
trousers
true

try
tunnel
turn (n)
turning (n)
TV
type
typist
typewriter
tyres

**U**

unable
uncle
under
underground
understand
unemployment
unfortunately
unimportant
university
unnecessary
unpleasant
until
unusual
up
upon
upstairs
upwards
us
use
useful
usual
usually

**V**

vacation
valley
valuable
value
veal
vegetable
very
view
village
violent
visa
visit
voice
volcano

**W**

wages
wait
waiter
waitress
wake
walk
wall
wallet
want
war
warm
was
wash
waste
watch
water

way
we
weak
wear
weather
week
weigh
weight
welcome
well
west
wet
what
wheel
when
where
which
while
whisky
white
who
whole
wholly
whom
whose
why
wide
wild
will
win
wind (n)
window
wine
winter
wish
with
woman
wonder
wonderful
wood
wooden
wool
woollen
word
work
world
worry
would
wreck
write
wrong

**Y**

yard (=3 feet)
year
yellow
yes
yesterday
yet
you
your
yours
yourself
young

**Z**

zero

# COLLINS ENGLISH LIBRARY Level 3

## Mystery/Adventure:

**BRAINBOX AND BULL**
Two boys visit an oil rig and find themselves in an exciting mystery.

**CLIMB A LONELY HILL**
Sue and Jack have to grow up quickly, if they want to stay alive in the Australian Desert.

**CUSTER'S GOLD**
In 1876, the news that there is probably gold in the Hills of Dakota leads to only one thing. War!

**THE GUNSHOT GRAND PRIX**
The racing car drivers know their sport is dangerous but suddenly a new kind of danger arrives.

**MAIMUNAH**
Maimunah, a Malay schoolgirl, begins an ordinary day, which becomes an exciting drama.

## Biography:

**FIVE GHOST STORIES**
Unusual happenings told by well-known authors.

**THE PICTURE OF DORIAN GRAY**
The classic tale of a double life.

**BRUCE SPRINGSTEEN**
The story of the world's most popular "rock and roll" singer.

**EMMA AND I**
The remarkable story of a blind lady and her guide dog.

**MARILYN MONROE**
The life of Marilyn Monroe from lonely childhood to world-famous actress.

## Classics:

**SIX AMERICAN STORIES**
Six great stories that are classics of 19th and early 20th Century American literature.

**LITTLE WOMEN**
The great classic tells the story of a year in the life of the March family during the American Civil War.

**DAVID COPPERFIELD**
This famous book tells the life story of a young English boy about 150 years ago – his sadness and happiness, and the interesting people in his life.

**AN AMERICAN TRAGEDY**
Clyde's dream of wealth and happiness – the American Dream – goes very wrong and ends in tragedy.

## History:

**THREE ENGLISH KINGS**
These stories are from three famous Shakespeare plays about English kings.

## Information:

**CINEMA STUNTS**
Find out how incredible things are made possible in films!

## Puzzles/Games:

**GRADED ENGLISH PUZZLES**
Crosswords, wordgames, vocabulary exercises, logic, spelling, map-reading, and lots more!